MONTAIGNE'S POLITICS

MONTAIGNE'S POLITICS

AUTHORITY AND GOVERNANCE
IN THE *ESSAIS*

Biancamaria Fontana

PRINCETON UNIVERSITY PRESS

PRINCETON AND OXFORD

COPYRIGHT © 2008 BY PRINCETON UNIVERSITY PRESS

PUBLISHED BY PRINCETON UNIVERSITY PRESS, 41 WILLIAM STREET,

PRINCETON, NEW JERSEY 08540

IN THE UNITED KINGDOM: PRINCETON UNIVERSITY PRESS, 3 MARKET PLACE,

WOODSTOCK, OXFORDSHIRE OX20 1SY

LIBRARY OF CONGRESS CATALOGING-IN-PUBLICATION DATA

FONTANA, BIANCAMARIA.

MONTAIGNE'S POLITICS : AUTHORITY AND GOVERNANCE IN THE ESSAIS /

BIANCAMARIA FONTANA.

P. CM.

INCLUDES BIBLIOGRAPHICAL REFERENCES.

ISBN 978-0-691-13122-1 (ALK. PAPER)

1. MONTAIGNE, MICHEL DE, 1533–1592. ESSAIS.   2. MONTAIGNE, MICHEL DE,

1533–1592—POLITICAL AND SOCIAL VIEWS.   I. TITLE.

PQ1643.F65 2008

844'.3—DC22   2007003796

BRITISH LIBRARY CATALOGING-IN-PUBLICATION DATA IS AVAILABLE

THIS BOOK HAS BEEN COMPOSED IN GALLIARD

PRINTED ON ACID-FREE PAPER. ∞

PRESS.PRINCETON.EDU

PRINTED IN THE UNITED STATES OF AMERICA

1   3   5   7   9   10   8   6   4   2

CONTENTS

ACKNOWLEDGMENTS

I wish to thank Raymond Geuss, Bernard Sève, and Quentin Skinner for helpful advice at the initial stages of this project; Antoine Compagnon, Neil Forsyth, Caroline Humphrey, Michael Moriarty, and Kevin Mulligan for their comments on all or parts of this text: the responsibility of the results is of course mine alone. For their encouragement, and for listening patiently as I talked endlessly about Montaigne on all conceivable occasions, I am grateful to Manuela Albertone, Bronislaw Baczko, Sandrine Baume, Pascal Bridel, Alberto Brunelli Bonetti, Romain Felli, Istvan Hont, Bela Kapossy, Silvia Kimmeier, Patrizia Lombardo, Bernard Manin, Pasquale Pasquino, Florence Passy, Ruth Scurr, and Sylvana Tomaselli. As usual, John Dunn has had to listen more often and at greater length than anybody else: I hope he will find in the book some reward for his endurance. Finally, I wish to thank Ian Malcolm of Princeton University Press for his help and enthusiasm. *Questo libro è dedicato a mia madre.*

B. F.
Lausanne, December 2006

MONTAIGNE'S POLITICS

INTRODUCTION

Montaigne: A Profile View

For over four hundred years, since his death in 1592, Michel de Montaigne has proved a difficult subject for portrait. The small group of loyal friends who first tried to celebrate his qualities and achievements—as the news that the author of the *Essais* was dead spread slowly across Europe—may have found some comfort in the panegyrics, tributes, and praises they lavished upon his memory.[1] But the man who invented a radically novel, breathtakingly modern way of writing about the self had fatally undermined the future efforts of interpreters and commentators, keeping for himself all the original insights, and leaving for posterity only the dry bones of conventional rhetoric and of standard literary formulas. There is simply nothing anyone can say about Michel de Montaigne, about his temperament, experiences, and ideas, that has not been said more interestingly and effectively by himself.

The choice that is made here of selecting one particular dimension of Montaigne's contribution—focusing upon those aspects of his reflection that are relevant to the understanding of politics—may also seem (and perhaps is) a self-defeating exercise. It goes against the spirit of the writer's work, which deliberately rejected any specialized approach to the understanding of human reality, and it contradicts his deliberate blurring of the contours of his private and public persona. The very nature of the *Essais*, which stand as an intricate, closely knit unit, in which the world is apprehended through the unique filter of the self, seems to preclude any clear separation of domains of inquiry. Jean-Jacques Rousseau claimed that what Montaigne offered as self-portrait was in fact just a profile, a carefully selected perspective;[2] whether he was right or not in his judgment, I intend to follow his suggestion: a profile view is what I shall be attempting in this book.

As a rule, those intellectual historians who are interested in the political and ideological implications of Montaigne's work prefer to avoid any direct confrontation with the intrusive personality of the author: they concentrate instead upon the text of the *Essais* taken as a distinct, disembodied entity, or upon the discursive contexts surrounding it. Such approaches offer the advantage of methodological coherence and can certainly help to clarify the language and structure of Montaigne's writings, but they still leave open the question of their interpretation. Recent attempts to place Montaigne's career in the context of sixteenth-century literary and political patronage have the great merit of injecting some historical substance into our reading of the *Essais*; such studies, however, are less preoccupied with Montaigne's own intellectual project, than they are with the definition of some wider category (patron, author, political professional) that he might be taken to represent.

Though the *Essais* are generally regarded as a landmark in the history of modern European thought, we have no clear understanding of what they represent or stand for in any ideological or political context; similarly, the labels currently employed to describe the author's position—such as skepticism, neo-stoicism, civic humanism or humanism *tout court*, individualism, libertinage—seem far too hazy, and remain on the whole peripheral to the actual content of his work. As a result, there is a lack of proportion between the elevated status of Montaigne the writer—established by a vast and ever growing stream of literary scholarship—and the uncertain reputation he enjoys as moralist, philosopher, and observer of the social and political reality of his time.[3]

Modern historians are not alone in finding Montaigne's work difficult to interpret and to classify; this state of affairs began long ago, possibly among the first generation of readers of the *Essais*. But instead of resulting (as one might expect) in a variety of conflicting pictures of the author, the uncertain responses of those early interpreters and commentators converged very early on upon a single, enigmatic persona. In fact, unlike other major intellectual figures, Montaigne has never been the object of much controversy, except perhaps on a few particular aspects of his work: the image of the writer promoted by his admirers, and the one set forth by his detractors, are surprisingly similar, and differ in tone and coloratura rather than in substance. This shared image has changed very little through time and the commonplace views currently held about the *Essais* were already firmly established in the interpretative tradition by the beginning of the eighteenth century.[4]

To the audience of his friends and imitators—from Justus Lipsius to Pierre Charron, from Jean-Jacques Rousseau to Voltaire—the writer appeared as a benevolent sage, a tolerant, compassionate man who kept his distance from partisan struggle; a sparkling intellect, perhaps a little too frivolous and aloof if one considers the dramatic historical events that formed the background of his life. Mme de Lafayette effectively summarized these sentiments when she described Montaigne as someone it would be nice to have as one's neighbor, thus promoting the reputation of the writer as the embodiment of renaissance refinement and gentlemanly virtues, to the detriment of any possible role as *maître à penser*.[5]

This same image of Montaigne as wise and witty occupant of his chateau can be found in the writings of his enemies, from Blaise Pascal and those *dévots* who followed his lead—Malebranche, Garasse, Berulle, Bossuet—down to Sainte-Beuve, with the difference that, far from wishing to have him living next door, they strongly disapproved of him and denounced his relaxed style and disengaged attitude. In their eyes the writer's levity and detachment appeared as a guilty lack of commitment, while the digressive, self-referential style of the *Essais* was stigmatized as an indecent display of authorial vanity.[6]

Admirers and detractors have also been united by a shared mistrust of the writer's Christian sentiments and of his professed loyalty to the Catholic Church. The question of Montaigne's religion is one of the few truly controversial issues in scholarly interpretations of his life and work. In the seventeenth century Pascal and the *dévots* accused Montaigne of hypocrisy, denouncing the *Essais* as an apology not just for skepticism, but for incredulity; their campaign of denigration led to the inscription of the book on the Index of forbidden works on the part of the ecclesiastical authorities in 1676, thus reversing the decision of the sympathetic Roman censors who had accorded it the *imprimatur* in 1580.[7] Protestant commentators thought that Montaigne's professed Catholicism was an excuse to avoid addressing any serious doctrinal issues, clinging instead to a religion of external forms and rituals. Freethinkers and libertines for their part were ready to rally to the judgment of the *dévots*, adopting Montaigne as a fellow traveler who had taken the prudent option of disguising his true opinions under the appearance of conformity. All parties harbored the uneasy feeling that the writer's real intentions eluded them; all chose to believe that he had deliberately misled or deceived them, thus promoting the tenacious legend of his ambiguity and duplicity.[8]

It would be easy to suggest that, when Pascal denounced Montaigne's obsession with self-analysis, or when André Gide dissected and exposed his ambivalence, they were in fact projecting upon the author of the *Essais* some intimate traits of their own.[9] Yet it remains true that Montaigne's credibility as moralist and as a political thinker has been seriously undermined by a double indictment that bears at the same time upon his work and upon his personal position. The first accusation is one of quietism. In short, it is claimed that, if Montaigne produced a series of lucid critical insights about contemporary society and about the exercise of power, he failed to suggest any remedy or propose some alternative political model. A conservative at heart, he disapproved of all initiatives directed toward the subversion, or even the radical reform, of existing institutions, either because he thought they would prove ineffective or because he believed they would generate disastrous side effects. In so far as he held "liberal" views, he did so from the purely negative perspective of the protection of the individual sphere of the self from external threats.[10]

The second accusation is one of concealment, the charge being that in the *Essais* the author deliberately failed to make explicit the most radical and subversive implications of his reflection, especially in sensitive matters such as religious belief, hiding them behind a smoke screen of ambiguous rhetorical formulas. A certain obscurity surrounds the relation between the first and the second accusation: it is not clear, for example, if Montaigne is supposed to have feared the philosophical implications of his views, or their practical consequences; whether a frank admission of his true beliefs may have resulted in an altogether different line of action in public life. Yet coherence is hardly the point here: what matters is the diffuse feeling, persistent through centuries of commentaries and interpretations, that the writer has somehow betrayed the expectations of his readers, by failing to fulfill the promise of his novel and provocative literary enterprise.[11]

In other words, if the *Essais* was the first great contribution to the critique of the *ancien régime* written in the French language—in line with works such as Bayle's *Dictionnaire historique et critique*, Montesquieu's *Esprit des lois*, or Diderot's *Encyclopédie*—it was a contribution that never really came into its own, because the author was unwilling or unprepared to announce his true colors. As to the promotion of the *Essais* to the status of a literary monument that transcends all particular historical and political context, this exalted position, in its blandness, is no compensation for the ideological battle (for which cause, against what enemies?) that was never engaged.

The Politics of Survival

The widespread feeling that, if Montaigne's work addresses a number of crucial social and political issues, it still falls short of its original promise, is partly based upon a misunderstanding of its intentions and significance. It is also sustained, in the first instance, by two external circumstances: firstly, the production of the *Essais* apparently coincided with the author's resolution to withdraw from public life by giving up his parliamentary office; secondly, it has generally proved difficult to associate Montaigne with one or other of the political factions involved in the protracted civil conflict that dominated most of his adult life.

The writer's professed intention of leaving all other business to serve the Muses—famously recorded in the inscriptions that appear on the beams across the ceiling of his library[12]—finds apparent confirmation in the chronological sequence of events: Montaigne began to work on the early drafts of the *Essais* after selling his office in the *parlement* of Bordeaux in 1570. The date itself is not without importance, since Montaigne "abandoned" his parliamentary post shortly before the tragic events of the Saint Bartholomew's Day Massacre: in particular, he was no longer a *conseiller* in October 1572, when the parliament voted, against the passionate pleadings of its *président* Lagebaston, the death of some three hundred Huguenots, who were held in custody by the town's authorities. Montaigne's subsequent reluctance to make any direct reference in his writings to the events of 1572 (refraining from any celebration of the massacre of the kind produced by some of his famous literary friends such as Guy de Pibrac or Pierre de Ronsard, but also from any explicit condemnation) is inevitably perceived by the modern reader as a disturbing omission.[13]

Montaigne's contemporaries would have recognized the image of the writer isolating himself from the world to pursue his vocation for what it was, a literary formula, embedded in classical rhetoric and in tune with the language of the learned academies that flourished under the Valois[14]—a conventional posture, which announced the writer's intellectual ambitions and his philosophical colors rather than describing his practical projects. Posterity, possibly influenced by the sequence of historical events, or simply oblivious of Renaissance literary conventions, has taken the idea of retirement more seriously, as an accurate description of the writer's position; it has also read the author's insistence on the "private" and "domestic" character of his work quite literally, as a profession of disengagement from public responsibility. Recent scholarship has done its best to correct this view, showing that Montaigne's "retirement" was far from being a quiet and sheltered retreat, and arguing that the writer continued to take active part in political life until his death over twenty years later. Yet these incontrovertible historical claims have failed thus far to reverse the impression transmitted by tradition, possibly because the surviving evidence on Montaigne's political contacts and diplomatic activities is patchy, and his role difficult to characterize.

Montaigne was twenty-nine years old when the first religious troubles broke out in 1562; when he died, thirty years later, in 1592, the conflict was only just approaching its conclusion; it would still take several years before the new king, Henry IV, achieved a complete pacification of the country, while the marks of destruction across French territory would remain visible for decades afterwards.[15] The protracted character of the French crisis—with civil war becoming a permanent and almost "normal" state of affairs—should be kept in mind, since it helps to explain how people in Montaigne's generation tried to shape their lives both away from and around public events, alternating moments of intense participation with intervals of disaffection and despair, falling in and out of the projects and initiatives that were subsequently hatched to provide a political solution.

Whatever his feelings about the political situation, Montaigne's resolution to sell his office in 1570 was largely circumstantial: at that particular time he had just inherited his father's estate and felt some obligation, as the eldest son, to look after the family's land and properties, an occupation of which, admittedly, he soon tired.[16] His activity at the Bordeaux parliament, limited as it was to the *chambre des requêtes*, was rather dull: unlike the *grande chambre*, the main assembly of parliament in which all the affairs of public importance were discussed, the *chambre des requêtes* was an administrative subcommittee that dealt essentially with ordinary litigation; Montaigne's office involved much tedious paperwork and offered limited possibilities of advancement, especially to someone whose family was already well represented within that same institution; the number of members of the same family who could sit in the *grande chambre* was in fact restricted by law, and Montaigne—who had married into a prominent parliamentary family, the de Chassaignes—had to face the competition of older relatives and in-laws.[17]

In a provincial, tightly knit community such as the magistracy of Bordeaux, Montaigne's domestic and parliamentary connections were inhibiting in other ways, in particular by associating him with a Catholic party which, since the beginning of the first religious war in 1563, had acquired an increasingly intolerant and aggressive profile. After his resignation he continued to provide legal advice to the parliamentary chambers, but was more at liberty to cultivate relations with the other pole of political power in the region, the one represented by the lieutenant of the Guyenne and his officials, men who were directly dependent on the king and the Parisian court, and who often found themselves in conflict with the different parliamentary factions. He also moved into higher social circles, and soon enjoyed the friendship and patronage of the de Foix-Candales, the grandest aristocratic family of the Guyenne, Catholics who had traditional bonds of kinship and feudal allegiance to the kings of Navarre. It was in their house that Montaigne first met Henry of Navarre; by the end of the 1570s he had been appointed "gentleman of the chamber" of both Henry III of Valois at his Parisian court, and Henry of Navarre at his provincial, but intellectually lively, court at Nérac. He also befriended a string of noble ladies who are associated with the composition of the *Essais*: Diane de Foix, Marguerite de Duras, Navarre's wife Marguerite de Valois, his sister Catherine de Bourbon, and his politically influential mistress Diane ("Corisande") d'Andoins.[18] It was thanks to the support of the de Foix entourage that Montaigne was appointed mayor of Bordeaux in 1580, a post for which he had not canvassed (he was traveling in Italy at the time) and which he held for four anxious years, spending a considerable amount of time and energy on the effort to keep the city free from unrest and military assaults.[19]

In retrospect, Montaigne's move out of parliament could be said to have marked the beginning, rather than the end, of his public career. Though power relations and allegiances shifted through time, the writer found a natural political niche among those members of the Catholic elite

of the Guyenne who patiently canvassed to limit the damages of the conflict and to keep their region—so dangerously enclosed between zones
under Protestant influence—as much as possible out of trouble. With
equally good connections in the Huguenot camp, he frequently acted as
go-between among the various parties involved in the conflict: the parliament of Bordeaux, the town council, the king's officials and military commanders, and their counterparts on the Protestant side. We also know,
though only by tantalizing hints (such as ambassadors' reports or contemporary memoirs) that he was entrusted with confidential missions by the
kings Henry III of Valois and Henry of Navarre, as well as by the leader of
the Catholic League, the Duke of Guise. Given the circumstances, he
proved altogether a deft and successful political operator; by the time of
his death, in 1592, he basked in the friendship and reflected glory of the
new king, Henry IV, the "heretic" enemy he had so stubbornly supported,
and who had finally emerged as the winner in the protracted dynastic
struggle for the possession of the French crown.[20] When he died, those
who had know him were unanimous in paying tribute to his ability to handle with confidence and experience "*les affaires du monde*," an acknowledgment that seems to contradict the writer's modern reputation.[21]

Far from being written in isolation and detachment from public life, the
subsequent drafts of the *Essais* accompanied Montaigne through the instructive, if distressing, experience of the religious wars. One important dimension to emerge from the layered structure of the book is precisely the
growing confidence the writer displayed in assessing political circumstances and lines of action. There is a visible shift from the bookish knowledge, largely derived from the study of classical historians, that characterized the early drafts, and the intimate understanding of the mechanisms of
power, born of direct observation and experience, that comes out of the
pages of Book III, written in the last years of the writer's life.[22] It is true,
however, that the *Essais* are difficult to classify in political terms, since they
do not speak with the voice of a particular ideology or faction. Montaigne
belonged to a generation, raised in the cult of classical history and literature, whose ambitions, political as well as intellectual, were wrecked by the
advent of the religious conflict. Before the conflict began, the writer had
found a congenial project in the proposed reforms of French institutions
set forth by the Chancellor Michel de l'Hospital: these involved a reform
of the Church, to eliminate those abuses in the administration of ecclesiastical benefits which had contributed to the development of heresy, and,
in parallel with this, a reform of the law, in particular the abolition of the
venality of offices and of other corrupt practices.[23]

This lofty Erasmian vision, which claimed that the Catholic monarchy
should confront the crisis of the Reformation not by attacking her heretic
opponents, but by amending her own ways, found predictably little sup-

port among the different segments of the French establishment, and especially in the parliamentary milieu to which Montaigne belonged; whatever precarious credibility this vision had gained throughout the 1550s was swept away at the beginning of the 1560s by the outbreak of the conflict. The premature death of Montaigne's beloved friend Estienne de La Boétie in 1563, besides having a deep emotional impact upon the writer, contributed somehow to his feeling of being one of the few surviving heirs to the best hopes and ideals of his own generation. By that time he had also outgrown his own professional role of magistrate: years of practice in the legal profession, the "*chicane*" as he contemptuously called it, had eroded any residual loyalty the young *conseiller* might have felt toward French parliamentary institutions and French justice—though paradoxically this negative experience would never entirely destroy his disposition to look at public issues primarily from the distinctive perspective of the man of law.

Unlike some of his siblings (one of his brothers and a sister converted to Protestantism), Montaigne was never seriously attracted to the ideas of the Reformation, which he failed somehow to recognize as a spontaneous religious movement, with genuine (if misguided) spiritual motivations;[24] what he saw instead was the manipulative action of a leadership of religious fanatics and ambitious warlords, who used the religious issue to promote their own interests, mercilessly exploiting the credulity of an impoverished and discontented population. Precisely because he was convinced that the French people had many good reasons to revolt against their rulers (such as poverty, exploitation, a ruthless and corrupt administration) Montaigne found it difficult to see the priority of a doctrinal dispute that, in his view, could hardly be understood by the mass of the people; his personal contacts with some of the leaders of the war on both sides probably contributed to reenforce his belief in the shamelessly opportunistic character of their motivations.

While he had no sympathy for the Reformation, Montaigne was unable to identify with the crusading spirit of the loyalist Catholics: being opposed on principle to the practice of torture and to cruel executions, he found the means employed in the persecution of heretics barbarous and horrifying, and judged the penchant for populist violence and feudal brutality developed by the Catholic party equally unacceptable. If Montaigne can be appropriately described as a "*politique*"—the name given to those moderates who, throughout the conflict, tried to reach some kind of settlement between the two religious factions—this label does not associate him with any definite political ideology. During the wars moderates were often accused by both religious parties of indifference and incredulity; modern historians have followed their lead, by associating the position of the *politiques* with the secular ideology of reason of state or with straightforward opportunism. This view is somewhat misleading: if some *poli-tiques* can be described as religious skeptics, the great majority of them were, like Montaigne, sincere Christians, who could not be reconciled to the idea of a fratricidal war fought on religious grounds. What united them in the search for a viable compromise was the spontaneous solidarity of people trying to survive a civil catastrophe of unprecedented proportions, without any common project or design beyond the immediate one of the limitation of damage.[25]

In the *Essais* Montaigne expressed a clear (if not overstated) preference for republican government: in the text republics were described as the most 'natural' and 'equitable' form of regime, while collective political decisions were judged safer than individual ones. Monarchy featured invariably as second best, a form of government imposed by particular historical circumstances and traditions.[26] There were probably a number of different reasons that led Montaigne to support the cause of Henry of Navarre: loyalty to his local patrons, a shrewd assessment of Navarre's superior abilities, cultural and temperamental affinities may all have played a role; but certainly a belief in the merits of monarchy, let alone absolute monarchy, was not one of them. As to the political initiatives associated with Henry IV's reign, while it is pointless to speculate about developments that occurred principally after Montaigne's death, it can be said that some of them, such as the king's conversion to Catholicism, or the establishment of religious coexistence, were certainly close to the spirit of the writer's own convictions; while others, such as the reform that turned the venality of offices into a permanent feature of French law, went against the advice that Montaigne had offered to the king in the years of their association.[27]

In a poignant passage of his work the writer observed, echoing Erasmus, that it was his fate to be alienated from both parties and to be regarded as "Guelph by the Ghibelline and Ghibelline by the Guelph."[28] In fact his position, far from being unusual, was probably common to many moderates confronted with a context in which conflicts were strongly radicalized and allegiances unstable. However, after Montaigne's death, the difficulty of associating him with any official faction in the universe of the religious wars and their aftermath—Catholics or Huguenots, partisans of royal absolutism or *monarchomach* anti-royalists, *politiques* or *ligueurs*, libertines or *dévots*—has deprived him of the support and credibility that come from being adopted within a recognized ideological tradition. On the whole historians have found Montaigne's lack of affiliation puzzling and have tried to explain it away as indifference, resigned submission to authority, or secret disaffection—attitudes that seem ill-suited to capture the fierce independence and highly individual vision of the world that characterized the *Essais*.

Intellectual Ambitions

But where did the vision come from, how did Montaigne come to adopt such a distinctive personal approach to the understanding of the world around him (or, as he would rather say, of himself through it)? At some fundamental level the question is of course unanswerable: no one can really explain a literary vocation or a particular impulse toward exploring the self through the medium of writing. Yet in a more superficial dimension it is at least possible to trace, in the development of the text, some converging paths through which the author came to focus upon his object.

The first of these paths to emerge is unsurprisingly the most obvious and conventional one: the attempt, on the part of a still inexperienced author, to produce an ambitious work of historical and juridical interpretation, testing his views against the established wisdom of both classical and modern authorities. It is difficult to tell to what extent this exercise was purely academic, or whether it was prompted from the start by the need to come to terms with contemporary French events, to find some explanation for the religious crisis, and to predict its possible developments. Probably all these factors played a role, but as the work took shape, contemporary reality kept intruding into the text, gradually conjuring up the sombre picture of a violent and corrupt European society on the brink of disintegration.

The most striking aspect of the first religious war that began in the early 1560s was, for those who experienced it (and there is no reason to think that Montaigne was an exception), its sudden and unexpected character. Though it was obvious to observers that French society was traversed by tensions which, in unfavorable circumstances, might destabilize it, the particular form taken by the conflict was on the whole novel and surprising. What was new was not the spreading of the Reformed faith (an already familiar phenomenon from the previous decades), nor the bouts of revolt and of ferocious repression that accompanied it.[29] The novelty was represented instead by the quick process through which a whole range of latent conflicts—social, economic, territorial, dynastic, institutional—were absorbed within the single mode and the distinctive rhetoric of the war of religion.

Confronted with an apparently new type of civil unrest, with communities, once united, now fighting furiously over chapels and burial grounds, holy images and stations of the cross, those in charge of public order reacted with due alarm, but without any great clarity of purpose; thus the measures adopted by local authorities, magistrates, and the king's officials were often contradictory, and were often made ineffective by paralyzing conflicts of competence. Montaigne must have been familiar with the report that his friend La Boétie had written on behalf of the Bordeaux parliament, after accompanying the king's envoy, the Lieutenant de Burie, on a tour of inspection of the region of Agen. In the months that preceded the outbreak of the war, the region had been the theater of serious incidents between Catholics and Protestants; against their best judgment, Burie and the other delegates had hastily introduced some measures of compromise to restore order, but in reporting to the *parlement* La Boétie expressed the view that their effect would not prove long lasting.[30]

On the whole the reaction of observers fluctuated between two alternative interpretations of the crisis: the first one saw the war as a struggle for the true faith, an epochal conflict of paramount spiritual significance; the second described it as the replaying, under new names and new pretexts, of old and essentially worldly disputes. Seen from the first perspective, Christian civilization in France, perhaps even in Europe, was coming to an apocalyptic end; from the second, the nation was just experiencing a particularly nasty display of ordinary vices—resentment, envy, greed, desire for revenge, and so on—which, if appropriately dealt with, would eventually subside again within the boundaries of social discipline.[31]

In the *Essais* Montaigne would explore both hypotheses, but to begin with he was engaged in the definition of a broader methodological perspective from which the question could be addressed. What we know about the evolution of the text shows that the early drafts, written in the first half of the 1570s, focused mainly upon questions such as the role of chance in military and political undertakings, the stability of regimes, the ambivalence of men's emotional responses, and other themes connected with historical prediction and causality. To confront these questions Montaigne mobilized a considerable mass of sources published in the four languages he read fluently (French, Latin, Italian, and Spanish), ranging from Greek and Roman historiography through modern commentaries, chronicles, and memoirs, down to travel narratives and to the fashionable modern genre of legal histories.[32] His command over such vast literature—artfully presented in the text as the product of casual, whimsical reading—did not fail to impress his early readers, so that a solid reputation for erudition and learning accompanied the author of the *Essais* through the centuries.

Yet this scholarly tour de force, initially undertaken with considerable energy and enthusiasm (typical perhaps of someone who had come relatively late in life to such systematic intellectual activity), would soon expose the weakness of those doctrines and theories from which he had initially hoped to fashion his own interpretation. By testing the range of explanatory models on offer, Montaigne was soon able to show that historical examples could be used in different contexts to support contradictory outcomes; that the search for primary causes runs into circular arguments; and that, more generally, individual as well as collective human responses defy all attempt at straightforward prediction. As a result, he rapidly lost his initial confidence in abstract models of classification and explanation and in the possibility of defining a general framework, within which the mechanisms regulating social consensus and social conflict could be understood.

Up to the initial stage of his investigation Montaigne's project was not very distant from the spirit of some of his most prestigious modern sources, works such as Machiavelli's *Discorsi*[33] or Jean Bodin's *Methodus.*[34] Like Machiavelli, Montaigne was fascinated by the experience of ancient republics, and held them as a paragon against which modern political events and circumstances should be measured. His legal background, his familiarity with jurisprudential discourse, his persistent concern with the origins and nature of the law, meant also that he felt an obvious affinity with Bodin's reflection. However, he remained no less unconvinced by Machiavelli's attempt to define, in near-scientific terms, predictable patterns of social and individual behavior, than he was by Bodin's ambitious synopsis, which linked different phases in the history of humankind with specific types of legal institutions. Both approaches seemed in the end too general and abstract to come to terms with the forever shifting, infinitely intricate reality of human interaction.

Montaigne's resolute departure from the conventional path of systematic inquiry turned the *Essais* into a novel, highly distinctive type of work, which no longer resembled any of its original models; but his approach did not lessen the work's commitment to some of the basic issues he shared with them, although these now appeared in a richer, more diversified context. The shift in methodology tends to hide this fact, as if in developing his new skeptical approach, the writer had given up addressing any specific questions about the structure of human societies and about political institutions, or as if he had lost interest in finding any specific answers for them, satisfying himself instead with a set of philosophical paradoxes.

Recent studies focusing upon the tradition of Pyrrhonism and Montaigne's philosophical views have helpfully stressed that skepticism need not imply an abdication from action, either in individual circumstances or in a social context. On the contrary, the adoption of the skeptical method may serve to break away from the constraints of theory in order to establish a more direct, flexible connection with reality and with living experience. In the case of the *Essais* this process is more visible if, instead of focusing exclusively upon the *Apology of Raymond Sebond*—Montaigne's methodological manifesto in Book II—as commentators have traditionally chosen to do, the impact of the skeptical approach is considered across the whole text of the *Essais*. Where the *Apology* presents in fact a general philosophical discussion of the limits of human reason, it is in dealing with a variety of social and ethical issues that the eminently practical scope of Montaigne's skeptical method becomes apparent.[35]

The new approach enabled the writer to expose the limitations of those established authorities who, by clinging to abstract schemes and models, failed to grasp the complexity and instability of human circumstances. Historians, for example, were misguided when they described the lives and characters of famous men according to patterns that make them look all the same, arranging the historical evidence to suit a set of ideal images of how great men should behave. Like all those who aimed at controlling and manipulating human actions, they were inclined to attribute to these a continuity and coherence that in practice was simply nonexistent.[36] In opposition to these schematic approaches, Montaigne revived the classical metaphor that compared any serious attempt to understand and influence human actions to the art of medicine: a practice ready to acknowledge the infinite peculiarities of living organisms and capable of adjusting to them.

What was in question was not simply the adoption of a novel intellectual strategy, but a radical change in the attitude and disposition of the person who, by speaking or writing, took up the role of authority. It was not sufficient to point out that the conventional discourses of philosophy, history, or jurisprudence were inadequate; one must be ready to adopt a type of language that might prove radically different in tone: less arrogant, less dogmatic, ready to question its own motives, simple; a language in fact that ordinary people might understand because it was close to their experience and to their sentiments, rather than addressing them from above. It was necessary, Montaigne claimed, to follow the example of Socrates by establishing a conversation with ordinary people such as artisans and manual workers, because it was with such persons—not with poets or philosophers—that we spend most of our lives, as it is on them that we depend practically for our everyday survival.[37]

Montaigne's growing anti-intellectualism had recognizable antecedents in the ancient and Christian traditions: beyond its skeptical mistrust of system, it could be associated with the Socratic insistence upon self-knowledge, with stoic and epicurean aspirations to restore nature and reject artifice, but also with the evangelical values of humility and love brought back into the contemporary debate by Erasmus.[38] In the *Essais* the figures of Socrates and Christ appeared blended in a single image of the philosopher-teacher capable of addressing, in simple language, his fellow men as equals and of speaking to their hearts before their minds.

In contrast with the more conventional anti-intellectual postures inherited from classical literature, the task Montaigne set for himself in the *Essais* was that of bringing the dimension of practice into the writing, "contaminating" as it were his prose with the eclectic and confused peculiarities of human experience, with the oddities, emotions, and trivial details of everyday life. He developed this provocative style with the same relish and dedication he had originally invested in accumulating bookish knowledge and academic credentials. His anti-intellectualism did not

develop as a mere rhetorical expedient: it grew instead into a militant vocation, boldly exhibited and charged with all the writer's personal emotions and sentiments.

Passions

Moving away from the more specifically intellectual dimensions of the *Essais*, a different point of entry into the work is offered by a set of the author's emotional responses: the growth of feelings of outrage, compassion,
and indignation, fed by the mounting horrors of the wars, represents an
essential support to Montaigne's analysis, though one that the writer
clearly decided not to emphasize. Whatever their attitude toward Montaigne's work, past and present commentators are in fact unanimous in
their appreciation of the author's moderation and detachment: they praise
his capacity to face with equanimity the most disruptive experiences and to
show no partisan animosity in response to the tragic events of his time. For
Montaigne's contemporaries this serene attitude was associated with a specific philosophical ideal—that of stoic wisdom and of philosophical detachment form the world—though it is possible that the writer's easy nature and friendly disposition might have contributed to the result as much
as any self-imposed discipline, Gascon bonhomie breathing new life into
the austere Roman stereotype.

This image of Montaigne as impassive, smiling sage has long survived its
original connotation, taking on different forms over time and reappearing
as Christian compassion, humane benevolence, skeptical irony, enlightened sympathy, liberal toleration, or postmodern indulgence, in tune with
changing cultural fashions. The paradox in this tenacious characterization
of Montaigne is that it is both genuine and misleading. It is genuine because it corresponds to the rhetorical strategy the writer deliberately
adopted in his book: if we cannot tell what the author of the *Essais* really
felt about a number of sensitive issues, we can at least recognize his determination to oppose moderate tones to partisan peroration, common sense
to fanatical preaching, modesty and doubt to dogmatic certitude, irony to
arrogance. It is misleading, on the other hand, because it conceals the passionate sentiments that sustain the whole enterprise: feelings of rage, disgust, indignation, outrage, carefully mastered under the smooth surface of
an easy, meandering prose, which only at unguarded moments flare up un-
expectedly like flashes of lightning across the page.

In itself Montaigne's choice of understating his emotions, steering away
from the tones of acclaim, invective, and peroration that characterized
French literary production in the aftermath of the Saint Bartholomew's
Day Massacre, is impeccable, and greatly enhances the impact of his writ-

ing. And yet the undercurrent of passionate involvement, however strategically concealed, gives body and animation to the text, turning it into something far more engaging than the erudite performance of an accomplished intellectual. As to the nature of his emotional response, this is best described as an overwhelming sense of outrage: the unnecessary, cruel suffering of innocent people on account of the willful actions of human agents offended him as an intolerable breach of natural justice, which nothing could ever legitimate or condone. In the *Essais* this sentiment of outrage appeared in a very wide range of contexts; though contemporary French events were naturally prominent in his narrative, Montaigne was not especially interested in denouncing abuses and atrocities committed by a particular set of political actors: the picture he conjured up showed the human race, across space and time, tragically divided between the socially privileged and those whose lives counted for nothing, the grossly rich and the abjectly poor, the victims of persecution and their oppressors, masters and slaves.

Montaigne did not regard this reality of injustice and domination as a natural state of affairs. Nature exposed men to sickness and death, to need and fear; in some very primitive forms of society close to the state of nature, such as primitive tribes, men would no doubt subsist in very deprived, precarious circumstances; their efforts to survive would be hard and painful, their lives short and brutish. But it was only in the more complex social setting of civilization that people would be left to starve on the doorstep of houses replete with food, that they would be sacrificed to the vanity and ambitions of the powerful or perhaps tortured and executed in order to prove some obscure point of doctrine. If men in their natural state were capable of violence and cruelty, it was only in the realm of civilization that they committed crimes under the pretense of serving justice or religion, insulting their victims with their hypocrisy and arrogance.[39]

This bleak picture of the evils of the civilized state had recognizable Augustinian undertones (Augustine's *City of God* featured very prominently among the sources of the *Essais*): in his struggle to elevate himself above his original near-animal condition, man could only magnify the most perverse features of his nature such as greed, deceit, cruelty, and ambition. Human society was flawed because humans were basically incapable of any consistent effort toward peace and justice and tended to slide back into a logic of spiritual and material enslavement—a reality that was of course even more damning for those generations and those nations who had enjoyed the benefit of Christian revelation and of God's grace through baptism.

If he was an attentive reader of the *City of God*, and if he brought into the *Essais* echoes of its tragic vision of humanity, Montaigne placed his own analysis upon rather different ground, in tune with the critical readings of Augustine's work promoted by the Erasmian school.[40] In his view neither the corruption of the individual, nor the decadence of human societies, should be regarded as predetermined results, dictated by man's sinful nature and inscribed in the experience of the Fall. For him, the most distinctive feature of human nature was precisely its plasticity. Man was double: he was what he was, but he was also what he might become; all one could hope to capture was not man's essence, but a passing state. Experience showed the existence of a wide range of human types, from the most brutish to the most elevated, to the extent that the very notion of "human" was difficult to associate with a set of definite features; even the discontinuity between "human" and "animal" species appeared problematic.[41]

To Montaigne the circumstances that caused such dramatic inequality of conditions among human beings practically everywhere on earth seemed neither necessary nor irreversible. He thought, like Rousseau, that such circumstances were manmade and largely accidental; but unlike the author of the two *Discourses* (who remained more faithful in this respect to the original Augustinian model) he did not regard history as the progressive fall of mankind into moral decadence and material enslavement, but rather as a cluster of confused and often contradictory movements. To assume otherwise, to think that the fate of mankind must unfold according to a predictable pattern, was an act of presumption (how can we expect to know what God has in store for us?) and suggested a lack of faith in God's infinite mercy. Since human nature was capable of change, and since history must be seen as a complex and essentially open process, one should never accept injustice as a historical or anthropological necessity. Whatever the circumstances that led to it, injustice was always the product of specific human actions and human choices; such human choices were always, in the last instance, individual ones, and it was this individual responsibility for evil actions, rather than some global sense of human perversity, that must be addressed.

Inevitably the main target of the writer's revulsion, as it emerges from the pages of the *Essais*, was the people in power, those who used their authority and privileges to crush the less fortunate: greedy officials, unscrupulous judges, vengeful aristocrats, fanatical religious leaders, deceitful rulers, ruthless colonialists. Such people would happily hang a peasant for a crime he had not committed, rather than taking the trouble to investigate his guilt; they were ready to torture some hapless servant who followed the new heretical faith out of loyalty toward his master, or to burn alive some harmless lunatic who thought she possessed magic powers. They might, like the king of Portugal, trick thousands of Jews into giving up their homes and properties on the promise of safety, only to leave them to die on rafts at sea; or perhaps, like the men in the service of the crown of Castile, they might be ready to massacre and enslave entire nations on behalf of the commerce of pearls and spices. Montaigne was convinced, like Erasmus before him, that the crisis experienced by French and, more generally, by European society in the time of the religious wars was largely to be imputed to the deficiencies of her ruling classes. The corrupt practices of the clergy had discredited religion in the eyes of many, leaving the people exposed to the preaching of zealots and the manipulations of demagogues. The greed and partiality of the magistracy had destroyed popular trust in the law and in justice. The violent habits of a brutal, ill-educated nobility, with no useful skills other than the combat for which they continually trained, were turning Europe into a vast feudal gangland.[42]

Yet, if he reacted vividly to the abuses of the men in power, Montaigne was convinced that the responsibility for the crisis did not stop at the higher levels of the social scale. No doubt those who belonged to the ruling elite were doubly guilty, because they were in charge of things and could influence people, and also because they should have known better. However, in a situation where injustice and violence were widespread, everyone carried a share of responsibility: not just those who initiated the abuses and their followers, but also those who, from cowardice, indifference, or simple inertia, stood by and did nothing to stop them (indeed the writer placed himself in this last category of passive bystanders). A craving for domination was not the exclusive vice of the rich and powerful, though of course they had greater opportunities to indulge in it than ordinary people: even the most humble and insignificant members of society were capable of oppressing those they perceived as more feeble than themselves, as in the case of parents who brutalized their children, of children torturing animals, or of able-bodied persons victimizing the crippled and the insane. Such instincts were deeply rooted in human nature, where they fought with the equally natural sentiments of sympathy and compassion, and must be eradicated early on by education and example, since they remained beyond the reach of the law.[43]

Montaigne did not consider domination (*maistrise*) primarily as the feature of specific political systems, though he suggested that some types of regime were more conducive to it than others; instead he portrayed the exercise of abusive power as a flaw that cut across the whole spectrum of human associations: it was present in the relations among individuals, families, social groups, tribes, nations, empires; it even extended to the relations between living species, since humans were inclined to exercise an arbitrary and often abusive dominion over animals and over their natural environment.

At moments, when the subject of domination is discussed, it is possible to recognize in the *Essais* echoes of the classical republican rhetoric that characterized La Boétie's influential "*Discours de la servitude volontaire*";

men are slaves because they choose to be, whenever, from lack of courage and virtue, they submit without resisting to tyranny; freedom comes from the absence of relations of personal dependence, and the only just polity is one in which all citizens are equal in front of the law. The obvious affinity between the *Discours* and some of the arguments of the *Essais* has led some scholars to suggest that Montaigne, rather than La Boétie, was its real author, or that he was at least responsible for redrafting it in the 1570s.[44]

Elsewhere in the text, however, the writer looks beyond the classical universe of the republic threatened by tyranny, to consider the reality of oppression in a much broader perspective: in the family, in the schoolroom, and in the village, wherever petty despots exercise their power; among those human groups, anywhere in the world, who are targeted for persecution; across the continents, in the relations between conquering colonists and the populations they enslave. Thus, halfway through building up his case, Montaigne moved away from the familiar ground of the defense of republican freedom to espouse instead the sentiments of Christian universalism: passionate indignation, the sense of scandal in the face of cruelty and injustice, and its counterpart, compassion, are among the most distinctly Christian features of the *Essais*, and this regardless of any assumption one might choose to make about the personal religious beliefs of the author. In his work Montaigne returned over and over again to the subject of justice, exposing the imperfections and limitations of all human laws and the flaws attached to the practice of their administration. Yet, beyond the inadequacy of their own rules and arrangements, he thought men were still capable, in the face of gross abuse, to glimpse the truth of God's justice: they might be unable to agree about its prescriptions and to follow them, but they could not entirely free themselves from its incumbent presence.

This move toward a superior conception of justice is not without consequences for the overall coherence and credibility of Montaigne's vision. The author's Christian sentiments propelled the *Essais* beyond the boundaries of the classical republican tradition; but the same sentiments made the work incompatible with those contemporary political doctrines that advocated the restoration, in Europe, of a Christian polity (monarchy or empire) placed under the guidance of the Church. The *Essais* have been occasionally associated by historians of political thought with the neo-stoic tradition of reason of state; if this association is partly justified by the fact that Montaigne shared with writers, such as his admirer Justus Lipsius, a common background in the Ciceronian and Tacitean heritage,[45] it rests nevertheless upon a misunderstanding of the essence of Montaigne's Christianity, which was radical, egalitarian, sternly opposed to violence, and made no concessions either to the secular ambitions of the Church or to the requirements of a superior statecraft. The passionate denunciation of the genocide of the Amerindian populations in Book III—where the conquering style of the king of Castile, "the greatest prince of the habitable world, to whom the Pope, representing God on earth, had given the principality of all the Indies," was most unfavorably compared to that of Alexander the Great—showed just how little trust the writer put in the ideal of a Christian empire.[46]

The problem with this universalistic approach is that it blurs to some extent the focus of Montaigne's original indictment; if the duty of the citizen confronted with the enslavement of the republic is clear enough—to fight against the tyrant or to perish—what is the appropriate ground to resist abuses committed in such diverse and complex settings across the planet? When sovereigns and entire nations are guilty, when oppression stretches across continents in intricate webs of interest and complicity, what possible redress could there be on this earth for the helpless victims?

Today, after the age of Marxist internationalism, this "global" vision has gained new credibility as a possible standpoint from which to address issues such as the defense of human rights, the equitable distribution of resources, or the protection of the environment. In this context some of Montaigne's insights sound much closer to contemporary preoccupations than to those political issues discussed by influential sixteenth-century works. But on the whole it is unsurprising that commentators should regard the *Essais* as rather marginal to the development of sixteenth- and seventeenth-century political theory and that they should place them instead in the no-man's land of "humanism," a philosophical ideal with no clear content beyond a set of liberal sentiments, and no obvious political implications, stretching conveniently from the "Renaissance" to "modernity."[47]

Yet some at least of the principles embedded in Montaigne's Christian vision of the world had clear practical implications. One of them was the belief that only a community founded upon cooperation, understanding, and peace was truly human: no doubt experience showed that other types of association were practically viable, but they did not correspond to the way in which men should live according to their moral potential and to God's design. In one of the most famous of the *Essais* (essay 31 in Book I), the writer described a community of savages (possibly inspired by contemporary accounts of Brazil), the Cannibals, comparing it polemically to contemporary French society: the Cannibals were pronounced less barbarous than the French, since their brutal habits (such as the practice of eating their enemies) were the expression of a primitive, near-animal nature rather than the product of corruption and deliberate cruelty. The Cannibals' society was practically viable, and yet nowhere in the text does Montaigne suggest that sharing their lifestyle would be a desirable state of affairs; such a primitive community, ruled by basic needs and appetites, corresponded perhaps to an early phase in the evolution of mankind, but it was nonetheless barbarous, and remained below the level of sociability that men could achieve in virtue of their reason.[48]

Another theme in the *Essais* that links the work with the "pacifist" currents in the Christian tradition was the mistrust of violence as a means toward redressing wrongs and restoring justice. Violence, even when employed in the service of a just cause, was always wrong, both because whoever resorted to it was bound to create new abuses, and because the exposure to violence, for example during a prolonged war, had the effect of corrupting society at large, by generating brutality and indifference to suffering.[49] Moreover, as the experience of the Reformation had shown, in any situation of conflict or civil unrest, it was the lives of poor, defenseless people that were most likely to be sacrificed. Crucial to Montaigne's vision was in fact the belief that the lives of all human beings were equally valuable, regardless of their personal abilities, their culture, or their status; in particular, the lives of ordinary people were as important to society— which they sustained and made viable by means of their menial activities— as those of distinguished and superior persons.

These Christian presuppositions in Montaigne's outlook suggested that the development of friendly, cooperative relations among human beings, or, in other words, the promotion of sociability, constituted a moral obligation for all people. Humans might be naturally sociable, if only for utilitarian reasons; but, in practice, achieving a reasonable degree of consensus and solidarity in any community required a collective effort, which must be even greater in circumstances in which public trust and civil peace had been thoroughly destroyed. There were of course ways in which sociability could be promoted from above, by well-meaning rulers, on a large institutional scale: for example, by formulating agreements, by introducing better laws, and by fighting against the corruption of public institutions; at a different level, by reforming education, developing commercial relations, offering better religious instruction, and so on. In the first instance, however, sociability represented a moral obligation for the individual: each person could contribute to make society more compassionate and just, in the same way in which, in bad times, each person contributed to make it more hostile and unlivable. Montaigne did not underestimate the importance of political and legislative intervention; indeed he considered that in the aftermath of the civil war some reforms (such as the reform of the legal system) would be essential to restore order and confidence within French society. However, what really interested him, the question he placed at the center of his reflection in the *Essais*, was not how society could be improved by legislative action, but how sociability was to be built (or destroyed) from the bottom up, how it could emerge from the murky, diversified, unstable world of individual experience.

The Individual Perspective

Whether we look at the development of Montaigne's work from the perspective of its intellectual background and references, or from the angle of its emotional motivations, we end up with the same notion of what is required to satisfy the writer's aspirations: the elaboration of a distinctly individual, personal approach to the issues that are being discussed. It is the choice to speak simply and immediately for himself that makes it possible for the writer to break with academic conventions and to abandon systematic presentation in favor of a more flexible, critical type of inquiry: an experimental style of writing aptly described by the equally novel title of "*essais.*"[50] The same choice allows him to address the reader not from a position of authority, but directly and modestly, as an equal; not voicing partisan views or dogmas but giving expression to the uncertainty of his own judgment.

To some extent this project of writing as *homo pro se* was part of the classical Ciceronian tradition, still very much alive in Montaigne's time. The model was that of the private citizen or public man in (hopefully temporary) retirement, who wrote for the instruction of his family and friends: such an author would compose his work in a simple, understated style, with the aim of leaving behind him a treasure of personal memories and wise exhortations. Montaigne subscribed to the conventions of this genre in the Preface of the *Essais*, where he claimed that the aim of his writing was purely "domestic and private," his intention being that of leaving to his family and friends something to remember him by after his death.[51] Elsewhere in the text, however, he stigmatized the complacent aspects of this type of autobiographical writing, and ridiculed those ambitious public men—such as Cicero—who expected to gain glory by the idle display of "chatter and verbiage," and who manufactured seemingly private letters, artfully crafted in impeccable style, for the sole purpose of putting them into circulation.[52] The effort of speaking for and about oneself was of no interest, if it remained confined to the exhibition of conventional sentiments and elegant prose: to be worth the effort such writing must explore in depth the essence of one's thoughts and experiences.

Thus Montaigne was not satisfied with recording exemplary memories or expressing well-considered opinions, but brought to the text the full stream of his experiences, fantasies, physical sensations, whims, and emotions—the magma from which he believed human opinions took their fluid and uncertain shape. As has often been pointed out, these self-referential elements were absent from the initial drafts of the *Essais*—which were modeled upon a more traditional (and impersonal) style of historical commentary; but once they were introduced, they completely transformed the work, giving it a new feeling of vividness and variety, as the distinctive personality of the author gradually invaded and took over the text. Book and writer complemented one another: the writer gave his own living form to the book, and at the same time adjusted his personality and behavior to the image of himself he was creating on the page.[53] As Montaigne famously observed in a letter addressed to Henry III of Valois, the king having graciously expressed his appreciation for his book, he must necessarily like the author, since author and book were one and the same thing.[54]

On the whole Montaigne's contemporaries were not impressed by his efforts to create a less conventional, more spontaneous style of address. They judged the prose of the *Essais* digressive, careless, and generally lacking in style (defects enhanced by the lack of purity of the author's Gascon French). If they were ready to admire the erudition and sound judgment of the writer, they also believed he took excessive liberties with his subject (whatever that was) and pronounced the book unpolished and poorly structured.[55] Modern (and especially postmodern) commentators have reversed this verdict, finally recognizing the extreme originality and depth of Montaigne's experiment; yet to a large extent this appreciation focuses upon the *Essais* as a literary work and as an aesthetic achievement. From the vantage point of political and moral reflection, Montaigne's solitary enterprise is still regarded with suspicion: interpreters have seen his insistence upon the individual perspective as an elusive strategy, an attempt to avoid public commitment by seeking refuge within the microcosm of personal sensibility. Though it is generally acknowledged that the ambivalence and circularity that characterize the argumentation of the *Essais* belong, like the suspension of judgment, to the strategy of skeptical discourse, there is still a tendency to see these fluctuations in the prose as the marks of a capricious and contradictory intellect, constantly seeking a way out of the conclusions of its own analysis.

Montaigne's ambition to construct an independent standpoint from which to express his critical judgment is obviously central to the project of the *Essais*, but the relation between his fictional independent author and his imaginary audience remains difficult to interpret. In the text he expressed disapproval of those authors who published in the hope of gaining money and glory, in the same way in which he distanced himself from those people who were ready to sacrifice their freedom for the sake of public advancement. He also confessed that the pleasure he derived from writing was so great, that it would be worth the effort even if his book failed to attract a single reader. This fierce profession of freedom and dignified self-sufficiency did not exclude the intention of taking position in a public debate; on the contrary, the main reason why a writer must not be influenced by instrumental motives, or by the desire for public approval, was precisely that only complete honesty and independence would give true authority to his views and make them worth listening to.

As Jean Starobinski argued in his classic study of Montaigne, the themes of the world as theater, of false appearance and hypocrisy as dominant features of human society, were central to the culture of the period.[56] In the *Essais* this broad philosophical question of the relation between reality and appearance, or truth and falsity, was also articulated in the form of a specific historical judgment about the practical consequences of deception. Montaigne was convinced that one of the greatest evils associated with civil conflict was the corruption of public discourse: after decades of propaganda, people were so disgusted by the voicing of partisan views, by the constant manipulation of truth, that they did not believe any longer anything they were told. Even the laws issued during those years avoided calling crimes by their real names and invented new, "gentler" terms to describe transgressions and abuses that had become commonplace.[57]

This policy founded upon deception was self-defeating, and those princes and leaders who practiced it must know that sooner or later people would see through their lies, and lose all confidence in their authority. But meanwhile the damage done to the community was beyond measure: words were an essential component of the fabric of human society; in relations between men, speech and persuasion represented the only viable alternative to violence. Whoever connived in their corruption did in fact "betray human society," undermining the foundations of peaceful coexistence and of public trust.[58] In this context the writer could offer a distinctive contribution to the reestablishment of public confidence: by showing, within the limited scope of his own individual work, that good faith and sincerity were possible, he might do something to restore the credibility of language. Thus, against the tide of debased, deceitful discourse, the author of the *Essais* was determined to speak "by his own universal being," not "as a grammarian, poet, or jurisconsult but as Michel de Montaigne"; the expression of a personal viewpoint, divested of any technical authority, would alone prove truly universal, as the diversity of their individual voices was precisely what all human beings could recognize as common ground.[59]

It is interesting to compare Montaigne's notion of the role of the writer as independent voice with that expressed by Voltaire during the preparation of the *Dictionnaire philosophique*. Writing to Mme du Deffand in February 1760, Voltaire explained that he was engaged in "giving to myself in alphabetical order an account of all I must think about this world and possibly about the next—all of this for my own benefit, and perhaps, after my death, for the benefit of honest people," and added: "I go about my task as frankly as Montaigne did about his."[60] Though Voltaire set forth the obligatory modest reservations as to the appeal of his work ("perhaps after my death . . ."), in his case one has no doubts that his voice would hit the desired target of the crowd of "*honnêtes gens*" ready to become his audience. His public was out there, marshalled in the ranks of the republic of letters, the very embodiment of enlightened public opinion, eager to be stirred up by his words; the existence of a receptive readership justified the writer's solitary effort, ensuring that what he had to say would make a difference.

In the case of Montaigne, on the other hand, things do not seem so straightforward. In a bout of ferocious self-irony the writer claimed that he published on the same principle that ruled the practice of public hangings: they did nothing for the improvement of those who were executed, but served as a warning to possible future offenders.[61] For all the rhetorical cautions about writing only for one's family, it is clear that the *Essais*, just like Voltaire's *Dictionnaire philosophique,* were in fact intended for public circulation. If Montaigne was sincere when he claimed that he did not expect money, advancement, or fame from his writings, it is clear that the reputation he acquired through his work engaged him, with each successive revision of the *Essais*, in a dialectical relation with his readers. As Rousseau once observed when comparing himself to the author of the *Essais,* the only difference between them was that he, Jean-Jacques, wrote only for himself, while Montaigne wrote for other people.[62] Somehow, however, the people who formed Montaigne's readership do not have the same solid collective identity as Voltaire's public (or as the identity we are inclined to attribute to an enlightened eighteenth-century audience). Whom did Montaigne write for? If he did attach to the exercise of writing a distinctive moral value, if he thought he was creating, in his own way, new bonds of human friendship and understanding, who were the people he wished to involve in this virtuous verbal exchange?

We know the identity of some of the early readers of the *Essais:* the circle of Montaigne's noble patrons (including the kings of France and Navarre); distinguished intellectuals who were personally known to him (like the jurist Florimond de Raemond, the poet Pierre du Brach, Pierre Charron); foreign writers like Justus Lipsius, who entered in correspondence with him after reading his book; a young woman from Picardy called Marie de Gournay, who fell in love with the author of the *Essais* and later became his "adoptive daughter" and literary executor, as well as a writer in her own right.[63] We also know that Montaigne was struck by the fact that, once the book was in circulation, his reputation as a writer was greater abroad than in his own domestic surroundings.[64] Yet neither this known audience of notables, professional intellectuals, and learned women, nor the shadow of anonymous readers that can be conjured up by looking at the number of subsequent editions, can tell us much about Montaigne's imagined public.[65]

In the dedication to the reader that introduced the book—possibly one of the most famous texts in modern European literature—Montaigne stressed the good faith of his work, its lack of artifice and his own readiness to appear "naked" in front of his public: he described in fact his own disposition, without making any assumption about his readership, apart from the fact that, whoever they were, they were probably wasting their time.[66] When Rousseau used a similar artifice in 1760 in the Preface to the *Nouvelle Héloise*, he actually pointed at the sort of people who were likely not to like his work (wits, *dévots*, libertines, and so on).[67] Montaigne did nothing of the sort, neither indicating a privileged audience (such as Voltaire's "honest people"), nor denouncing potentially hostile critics. His negative rhetoric left in fact the question of the recipients of his work completely open.

Did he actually imagine that, by writing a new and provocative type of book, he might reach a different public from the one he would have attracted with a more conventional work? Possibly not (after all, there were not so many readers out there in 1580); he might, however, hope to make a different kind of impact upon his audience. Directness, sincerity, the reckless exposure of self, might leave the readers indifferent and even disgust them, but might jolt some of them out of their mental habits and perhaps kindle somewhere a sparkle of imaginative sympathy. The dubitative mode is important here, since Montaigne had no confidence that his strategy would succeed: to the end of his life he was unable to stop writing and yet his doubts about his work grew with each new draft and new revision. Writing was an individual act of faith, in which the writer would bare his soul in the hope of becoming the catalyst of some human response. He did not write in order to reach an audience as much as to create one, in the same way in which he had fashioned himself through his book. This was the visionary challenge of the *Essais*: that out of the ruins of a decomposed, acrimoniously divided society it might be possible to piece together the fragments of a rational human conversation.

Chapter 1

THE SPIRIT OF THE LAWS

THE NATURE of the laws—both in the sense of customary human norms and of positive, written codes—is a central theme in Montaigne's *Essais*. For a substantial part of his adult life—from the mid-1550s to 1570—the practice of the law represented Montaigne's main public activity. If during that period he developed a deeply felt revulsion for the French legal system and all it stood for, his concern with the general issue of the nature of the laws, far from fading away, continued to resurface in the subsequent drafts of his work.

The French Experience: "N'y avoir qu'une justice"

Hardly any evidence has survived about Montaigne's legal studies. He may have been a student at the universities of Paris, Toulouse, or Bordeaux (of these, Toulouse—at the time a more prestigious institution than Bordeaux—seems the most likely); alternatively, he may have studied privately, since it was common practice for aspiring magistrates (especially those who came from parliamentary families) to work in small groups under the supervision of a lawyer—an informal training that was often completed by a period of attendance at parliamentary sessions.[1] Whatever the particular context of his formation, it is perhaps significant that Montaigne should begin his career as the member of an institution that illustrated all that was dysfunctional and corrupt about the French legal system. Sometime between 1554 and 1557[2] he inherited from his uncle, Pierre Eyquem de Gaujac, the post of *conseiller* at the *cour des aides* of Périgueux, a new fiscal court created by Henry II as part of his policy of increasing the number of judicial offices that could be sold for ready cash. Unsurprisingly, the jurisdiction and competences of this new court—carved out from those of the *cour des aides* of Montpellier and of the *parlement* of Bordeaux—were ill-defined, if not altogether redundant. After a protracted dispute, made more acrimonious by the fact that the new posts had been sold on more advantageous terms than the old ones, the *cour des aides* of Périgueux was suppressed, and its members (Montaigne among them) were finally admitted into the *parlement* of Bordeaux.[3]

The greater part of Montaigne's subsequent parliamentary career was spent serving on the *cour des requêtes* (later *cour des enquêtes*), one of the four subsections of the Bordeaux parliament, which dealt mainly with private litigation: a rather tedious and uninspiring office, which made him more than familiar with the daily routine of legal administration.[4] From that position he had ample opportunity to experience the inadequacy of the existing body of French codes and legal traditions, and was able to observe the vices which characterized their interpretation and application. In the reconstruction he sketched later in the *Essais*, an unfortunate combination of Roman law and feudal custom had produced in France an aberrant result, a judicial monstrosity, which subsequent interventions on the part of the crown had only succeeded in making more incoherent and unmanageable. To begin with, France had far too many laws, as if her legislators had pursued the insane design of creating a specific law for each particular case that could conceivably present itself, not just in our world, but "in all the worlds imagined by Epicurus." Predictably, a hundred thousand laws of this kind would still be too few to legislate for "the infinite diversity of human actions"; moreover, many of these laws were obsolete or redundant, some contradicted one another, and all were expressed in a characteristically cryptic jargon, in such a way that the French language, which proved adequate for all other purposes, became obscure and unintelligible in the drafting of a simple document like a will or a contract. In short, the state of French legislation was so lamentable, that living in a lawless society would be preferable to being subjected to it.[5]

Montaigne did not take sides in the dispute that opposed the partisans of Roman law—a tradition that was particularly influential in the juridical practice of the Guyenne—and those jurists who supported French common law. He just stressed that the vertiginous accumulation of interpretations and commentaries of ancient legal documents had turned the practice of the law into a philological exercise, on which, unfortunately, the lives and properties of the subjects had come to depend. Roman legislation had at least the merit of being accessible to the Roman people: the laws were in fact inscribed on tables, on display in the public square, where anyone could read them. French law, on the other hand, was distinguished by its remarkable obscurity: people were governed by codes that were not even written in their own language, and that they could neither read nor understand without the costly assistance of specialists.[6]

The incoherence of this body of legal prescriptions was well matched by the "disorder and corruption" of the institutions responsible for their interpretation and administration.[7] Montaigne was strongly opposed to the venality that characterized the French judicial system. To begin with, he disapproved of the fact that magistrates generally expected to be remunerated for their services by the parties involved in trials: payments ranged from simple fees (*épices*), in themselves rather modest, to far more substantial benefits, such as pensions, appointments, or gratuities. More im-

portantly, he denounced the expanding business represented by the sale of
offices: though officially the French crown forbid the commerce of judicial
posts, under the reigns of Henry II and his successors the financial crisis,
brought about by the Italian campaigns and, later, by the religious wars, led
to a steady growth of this market, which the monarchy itself promoted, in
its eagerness to secure a steady supply of cash. The result was a proliferation
of offices, accompanied by paralyzing conflicts of competences, such as
those experienced by the writer in the affair of the *cour des aides* of
Périgueux. Because the conditions of sale varied with each new allocation
of posts, and the king reserved the right to "recall" certain posts and sell
them again,[8] the system did not even offer the advantage of creating a stable class of magistrates relatively independent from the crown, a positive
side effect of venality that would later be stressed by Montesquieu.[9]

In Montaigne's view, the practice of turning the law into a commodity
available only to those who could pay for it undermined any claim to impartial justice. Not only were laws generally made by idiots (*sots*), they
were also made by men who could not be just and impartial, because they
loathed equality. In France the magistracy represented a powerful caste, a
"Fourth Estate"; yet in practice only the lowest ranks of the population
were subjected to their authority and to the prescriptions of the law. The
nobility followed a code of honor of its own, which often clashed with ordinary legislation and was deemed superior to it; among the members of
the Third Estate, the rich could pay to secure a favorable treatment from
judges and tribunals, so that only the poor were exposed to the full rigor
of the law. Some peasants who had discovered, on Montaigne's own land,
the body of a man viciously attacked, would neither give him assistance,
nor report the crime, for fear of being accused of it—a fear the writer
thought fully justified; in a town nearby some "poor devils" would hang
for a crime they had not committed, because the court that had acquired
proof of their innocence did not wish to contradict the sentence of another tribunal, which had previously sentenced them to death. Everywhere justice was sacrificed to greed, to stupidity, to social privilege, and
to empty legal forms, producing as a result "condemnations . . . more
criminal than the crime."[10]

Another especially odious feature of French justice was the unnecessary
cruelty of its penal code, with its panoply of ferocious torments and executions. Far from being abandoned, these barbarous punishments had become more frequent and atrocious since the 1540s, as a consequence of
the subsequent waves of persecution against the Huguenots; in particular,
torture, which in the past had been used only episodically and exception-
ally, had become a routine practice in the investigation of heresy and of
other serious accusations.[11] Montaigne was appalled by these developments, which offended Christian conscience and violated the common

feelings of humanity, without bringing any practical advantage in the pre-
vention or repression of crimes. If the customs of those distant tribes who
ate human flesh, wore rings through their lips and noses, and sacrificed
slaughtered animals to the gods seemed savage and barbarous, how should
one qualify the behavior of those Christian magistrates who manifested
their religious zeal by inventing new appalling torments to inflict on their
victims?[12]

While Montaigne's passionate critique of French law was expressed in
especially vivid and explicit terms, with unusually radical undertones, on
the whole the writer's views on the corruption of justice were widely
shared within the milieu of the magistracy. The real question was whether
the judicial system could be reformed, and if so by what means, given that
the monarchy was hostage to its growing financial needs, and that the
courts systematically resisted all attempts to interfere with their corporate
interests.

At the outbreak of the religious wars, an ambitious plan of reform of
French institutions had been undertaken by the new chancellor, Michel
de l'Hospital. On his appointment, in June 1560, l'Hospital seemed an
unlikely candidate for ambitious and radical political initiatives. A magistrate, educated at the University of Padua, he had served for a long time
in the *parlement* of Paris (where he was a rather low-profile *conseiller* between 1538 and 1554), before moving on to a political career. A client of
the Guises, he owed his advancement to the patronage of Charles de
Guise, cardinal of Lorraine, and to the general feeling that he would be a
"safe"—that is to say a prudent and docile—appointment. Probably his
patrons did not expect that he might engage in any substantial project of
reform: yet soon he became the initiator of a wide-ranging set of measures designed to fight against the corruption of the Church, of justice,
and of public administration.[13]

These initiatives, which included a series of measures of religious toleration introduced by the Edict of Saint-Germain of January 1562 (also
known as the *édit de janvier*), were the last attempt made by the Valois
monarchy to forestall a civil war. Following the massacre of the members
of a Protestant congregation at Wassy, perpetrated by the Duke François
de Guise on the first of March, 1562, the first of the religious wars began,
making vain all efforts of legislative intervention and political compromise.
By December 1562 Montaigne and his fellow councillors at the *parlement*
of Bordeaux—who until then had deployed considerable diplomatic efforts to smooth out tensions and keep the region out of trouble—began
to raise troops for the city's military defense.[14]

In the *Essais* Montaigne paid a retrospective tribute to Michel de l'Hospital: the chancellor was one of few contemporary political figures to be
mentioned in the text, where he was described as "an able man of uncom-

mon virtue."[15] Though we have little information on Montaigne's response to the events of the early 1560s, we know that he was close to the
circle of the supporters of the chancellor and shared some of their views on
peace and reform: it is therefore reasonable to assume that the failure of
their policy had some impact upon his own hopes and expectations.[16] The
defeat of l'Hospital—who was gradually marginalized and retired from
politics in 1568—also raised the question of the credibility of his vision of
the French state as a Christian polity founded upon the preservation of
justice, and questioned the viability of the instruments of governance at
the disposal of the crown.

L' Hospital's projects of reform—which he presented in a series of significant public speeches and, later, in his writings—combined the traditional "legal" interpretation of the French constitution with an Erasmian
understanding of the phenomenon of the Reformation. The chancellor
saw the king and his magistrates as the joint custodians of God's justice,
which was embodied in the laws of the kingdom; however, he made a distinction between the role of the magistracy—which was confined to the
administration and preservation of traditional law and to current legal
practices—and that of the king, who could and should, if necessary, amend
and reform the existing legislation. In other words he endorsed the separation of the legislative function—exercised by the king with the assistance
of the Estates in a consultative capacity—from the judicial one, which was
entrusted to the *parlements*.

If the vices of the clergy and the degradation of the moral standards of
the Church had led many to embrace heretical doctrines, in the same way
the corruption of the magistracy and the perversion of justice had opened
the path to civil discontent and to rebellion. Persecution and punishment
were inappropriate as well as ineffective, responses to a phenomenon (religious dissent) that found its origins in the combined failings of Church
and State. The best strategy against heresy was the humble recognition, on
the part of all good Christians, of their share of responsibility, and their
sincere disposition to make amends, by offering a good example to those
who had left the right path. The equivalent of this strategy, in the domain
of civil administration, was the renewal of political institutions and the improvement of the morality of public officials, reforms that must develop in
parallel to the regeneration of the Church.[17]

On the whole the correction of the most blatant abuses in the administration of ecclesiastical benefits—endorsed by the Estates of Orleans in
1560—did not meet with serious opposition; the policy of tightening the
conditions of residence for the higher clergy, in order to avoid the phenomenon of absentee bishops, was also widely accepted. Though in the
past the Crown had largely exploited ecclesiastical benefits, allocating
them to laypersons (including women and minors) designated by the king,

the advantages of this particular malpractice were marginal and altogether less important than the opportunity of reasserting a stricter royal control over the Gallican Church. On this point at least the crown and its chancellor could count on the support of the *parlements*.

In contrast with these adjustments on matters of ecclesiastical administration, the reform of judicial institutions was to prove an impossibly controversial task. The chancellor's plans included such measures as the abolition of the fees paid to magistrats by the parties involved in litigation, routine checks over the financial circumstances of *conseillers* and judges to root out corruption, and the creation of a system of appeal to independent courts, as a corrective to any miscarriage of justice. Crucially, l'Hospital was determined to suppress once and for all the sale of judicial offices, reducing the number of existing posts, and abolishing those created since the death of Louis XII; by proposing the suppression of the so-called "perpetual" offices, he also rejected the principle of the irrevocability of magistrates, stressing instead the provisional nature of their mandate, and reasserting the fact that they were answerable, for their conduct, to the higher courts and ultimately to the king.

As was perhaps to be expected, the most vigorous resistance against the *ordonnances* presented by the chancellor at the Estates of Orleans (1560) and Moulins (1566) came from the judiciary itself—most prominently from the *parlement* of Paris—an indication that, on the whole, magistrates were not prepared to endorse any substantial change in their prerogatives and privileges. The chancellor's attempts to appeal to other institutions (first the Estates, subsequently a specially designated committee attached to the King's Council) were equally unsuccessful. The growing tensions between the religious communities and the beginning of the conflict helped to divert public attention away from this issue, to the general relief of all those concerned.

Predictably, after the outbreak of the first religious war, the French legal system deteriorated even further. In its anxiety to control religious dissent, the crown alternated bouts of repression against the Huguenots with halfhearted attempts at toleration. These ineffective fluctuations in religious policy, marked by a succession of royal edicts that were never enforced, accentuated one of the structural weaknesses of French law, its instability. As Montaigne observed, laws kept changing with the same speed as fashion in clothing.[18] The language of the law became so debased that the same actions would sometimes be qualified as "crimes," and sometimes described instead in "gentler" terms, for the sake of political opportunity: a situation reminiscent of the darkest periods of the Roman civil wars.[19] At a different level, the enormous damage inflicted upon the French economy and royal finances by the conflict—through the collapse of agricultural production, the dramatic rise in prices, and the steady decline of fiscal revenue—made the prospect of the abolition of corruption and venality increasingly unrealistic.

Twenty years after the beginning of the wars, in 1583, the political and social implications of the deterioration of French justice were set forth in a letter addressed by Montaigne, at the time Mayor of Bordeaux, to the king Henry III. The letter, drafted as an extensive and detailed *cahier de doléances*, described the conditions of extreme distress and destitution into which a large portion of the town population had been plunged by the wars, a phenomenon made apparent by the growing crowd of beggars, "a frantic multitude of poor people." The text identified, as the main cause of this new poverty, the unfair distribution of the burden of taxation.

The wars had considerably increased fiscal pressure, and yet this growing charge was not sustained—as the laws of the kingdom and those of reason dictated—by the richest and most prosperous citizens, with the working population contributing in a lesser measure, "the strong supporting the weak." On the contrary, it was mostly the working poor who paid, since all the wealthiest families in town enjoyed some form or other of tax exemption, by gracious concession of the crown. The list of the beneficiaries of this royal largesse was very long, and was reported in detail: it included officials of justice and their widows, financial officials, lieutenants, vice-seneschals and their subordinates, people who held posts in the two royal households of Valois and Navarre, members of the chancellery, officials in charge of the artillery, of supplies, and of military defenses; the children of presidents of parliament and of *conseillers* were also declared noble, and came to join the happy crowd of those who were exonerated from taxation with the king's blessing.

Another important cause of distress for the population denounced in the letter concerned one of the major trades in town, the sale of wine by "the sworn keepers of taverns and public houses": in the past all licences necessary for the exercise of these trades had been allocated by the town authorities free of charge, as prescribed by the law; now they were subject to exorbitant payments, in virtue of some new edicts obtained '"by circumvention and heavy pressure" (the letter did not specify who had exercised this pressures, but mentioned the interest of "certain private persons"). These new practices were clearly illegal, and could probably be challenged in a court of law, but the people who suffered from them lacked the resources necessary to obtain legal redress for the abuse. Legal expenses had in fact also increased, and where before it was sufficient to pay a single court clerk, it was now necessary to provide for two or three different officials, against the basic principle that "kings rule by justice," and that justice must be administered "gratuitously and with as little burden on the people as possible." By perpetuating the practice of fiscal privilege, and by making legal pursuits inaccessible to the poor, royal justice was thus failing in its essential task, which was "the preservation of all estates" of the kingdom.[20]

A year later, in 1584, Montaigne drafted a set of comments on a project of judicial reform, intended for Henry of Navarre. Some of his suggestions echoed the preoccupations of Michel de l'Hospital about the creation of mechanisms of control over judicial decisions: they advocated a plurality of judges at trials, and opposed the limitation of the number of lawyers. More crucially, the writer reiterated his belief that there should be "one single justice," and that consequently legal services should be free of charge and equally accessible to all, regardless of wealth and social position. It is not known how Henry of Navarre responded to these suggestions. Before he became king of France, he did express publicly views that went in the direction of Montaigne's own preoccupations. In a letter addressed to the parliament of Tours in 1590, for example, he wrote:

> Justice, when it is well and scrupulously administered, allows kings to reign happily, and preserves their subjects in the obedience they owe to their sovereign, making them live in unity, concord, and friendship. This justice is the main pillar upon which we wish to rest the foundations of our state, which could not subsist otherwise; our greatest care, besides honoring God, being that of dispensing it equally, and at all times, to our subjects, as it is our duty.[21]

However, when a major reform of the system of venality was finally undertaken in 1604, a few years after Montaigne's death, the king, together with his minister of finance Maximilien de Béthune, Duke of Sully, backed the option of stabilizing rather than abolishing the sale of offices, against the vote of a large minority of the King's Council. The disastrous financial situation of the new monarchy, after the ruinous years of the wars and the costly settlement with the Huguenots, was in itself a more than sufficient reason to justify this choice.

The 1604 reforms, largely designed by Charles Paulet de Coubéron, succeeded in bringing under control the jungle of existing offices, making the structure and allocation of posts more coherent. They also abolished a maze of contradictory regulations, which in the past had allowed the king to "recall" certain posts in order to sell them again: instead, the buyer was now granted a stable possession through the payment of a yearly fee (*paulette*).[22] The new system offered obvious advantages: it simplified the hierarchy of offices and provided the crown with a regular yearly income. Because the new mechanism of payment was financially more onerous for the buyer, the reform gradually restricted the tenure of public posts to smaller and richer social groups, thus making the French magistracy, in the long run, more exclusive, as well as more independent from royal authority. But the ideal of a public service uncontaminated by wealth, and of a justice equal for all, which had inspired Montaigne and some of his contemporaries, disappeared from sight for the centuries to come.[23]

The preservation of a reasonably equitable system for the administration of justice represented, in Montaigne's eyes, a vital political requirement: while French law, such as it was, had little to recommend itself, it was still the only barrier that stood between the French people and the arbitrary power of particular individuals and groups. Nothing could be worse than a situation in which "wickedness became legitimate, and assumed the cloak of virtue with the approval of the authorities."[24] Only a fair application of the law could guarantee that the subjects' basic entitlements were respected and that the people might enjoy a degree of safety and freedom. The alternative was an intricate system of personal bonds, founded upon the exchange of favors and threats—a type of human interaction which the writer evoked with considerable distaste: it was, for example, thanks to the protection of powerful patrons that during the wars he could live unmolested in a region controlled by Protestant troops, and continue to observe the Catholic rituals in the chapel of his house (all neighboring churches having been vandalized or closed down); this state of affairs, however fortunate for him, was still intolerable, since we should live "by right and authority, not by reward or favour."[25]

It is interesting to compare the account of the consequences of the corruption of justice outlined in the *Essais* with the approach to the same topic sketched in the *Discours de la servitude volontaire*. After decades of erudite disputes, the relation between these two texts remains uncertain and fiercely controversial. In the absence of new evidence it seems impossible to establish conclusively whether Montaigne was—as he himself claimed—entrusted by La Boétie with the manuscript of a text written by the latter before they became acquainted (possibly in the late 1540s or early 1550s); whether he edited or redrafted the text after La Boétie's death in 1563; or whether he was in fact the only and real author, as it is claimed by some scholars. The reasons why the *Discours* was not included, as apparently planned, in the body of the *Essais*, and the circumstances of the publication of parts of the text, under the title *Contr'un*, in the *Reveille-matin des françois* (a collection of anti-monarchical pamphlets) in 1574, remain also a matter of conjecture. Whatever the truth about Montaigne's role—as mere literary executor, editor, or author—there is an obvious convergence in the way in which both the *Discours* and the *Essais* associate the progressive debasement of the magistracy and the sale of offices with the transformation of the French monarchy into a despotic regime.[26]

In the *Discours* the establishment of new magistracies under Julius Caesar (generally interpreted as a reference to the reforms introduced by Henry II in 1552, which extended significantly the number of saleable offices) was described as an initiative which, rather than serving justice, offered new supports to tyranny. Far from reinforcing public service, the new posts would bring into the system a crowd of men, bound by personal obligation and dependence, who believed they could profit from the regime "*par les faveurs et soufaveurs.*" The growth beyond measure of this network of patronage was denounced by the author as an essential step toward the establishment of servitude.[27] It is important to stress this point, because in the rhetoric that characterized the anti-monarchical pamphlets of the 1570s, this attention to the issue of the modes of access to public posts seems to have disappeared altogether, to be replaced by a messianic vision of the magistracy as custodian of divine law against a godless sovereign.[28]

Montaigne was well aware of the fact that the law itself was, to a large extent, the reflex of power relations within society—a truth well illustrated by phenomena such as the strong class bias that characterized the administration of justice, or the dramatic shifts in the attitude of the French monarchy toward religious dissenters. However, when legislation was stable, reasonably transparent, and administered by non-corrupt institutions, the law acquired a degree of autonomy from power: it became the expression of social consensus, of shared prejudices and agreements, rather than a naked instrument of domination. By allowing the degradation of both the letter and the practice of the law, French society had inflicted an incalculable damage upon itself, replacing a potentially benign rule of legal codes and conventions with a brutal one of force and savagery.

The Empire of Custom

Montaigne's overall view on the origin of the norms ruling human societies was that these were the product of custom, which he described, quoting Pindar, as "queen and empress of the world."[29] In every society norms emerged at random from a diverse background of local experiences, historical circumstances, and accidental events, which led to the adoption of certain practices in preference to others. Once a set of rules was established, people became attached to them, without ever stopping to question their utility or wisdom: habit gradually transformed social conventions, which in themselves were indifferent, arbitrary, or even aberrant, into valued precepts and honored traditions. As to positive laws, they took shape as the consolidation and transcription of customary norms (either existing locally, or imported by foreign conquest), though the passing of time and the evolution of language might eventually blur their origin. Thus laws were generally rooted in the past: they reflected the mentalities, habits, and agreements of previous generations, and were frequently at odds with the present circumstances of the societies they governed.

The view that legal structures were best understood in historical perspective, and that a similar method of investigation could be applied to the study of history and of the law, was a distinctive feature of the so-called "humanist" or "civic humanist" legal tradition. In France (as in other European cultures) this historical approach had been used, on the one hand, to correct and clarify the content of Roman law, often obscured by centuries of local usage and misinterpretation; on the other, to investigate the origins and validity of customary laws, establishing their credentials as a body of national legislation. During the 1560s, the project for a new historical method applied to jurisprudence had seen a further development with the publication of seminal works such as François Baudouin's *De institutione historiae universae* (1561), Jean Bodin's *Methodus ad facilem historiarum cognitionem* (1566), and François Hotman's *Antitribonianus, sive dissertatio de studio legum* (1567). Though Montaigne may have read all of these texts, he would have been especially familiar with Bodin's *Methodus*, which he discussed, and actually borrowed from, in various sections of the *Essais*.[30]

Like critics of the juridical tradition, Bodin identified the comparative study of the law as a ground for a potential conflict between customary law and Roman law, a conflict loaded with political consequences, as his and Hotman's later works would show. But the central ambition of the *Methodus* was to prove that the study of the laws and customs of different peoples, in different historical ages, could form the basis of a general theory of legislation. Comparative historical evidence could indicate which social norms and political constitutions emerged as recurrent and stable through time, thus leading to the formulation of a system of universal right:

> Indeed the best features of universal right are hidden in history itself, if we consider that we can find there that evidence, so important for the evaluation of the laws, represented by the customs of different peoples, as well as the origins, growth, and functioning, the transformation and the aim of all public affairs, that is to say, the main object of such historical method.[31]

In order to perfect this comparative approach, the author of the *Methodus* indicated a set of criteria that should be adopted to assess the validity of historical evidence, separating objective facts from myth and legend, and discussed, from this perspective, the performance of various classical writers. The wide historical scope of Bodin's intellectual project was obviously appealing to Montaigne, as was the idea that history might provide a critical angle from which to assess judicial practices; but while he was attracted to the comparative study of the law, from the start his analysis took a different direction, away from the systematic approach developed in the *Methodus*. In the essay "Defense of Seneca and Plutarch" (II, 32), written probably around 1578, Montaigne made explicit the grounds of his disagreement with Bodin, in terms that were as appreciative of the latter's work as a whole as they were critical of its specific claims.

In the *Methodus* Bodin stigmatized some of the accounts of Spartan customs provided by Plutarch as "incredible and entirely fabulous," a judgment that Montaigne found impertinent and misguided. It was of course possible that some of the evidence related by Plutarch was simply false; but Bodin's accusation of credulity, addressed to Plutarch, betrayed the prejudices of the modern historian. Plutarch himself, "the most judicious author in the world," had rightly kept an open mind. In the Spartan example, people belonging to an ancient military culture were apparently capable of enduring great physical suffering in a manner that, to the modern French mentality, seemed so barbarous and futile, that it was disbelieved. The same cultural distance could be observed, in contemporary France, between the urban and educated elites and the peasantry: Montaigne cited the case of peasants who, during the wars, would rather suffer torture than reveal the hiding place of their scanty valuable possessions.[32]

Montaigne's critique of the notion of "objective" historical judgment may have been influenced by Cornelius Agrippa's influential work *De incertitude et vanitate scientiarum* (1530), a leading contribution to the revival of Pyrronian skepticism.[33] Yet his spirited defense of Plutarch (one of his favorite authors) was entirely his own, as was the leading intuition behind his response to Bodin: the *Methodus* assumed that a comparative study of history would bring to light the basic rules and principles common to all human societies, and thus help to identify the universal principles of legislation; however, experience showed that different cultures and communities often endorsed opposite or contradictory practices, so that, in the end, the diversity of social norms had no coherent design to reveal, nothing beyond the volatile and arbitrary nature of all human arrangements.

In the essay "Of Custom and Not Easily Changing an Accepted Law" (I, 23), the first draft of which was probably written as early as 1572, habit was described as a dominant factor shaping human behavior. Humans tended to adjust to attitudes and practices they had acquired in early infancy, or absorbed from their environment, without questioning their value. This was true not only of individuals throughout their lives, but also of entire communities over the time span of generations. Human societies perpetuated practices and rules they had inherited from their ancestors, as if these were the only possible models of behavior. The origin of these rules (as in the case of reflexes acquired in early infancy) was generally quite accidental, a unique combination of local circumstances, external influences, or particular events, although the passing of time and the loss of historical memory generally contributed to obscuring this fact.

The illustration presented in the essay of different human customs across space and time tends to emphasize the unnatural, indeed almost freakish character of many of these practices, as in the telling example of the cripple from Nantes, who, having no arms, had learned to use his feet as if they were hands. The distance of social norms from any common "natural" pattern was confirmed by the fact that different cultures endorsed contrary types of behavior, as in the case of those peoples who turned their back to those they wished to greet, rather than facing them as we do. In the subsequent additions to the text, Montaigne mobilized a considerable range of historical and ethnographical materials, accumulating with relish the examples of practices—ranging from the odd to the picturesque and the monstrous—that patently contradicted our own notions of normality and propriety: shaving only half of one's head, living in houses without doors, allowing marriages between men, circumcising women, offering one's wife and children as sexual partners to guests, eating human flesh, killing the old, and exposing infants.

The pages of the *Essais* dedicated to the variety of human customs, with their unique combination of legends, ethnological narratives, travelers' tales, and paradoxical anecdotes, are possibly among the most familiar sections of the book, those that have exercised the greatest impact upon the imagination of readers through the centuries. The crucial feature, in this exotic kaleidoscope of human practices, was precisely the absence of common patterns: the same behavior encouraged by one community would be punished as criminal by another; actions that one tribe judged exquisitely polite, their neighbors would reprobate as positively offensive. On the whole, experience failed to reveal any set of shared rules or fundamental principles, acknowledged by all nations: there was in fact no "opinion so bizarre" not to have been adopted somewhere as a public norm.[34]

Each person, and each culture, regarded their own customs as eminently "natural"; since the customs of different nations were frequently opposed or incompatible, this intimate belief of acting according to nature was clearly deceptive, unless the word "natural" was stretched to cover the totality of existing human practices; and yet it was extremely difficult for people to reflect objectively on the value of their own norms:

> The laws of conscience, which we say are born of nature, are born of custom. Each man, holding in inward veneration the opinions and the behaviour approved and accepted around him, cannot break loose from them without remorse, or apply himself to them without self-satisfaction . . . But the principal effect of the power of custom is to seize and ensnare us in such a way that it is hardly within our power to get ourselves out of its grip and return into ourselves to reflect and reason about its ordinances.[35]

Montaigne did not deny altogether the existence of a law of nature, which he associated with the primitive, near-animal condition of mankind:

occasionally, in observing the life of savage tribes or the behavior of very simple, humble people, it was possible to recapture the flavor of this pristine human state. In practice, however, mankind had developed in too many directions, too far from its primitive circumstances, to retain any substantial attachment to this original form. In some cases the exercise of looking back toward nature may be turned into a powerful critical device to expose the flaws of modern civilization: Montaigne famously resorted to this strategy in his provocative essay "Of Cannibals" (I, 31), but there the notion of nature was employed as a philosophical ideal or methodological device, not as the description of a historical reality to which mankind may return.

In the design of Creation, men were not meant to be, like beasts, passively subjected to nature: they must choose, of their own free will, which precepts and which line of conduct to follow; their ultimate guide was not nature, but reason:

> Since it has pleased God to give us some capacity for reason, so that we should not be, like the animals, slavishly subjected to the common laws, but should apply ourselves to them by judgement and voluntary liberty, we must indeed yield a little to the simple authority of Nature, but not let ourselves be carried away tyrannically by her: reason alone must guide our inclinations.[36]

Men treated nature as makers of perfume treat essential oils, adulterating the original components by the addition of so many new ingredients, that the final result was in each case unique, different not just for each human group, but for each individual.[37] The authority of the laws was not based upon their link with some or other universal principle dictated by nature: what really mattered about them was not their content as much as their form. The content may lack any intrinsic merit, while the form—their acceptance by a given community—was an essential condition of human sociability: laws were respected not because they were just, but because they were laws. That, and nothing else, was "the mystic foundation of their authority."[38]

Unlike other writers who have stressed the importance of tradition in human societies, Montaigne was inclined to describe the "empire" of custom in strongly negative terms. He explained for example that, in his capacity as magistrate, whenever he had tried to investigate the origins of some customary laws, he had been shocked and disgusted by their lack of substance, and had resented the task of enforcing rules, that clearly had such weak foundations. Traditions had nothing whatsoever to recommend them other than age; and the passing of time, rather than lending them a venerable aura of dignity, exposed their "hoary beard and wrinkles," revealing their decrepitude. Custom was not only intrinsically worthless; it also exercised an unhealthy and stultifying influence upon human beings;

its authority was that of a "violent and treacherous schoolmistress"; it crept gently into peoples' lives only to show in due course "its furious and tyrannical face," gripping them with its claws, the caring teacher suddenly transformed into a monster.[39] As a consequence, the effort of distancing oneself from the established rules, bringing matters back to "truth and reason," was an especially difficult exercise. When children manifested vicious tendencies, the wise mother or teacher would do her best to repress these, before they grew into lifelong habits. But how could one hope to correct the errors and prejudices of an entire society, to which the practice of centuries had given a settled form?[40]

If he had serious reservations about the "'tyranny" of custom, which kept human societies prisoners, as it were, of their own past, Montaigne expressed nonetheless a marked preference for continuity in laws and institutional practices over change and novelty. He justified his position by contrasting the slow sedimentation of habit and opinion on the one hand, with the sudden tearing of this connective tissue by a divisive intervention on the other. If the sedimentation may have negative effects, producing uncritical acceptance and inertia, the tearing could bring unforeseen disruption and suffering. An essential feature of established systems of rules, whatever their intrinsic merits, was their capacity to elicit sentiments of trust and solidarity within the community. The ethos of the cannibals, for example, was limited to two simple precepts, extensively celebrated in their songs: bravery at war and a warrior's love for his (several) wives. This credo may seem a little simpleminded, but it was accepted with enthusiasm by all concerned. (Christians, it was implicitly suggested, who benefited from a far superior set of precepts, were unable to find in them in the same way a source of peace and unity.)

In stable political regimes, the rule of law was not just a system of empty rituals, of obscure codes and regulations imposed on an uncritical audience; it was a rule recognized by all as fair, wise, and worthy of respect. By contrast, radical changes and reforms, however desirable, could not be enforced merely by consent and persuasion, which alone could guarantee civil peace. Any too hasty transformation of the status quo would be likely to prove the work of a militant, factious minority, ready to impose their views by intimidation and even violence upon the mass of the population. Thus sudden change would easily lead to disruption and abuses, causing in the end greater damage to the community than any faults that might originally have been present in the old system. It might also, in the end, prove quite pointless, since people were likely to relapse into their old ways as soon as they had the opportunity of doing so. For example, in the same way in which they reproduced other norms of their collective life, men considered "natural," and were inclined to reproduce, the kind of political institutions they had always known. Those raised under republican gov-

ernment thought republics were best, and those who had always lived
under a king favored a monarchical regime; should their present government be removed by some major upheaval, they would each seek to replace it by a similar one:

> Nations brought up to liberty and to ruling themselves consider any other
> form of government monstrous and contrary to nature. Those who are accus-
> tomed to monarchy do the same. And whatever easy chance fortune offers
> them to change, even when with great difficulties they have rid themselves of
> the importunity of one master, they run to supplant him with another, with
> similar difficulties, because they cannot make up their minds to hate domina-
> tion itself.[41]

It followed from these considerations that, even if one disapproved of
some features of established institutions and laws, it would be wiser on the
whole to submit to them, abiding to legality, rather than taking the law
into one's hands and stirring up civil trouble. Insubordination to the law,
even on the part of a single person or of a small minority, would inevitably
have repercussions beyond its initial scope: the complex interdependence
of human practices and relations within any political community meant
that disobedience would sooner or later unsettle the fabric of society, since
polities, like buildings, were made of different components interlocked together, in such a way that it was impossible to move one of them without
disrupting the whole structure. What a minority of people might initiate in
the belief of acting for the best, would then end up causing unforeseen
and widespread disruption.[42]

While Montaigne's response was largely dictated by the traumatic experience of the impact of the Reformation upon French society, it is easy to
see why later commentators should interpret his views an expression of
deeply ingrained conservatism, attributing to him a skeptical mistrust of
any form of change and improvement. Montaigne was well aware of the
fact that custom and laws represented a form of rule of the past over the
present, a rule that sooner or later would prove outdated and inadequate;
he was, however, unable to identify, at least within the horizon of contemporary French society, any possible agents of change other than the au-
thoritarian intervention of the sovereign or the sectarian initiative of a minority, neither of which he regarded as especially reassuring.

In classical republics, the individual who wished to propose a change in
the established laws might hope to persuade his fellow citizens, by submitting his views to the governing assembly: no doubt his initiative would be
regarded with suspicion, and severe penalties may be attached to his gesture if he failed: but at least in ancient polities there was a practice of public discussion. In France the legislative initiative belonged to the sovereign
alone: only the king could make or change laws, and it was left to his indi-

vidual responsibility and judgment to decide on a new course. In circumstances where the gap between the old conventions and the present circumstances of the nation had become too wide, such royal intervention would involve an abrupt transition, from the observance of fixed laws and practices to an arbitrary interpretation on the part of the king of what new measures the country might now need.[43]

Montaigne was prepared to admit that, in circumstances of great public unrest, the sovereign should decide to endorse change, bending to the pressure of necessity: for a ruler the policy of remaining faithful to the letter of the law, while confronting rebels who were openly violating it, meant placing oneself in a situation of great disadvantage; in such cases it was perhaps prudent to acknowledge the status quo and to accept a change in the existing legislation.[44] At the same time the writer could not help reacting to this perspective with the magistrate's instinctive distrust of any royal initiative that led to a breach of the established law. Whenever momentous decisions of this kind became arbitrary, being left to the intelligence and initiative of a single individual, the risk was great: in order to make the right choice, the person responsible would need superior judgment and ability, while in practice rulers were seldom capable of greater wisdom or possessed greater talents than ordinary people.[45] The performance of the Valois monarchs in this respect had been a dismal combination of weakness, incoherence, and ill judgment: in their handling of the religious conflict they had begun by trying to make laws do what they wished, and had ended up pretending to wish what the laws enabled them to do.[46]

The Shadow of Justice

Montaigne's interpretation of the origin and nature of the law apparently led to a paradoxical conclusion: on the one hand he argued that laws were mere conventional arrangements, of no intrinsic value, subsisting only in so far as they embodied the prejudices of a particular human group; on the other hand he claimed that laws must be respected and maintained at all cost, to preserve the community and to avoid the risk of arbitrary rule. But how far should anyone carry the observance of norms that had no greater authority than that of common prejudice? To what extent should we be prepared to sacrifice our convictions and interests on the altar of consensus and sociability? Should we, like Socrates, be prepared to die rather than break the established law, whatever that law happened to be?

In his work Montaigne gave an indirect answer to these questions through a series of practical examples. In his activity of magistrate, not only would he refuse to do anything "dishonorable" (such as tricking a suspect into making a confession by a false promise of pardon) in the service of justice; he would actually disregard the letter of the law rather than inflict a cruel punishment upon another human being, however guilty. More generally, for all his reverence for the law, he would never continue to live under laws that threatened even minimally his own life or his liberty. In other words, there were obviously circumstances in which the established conventions of society must take second place, while the imperatives of individual reason and conscience—whatever these might be—prevailed.[47]

Men needed conventional justice, because the instability of their judgment and opinions would make life in a community impossible unless they could agree upon some common rules. But this artificial justice—the only one of which they were capable—had obvious limitations: its validity was restricted in time and space, its wisdom was often dubious, and its exercise was open to errors and abuses. Precisely because it was human—Montaigne claimed, borrowing an image employed by Cicero in the *De officiis*—it was the mere reflex and shadow (*umbra et imago*) of that superior justice that was dictated by nature and, ultimately, by God:

> Justice in itself, natural and universal, is regulated otherwise and more nobly than that other, special, national justice, constrained to the need of our governments. "*We have no solid and exact image of true law and genuine justice; we use the shadow and reflections of it.*"[48]

The study of the origins and foundation of the law had carried Montaigne very far from the prevailing view that French legislation was the earthly embodiment of divine laws.[49] For him an insuperable gap separated God's justice from the justice of kings and nations. The Augustinian tradition had stressed that men's sinful nature and unruly passions prevented them from following the law of God; positive law and political authority had precisely the role of compelling them to respect those precepts they were unable to obey by themselves. Montaigne accepted the point about human imperfection, but failed to recognize the role of authority as the channel through which God's law asserted itself.

He believed that human beings had simply no access to a certain knowledge of the law of God and could never reach an agreement about its content. It was only in the inner forum of their conscience that they could experience its imperatives, by recognizing instinctively when some obvious instance of injustice, abuse, or cruelty had occurred. In such cases the laws and conventions of nations became irrelevant, when set against the evidence of blatant abuse and injustice, causing real suffering to innocent human beings.

This recognition, this inner sentiment of justice, may be episodic, and the person who experienced it may fail to act upon it; yet its existence showed that human justice operated in the shadow of a supreme justice that could never be entirely eradicated from man's conscience. It is impossible to separate in the *Essais* the shrewd anthropological dissection of the artificiality of laws, from the overpowering sense of a transcendent moral imperative. Montaigne's analysis was sustained by the tension between these two poles: on the one hand the obligation to share the prejudices of our fellow human beings; on the other the absolute autonomy of the individual conscience, guided and justified by its exclusive relation with a superior spiritual awareness.[50]

The reflection on the law, so rich and well articulated in the text of the *Essais*, was employed by the writer as a powerful critical tool in a variety of different contexts. In the first instance Montaigne drew upon his personal legal experience to mount a frontal attack against French justice, to denounce its abuses and the transformation of the law into a system of corruption and domination. His criticism was directed against the policies of the French monarchy, which multiplied venal offices, recruiting into the magistracy scores of clients and social climbers; but it targeted at the same time the magistrates themselves, who forgot their duties in their pursuit of privilege, money, and advancement. By exposing the artificial, limited value of all human conventions, he demolished at the same time the traditional view that French law was the embodiment of superior Christian principles, entrusted by God to the king and his parliaments. Through the comparison between the legislation of "civilized" and "primitive" nations, he showed how the latter could achieve levels of moral unity and solidarity unknown in a divided Christian world. At a different level, Montaigne's distinctive use of the comparative historical method that characterized humanist jurisprudence, led to subversive results, undermining all systematic approaches and discrediting the notion of a universal legislation.

While he developed these different critical perspectives, Montaigne placed the law at the center of the experience of human sociability: for all their faults and limitations, laws represented an essentially benign dimension of human interaction, one based upon trust and consent. Thus his constant defense of the rule of law throughout the decades of elaboration of the *Essais* had very different motivations from those which had guided the reforming initiatives of l'Hospital: his was not the defense of a divinely inspired Christian order, but that of a fragile earthly frontier, the borderline that separated the territory of human community and of the rule of law from a landscape devastated by war and the abuse of power.[51]

Chapter 2

IN A LEADEN CENTURY

THE DECLINE OF VIRTUE

IN THE ESSAY "Of Cato the Younger" (I, 37), written as part of the first draft of the text, probably around 1572–74, Montaigne commented upon the absence of any sense of virtue from the experience of his contemporaries, particularly if by "virtue" was meant a practical moral ideal rather than some abstract philosophical notion:

> This century in which we live, at least in our part of the world, is so leaden that not only the practice but even the idea of virtue is wanting; and it seems to be nothing else but a piece of school jargon . . . There are no more virtuous actions to be seen; those that wear virtue's appearance do not for all that have its essence; for profit, glory, fear, habit, and other such extraneous causes lead us to perform them.[1]

In the "leaden" climate of the civil wars the decline of the standards of public morality, the corruption of justice, and the escalation of partisan violence had emptied the notion of virtue of any content; virtue was constantly confused with attitudes (such as the display of military valor or the fanatical attachment to a partisan cause) that had nothing to do with it; it was also seen by many as a remote, academic ideal that no longer had a place in modern society.

Hostages to Fortune

The reflection on virtue in the *Essais* was developed from the start against the backdrop of dramatic historical events and vividly illustrated through an escalation of coups d'état, military disasters, sieges, massacres, revolts, conspiracies, and assassinations. Thus Montaigne's approach to the issue was clearly guided by broad historical preoccupations: virtue was presented both as an individual quality and as the collective property of particular nations and cultures in given historical contexts, while the issue of moral corruption appeared intimately associated with the question of the progress and decline of political societies and of human civilization on earth.

  The writer's treatment of the topic showed his familiarity with a variety of classical philosophical sources, especially Plato, Plutarch, Cato the

Younger, Cicero, and Seneca. Like many of his contemporaries, Montaigne was especially influenced by the classification of human qualities and the ranking of virtues set forth in Cicero's *De officiis,* but in the *Essais* he combined Cicero's moral and political ideals with elements derived from a variety of Christian sources. Thus his reading of the classical moral tradition was filtered through the critique of pagan philosophy outlined by Augustine in the *City of God,* and was influenced by the discussion of the same themes set forth by modern Christian writers such as Erasmus, Cornelius Agrippa, and especially Juan Luis Vives, Augustine's sixteenth-century Spanish commentator and critic.[2] Characteristically, however, Montaigne was not interested in any academic discussion of the interpretation or analytical coherence of these contributions, but used them freely to find illustrations for his arguments or to highlight relevant points.

In this eclectic collection of classical and Christian sources, it was above all the *City of God* that provided the chief inspiration and the main critical target: in his work Augustine described how the Romans had left to posterity a remarkable example of what was regarded by pagans as "virtue"— that is to say an ideal of austerity, self-sacrifice, and dedication to the republic—and had been rewarded by God with centuries of power and grandeur for their city. In the long run, however, this false pagan virtue, motivated by ambition and by the desire of glory rather than by the love of God, had revealed its intrinsic flaw, leading Rome down the path of corruption and decline to her final ruin.[3]

Reconsidering this judgment over a thousand years later, it was difficult not to be struck by the fact that the nations of Christian Europe seemed incapable of providing even that limited, imperfect form of "pagan" virtue that had distinguished the Roman republic. As Montaigne argued, whatever the limitations and errors in their doctrines, the ancients had been able to provide real, living examples of virtuous individuals and virtuous deeds. Modern wits, on the other hand, used "their ingenuity to obscure the glory of the beautiful and noble actions of antiquity," while being unable to perform any of their own.[4] Indeed the ingenious arguments they produced to denigrate the achievements of the ancients showed that they were entirely wrapped up in a set of purely scholastic notions, and were unable even to fathom the meaning of public duty and of shared moral commitment.

Naturally one would expect Christians to uphold altogether different ideals of virtuous behavior from those pursued by pagans; Christians should not seek glory and conquest, but must labor to bring about peace, justice, and charity. Yet in contemporary society—and in France in particular—the products of such superior wisdom were yet to be seen:

> Compare our morals with a Mohammedan's or a pagan's; we always fall short of them. Whereas, in view of the advantage of our religion, we should shine

with excellence at an extreme and incomparable distance, and people ought to say: "Are they so just, so charitable, so good? Then they are Christians." All other signs are common to all religions: hope, trust, events, ceremonies, penitence, martyrs. The peculiar mark of our truth should be our virtue.[5]

Sadly, nobody could possibly formulate such a judgment in relation to France, where Christians—that is to say Catholics and Protestants engaged in a sectarian war—had largely surpassed pagans and Muslims in unprecedented displays of ferocity, so that one could find nothing in ancient history more extreme than what the writer and his contemporaries were forced to witness every day.[6]

One way of accounting for this eclipse of virtue in the modern world was to endorse, with Augustine, a radically pessimistic view of the destiny of human civilization on earth: because human beings were intrinsically corrupted by sin, human societies could only progress toward a greater degree of iniquity and suffering; the fact that this should be true also of those populations who lived after, rather than before, the Revelation, was an additional proof of man's moral inadequacy. If Montaigne was ready to admit that the present circumstances of Europe seemed to confirm Augustine's pessimistic expectations, he was nevertheless reluctant to endorse the view that mankind was doomed to decadence and decline.

To begin with, he did not fully share Augustine's vision of man as fatally marked by sin and evil: though very sensitive to the reality of human imperfection, he was closer to the Franciscan tradition led by Saint Bonaventure, an intellectual current within Christianity that was characterized by a benevolent vision of human nature, by the insistence upon the emotional aspects of the religious experience, and by a militant commitment to charity.[7] Setting aside his differences from Augustine, Montaigne's problem was essentially methodological: the moral superiority of Greco-Roman polities over modern European states was a single historical instance that could not be regarded as the conclusive proof of the existence of a general trend: in fact, it was not at all clear that historical evidence, however instructive, could ever produce the kind of broad predictive results that some theorists were inclined to attribute to it.

Although Montaigne's intellectual interests, when he began writing the *Essais*, ranged across a wide variety of subjects—including poetry, philosophy, theology, and geography—history occupied a central place in the preliminary research he undertook toward the preparation of his text in the late 1560s and early 1570s. If he continued to peruse his favorite classical authors—such as Seneca, Cato, and Plutarch—his readings for that period showed a marked preference for works of modern, especially French, history. These included chronicles of the French kingdom (Gilles, Froissart, Monstrelet, Joinville), regional histories (like Jean Bouchet's *Annales d'Aquitaine*), memoirs such as those of the brothers Du Bellay, but also

Francesco Guicciardini's *La historia d'Italia* and Paolo Giovio's *Commen-tarii delle cose dei Turchi*. At the time he was obviously already familiar with the works of ancient historians such as Herodotus, Xenophon, Cae-sar, Livy, Tacitus, and Sallust, which he must have read in his youth (as he had a poor knowledge of Greek, he read Herodotus in a French and Xenophon in a Latin translation); however, the majority of the references to these authors which feature in the *Essais* did not appear in the first edi-tion of 1580, but were added to the later ones, possibly to lend substance and authority to some of the arguments.[8]

The historical orientation and engagement with contemporary sources of Montaigne's early work is apparent in what is generally identified as the first body of the *Essais*, the sections composed between 1571 and 1574—roughly the 1580 version (A text) of 94 "essays," some very short, which occupy most of Book I and the first part of Book II. The model of these early compositions was that of Plutarch's *Moralia* and Aulus Gellius's *Noctes acticae*, with the development and illustration of a single theme through a string of historical examples; works like Machiavelli's *Discorsi*, Antonio de Guevara's *Golden Epistles,* and Pedro de Mexa's *Forest of Var-ied Lessons* provided modern examples of the same genre.[9]

The favorite topics were the conduct of war, military leadership, diplo-matic relations, and the religious practices, customs, and institutions of an-cient and modern nations. Even those sections of the text that focused upon human sentiments—imagination, fear, idleness—were illustrated by historical anecdotes, in contrast with the more personal observations that characterized the later drafts. In this early version of his work Montaigne also introduced several references to contemporary French events—the siege of Rouen (which he had witnessed), the assassination of the Catholic leader François de Guise in 1563, various battles in the first and second re-ligious wars, such as Dreux, Mussidan, and Jarnac—in a manner that imi-tated the anecdotal narrative of ancient chronicles, a practice he aban-doned in the subsequent drafts.

It has often been noticed that these early chapters suffered from a lack of spontaneity: the style was somewhat derivative, the autobiographical di-mension almost absent; the writer had not yet found that relaxed, personal tone that makes of the *Essais* such a uniquely individual work. These aes-thetic shortcomings were associated with a certain intellectual hesitation, a lack of clarity about the focus of the argument, and an apparent fluctua-tion in the author's critical intentions. In several of these essays the histor-ical evidence led to ambiguous results: the same line of conduct may gen-erate victory or disaster; opposite strategies produced identical outcomes; similar circumstances may prove providential or catastrophic. In most cases judgments about failure or success could only be formulated post facto: once accidental circumstances had led to a particular outcome, this outcome would then be ascribed to a deliberate line of action or to the intentions of the agents, while it was in fact just the product of chance.[10]

Whether the subject discussed was Alexander's conquests, the Roman civil wars, or the Italian campaigns of François I, the picture that emerged from these early investigations was that of a world where Fortune ruled, where human initiatives were hostage to unforeseen accidents and to the instability of passions, where the only lesson history could teach was that no outcome could be expected with any degree of confidence. Historical knowledge was very difficult to systematize, because the evidence from the past was contradictory, and could be interpreted in different ways according to the judgment of the historian. In historical writing, as in the practice of the law, the evidence of facts would always be filtered through the interpretation of individual human agents: like magistrates, historians sat in judgment upon the past, and like judges at trials, they were bound to succumb to their own prejudices and to the limitations of their own experience.

The authority of historians, like that of jurists, aimed at establishing regularities: if laws were too few and too general, they would fail to account for particular cases; if, on the other hand, they were designed to adjust to a large variety of individual situations, they would prove far too numerous to be usefully applied, and yet still too few to cover the entire range of possible occurrences. An additional limitation of historians' interpretative skills was the restricted scope of their area of interest: what European observers regarded as the history of mankind, was in fact the history of one particular civilization, our own, and perhaps of a few others within our reach. Yet there were on earth other human populations of which Europeans knew very little, some perhaps as yet undiscovered and totally unknown to us. It was quite possible that, while Europe was torn by fratricide wars, other distant nations were living happily in peace and harmony, and perhaps those historical ages we remembered as marked by greatness and glory had proved calamitous to other peoples.[11]

In the essay "Of Presumption" (II, 17), Montaigne made explicit his reservations about the usage of history in his only direct comment upon Machiavelli's work: in the *Discorsi* Machiavelli's arguments were "solid enough for the subject": yet his work had become an easy target of criticism, and, unsurprisingly, those who attacked it exposed themselves to be similarly criticized. In this kind of discussion there was always scope for "answers, rejoinders, replications, triplications, quadruplications," because such reasoning had no other basis than experience, while the diversity of events offered an infinity of examples of every kind.[12]

On the whole, Montaigne found more convincing the methodological approach set forth by Francesco Guicciardini. In *La historia d'Italia* (1567), as in his *Ricordi* (1576), the Italian writer denounced the limited predictive value of the exempla taken from ancient history, insisting instead upon the diversity (*differenza*) that characterized real historical contexts and events, making everyone of them distinctive and unique. In the face of such diversity it was important to adopt an intellectual strategy of discretion (*discrezione*): not exactly a suspension of judgment in the Pyrronian sense, but something practically quite similar to it, that is to say a prudent avoidance or postponement of conclusions, based upon the capacity to look beyond the appearance of things and to recognize differences (*discriminare*).[13]

In a similar spirit the *Essais* would describe the evolution of human history as an intricate, opaque process, involving a multiplicity of causes and open to all hazards. Only past events and local, short-term effects could be analyzed with some accuracy, while the shape of broad, long-term developments generally defied human ingenuity. The questioning of ancient and modern historiography convinced Montaigne that, if much could be learned from history, it would still be impossible to predict with any degree of accuracy the consequences of given political or military undertakings, or to assess the viability of particular regimes, simply by applying broad general principles. Human groups and communities were similar to living organisms, which could not be understood simply by taking them apart, and analyzing or comparing their different components; like people, polities were unique in their makeup, and proved fairly unpredictable in their responses to a prolonged crisis.

The theory of a steady decline of civilization, like any broad hypothesis about human history, stood on shaky methodological grounds: it was too general and farfetched, and could never be confirmed by experience. Moreover, in addition to these methodological considerations, there was another crucial reason for keeping an open mind about the prospects of mankind: for the Christian, assuming that mankind was doomed to ruin meant claiming a kind of knowledge to which men, in their finite nature, could never aspire; God alone could see through the appearance of historical events and penetrate their ultimate implications; for their part, men could only set their trust in His infinite goodness and mercy. Thus setting one's hope in the future and believing in the possibility, however remote, of moral recovery was both a logical necessity and a moral obligation.[14]

False Virtues: Military Valor

If he found contemporary circumstances deeply distressing, Montaigne came to see the crisis of French society as a passing phase: a "condition" that had specific causes in the recent and less recent history of France, and from which the nation, for all its appearance of being terminally ill, would eventually recover. Montaigne's favorite targets in explaining the origins of this diseased condition were the corruption of public institutions, the uncontrolled spreading of patronage, the inadequate education and poor administrative skills of the aristocracy, the oppression of the laboring poor, and the debasement of Christian religion to popular superstition. In discussing these factors of decadence, the *Essais* focused in particular upon some false notions regarding virtue, influential fallacies that had come to dominate public discourse and popular opinion, contributing to the disintegration of the community and to the decline of public morality. The first of these fallacies was the identification of virtue with military valor, that is to say with physical courage and the ability to fight.

Following a line of argument originally set forth by Erasmus, Montaigne suggested that this reduction of virtue to valor in combat had its origins in the progressive militarization of European society, a process that had probably begun at the time of the fall of the Roman empire, and had steadily developed through the centuries, finally culminating in the mass violence and atrocities of the religious wars. In France, more particularly, the feudal aristocracy had adopted an increasingly military profile, neglecting all civil and administrative skills, and restricting the education of young noblemen to the training for combat.

Because of this military disposition of the nobility, who were convinced that their honor and dignity depended on their ability to fight, the ideal of virtue had become identified in people's minds with physical courage and with a readiness to kill and to be killed. This modern confusion between military valor and virtue led back to a philosophical topos that had been extensively discussed by both classical and Christian writers, namely the relation between virtue and glory. The desire for glory led individuals to perform heroic, self-sacrificing actions: but such gestures, motivated by ambition—as was typically the case with military exploits—could not be described as truly virtuous, since virtue must find its own reward in the awareness of acting well, not in other people's admiration or praise. The only true glory came from goodness and belonged to God alone:

> God, who is himself all fullness and the acme of all perfection, cannot grow and increase within; but his name may grow and increase by the blessing and praise we give to his external works. Which praise, since we cannot incorporate it in him, inasmuch as he can have no accession of good, we attribute to his name, which is the part outside him which is nearest him. That is why it is to God alone that glory and honor belong. And there is nothing so remote from reason as for us to go in quest of it for ourselves.[15]

In the *De officiis* Cicero used the distinction between virtue and glory to argue that civil magistracies were more conducive to virtue than, and therefore superior to, military ones. If military deeds were of course necessary in the service of the republic, those who performed them were generally inclined to do so in the pursuit of personal glory and success, rather than for the sake of the common good. The temptation was just too strong, since military success could confer to a citizen a degree of fame and power, which it would be much harder to obtain by dealing with ordinary administration in time of peace. The greater merit of serving the republic in a civic, rather than in a military, capacity was precisely the fact that, as a civilian, one had far less visibility: one was therefore more likely to be motivated by a genuine sense of duty than by personal ambition.[16] In the *Essais* Montaigne echoed this Ciceronian theme in his discussions of the personality and career of Julius Caesar (a historical character with whom he entertained an intense love-hate relationship): a man naturally possessed of all the greatest qualities, but driven by immoderate ambition, Caesar had sacrificed everything to his own military success and personal glory, to the extent of destroying the free institutions "of the most powerful and flourishing republic that the world would ever see."[17]

Unlike virtue, which was not dependent on recognition, fame was largely the product of circumstances and of chance. In war, most particularly, valor was not always rewarded, and many splendid, heroic actions were regularly ignored, or fell into oblivion since "making certain actions seen and known was purely the work of Fortune." Even those heroes of antiquity who filled our imagination with admiration and envy were probably only a small, random selection of a much greater number of distinguished individuals whose names and deeds had failed to be recorded by some Homer or Virgil, and were therefore unknown to posterity. In the modern world the religious wars were a good illustration of this phenomenon, since of the many who had died, only a negligible number would be remembered by future generations; indeed it was not even certain that the whole experience of these wars, so momentous for those who happened to live through them, would leave a significant mark on the future memory of mankind: soon perhaps the names of leaders and battles, just like the bodies of the many who had perished, would lie buried forever.[18]

If the glory acquired through military deeds proved ephemeral, the damage caused to public morality by the spreading of military values and culture was unfortunately a lasting one. When the Romans first initiated the practice of staging gladiators' fights, their aim was to offer to Roman citizens (who sooner or later would be called to serve in the army) some instructive examples "in valour and contempt for dangers and death." Originally gladiators were prisoners and slaves, and their death in combat was treated by the Romans in the same spirit in which the moderns would regard the use of the bodies of executed criminals for anatomical experiences: as a practice which was in itself distasteful, but potentially useful to society.

Yet gradually the whole exercise got out of hand: circus fights became a popular entertainment for the Roman population at large, and delighted many who had no need to learn combat techniques (for they would never be called to fight), but simply took a perverse pleasure in the display of violence. Gladiators themselves were no longer slaves, but professionals, free citizens from all social classes, and even women, who chose to fight for the sake of money and fame.[19] A proof that this popular taste for bloody sports had not died out was that, as late as 1559, a king of France (Henry II) had been fatally wounded while taking part in a tournament.[20] The presence, in modern Europe, of entire armies of mercenaries, ready to fight in the civil wars not because they were in any way implicated in these disputes, but for gain, was a belated heritage of this corruption of the military spirit.[21]

This familiarity with violence and killing, and the readiness to risk one's life for money, had all sorts of negative consequences for society at large: people became fatalistic, careless of danger, indifferent to the sufferings of others as well as to their own, insensitive to cruelty. Describing the atrocious executions of religious dissenters, for example, Montaigne found remarkable not only the ferocity of the tormentors, but perhaps even more, the endurance of some of the victims; the sight of common people, who went without fear or complaint to the gallows, showed how anybody was capable of dying with the dignity of Socrates, but was also indicative of a collective loss of the sense of self-preservation:

> How many low-born people do we see led to death—and not a simple death, but mingled with shame and sometimes with grievous torments—bringing to it such assurance, some through stubbornness, others through natural simplicity, that we see no change from their ordinary manner: settling their domestic affairs, commending themselves to their friends, singing, preaching and keeping up a conversation with the people; sometimes even joking and drinking to their friends, yielding in nothing to Socrates . . . Any opinion is strong enough to make people espouse it at the price of life.[22]

A less dramatic, yet in Montaigne's eyes equally serious indication of the perversion of current mentality was the tolerance that parents and educators displayed when confronted with precocious exploits of cruelty on the part of children (torturing animals, bullying younger children, servants, or cripples): all dangerous signs of moral deviance, which were generally treated with indulgence and even amusement, when they should have been promptly and severely repressed.[23] As well as encouraging cruelty, this culture of violence rendered people essentially incapable of settling any civil or political conflicts without resorting to intimidation and aggression, by the peaceful means of discussion, negotiation, and compromise. Thus the aristocratic practice of dueling, which, though barbarous, had at least a limited scope, was now replaced by an escalation of vengeance and retaliation that implicated entire families and clans, and transformed single combats into battles.[24]

Possibly the most significant fallacy associated with this culture of violence was the belief that valor was an aristocratic quality, indeed the aristocratic quality par excellence. For centuries the French nobility had founded their identity upon this military self-image: convinced that they possessed a natural entitlement to protect their prestige through the use of force, they had in fact created a special code of honor, which they followed against the prescriptions of ordinary law. Thus instead of employing their military skill to uphold and defend the laws of the realm, they used it for the purpose of transgressing them.[25] But if the aristocracy regarded military valor as their exclusive prerogative, the experience of the civil wars had proved just the reverse: people of all social conditions—such as "merchants, village justices, and artisans"—were as capable of fighting and as knowledgeable in the martial arts as any member of the high nobility; in fact, as Erasmus had already pointed out, the ideal soldier was someone who was physically strong, poorly educated, and possibly rather stupid. Not only did military valor prove a most ordinary quality, it was also very easy to transmit: practically any physically able individual could learn to kill and to be killed, and turning men into violent thugs required far less time and effort than teaching them a useful trade.[26]

False Virtues: The Useful and the Honest

Together with the confusion of virtue and valor, another widespread contemporary fallacy was the belief that virtue—in the basic sense of "honesty," "moral righteousness"—no longer had a place in modern society and public life. This view manifested itself in various forms and ramifications: it began with the classical *raison d'état* claim that the sovereign was authorized to violate the precepts of morality in order to preserve the safety of the realm in times of crisis; it escalated into the conviction that anyone was entitled to a similar exemption from the rules of ordinary decency, when acting in the service of a supposedly just cause (such as the defense of what he regarded as the true faith); it finally turned into the crasser, commonplace belief that the useful must be preferred to the honest, that honesty represented an obstacle in private as in public undertakings, and that, like individuals in the pursuit of their interest, communities would be better off without it.

Montaigne admitted that the astonishing resilience of the French polity—which seemed to survive in spite of the appalling deterioration of its public morality—might lend some credit to the argument that virtue was indeed superfluous to the preservation of states. A state could be rotten to the core and yet remain afloat: witness the example of Rome, surviving by centuries the decline of her old republican virtues. Communities, like organisms attacked by some infection, often possessed hidden resources that allowed them to resist the poisonous effects of corruption: this, however, was only an indication of the strength of their inner structure, not a proof of the fact that vice exercised a beneficial influence.

Once again Montaigne mobilized his skeptical approach to historical prediction to denounce the current preference for the useful over the honest, and to undermine the credibility of those utilitarian conceptions of morality that focused upon the consequences, rather than the intentions, of an individual's actions. If it was true that virtuous conduct would not guarantee the success of any undertaking, it was not clear, on the ground of historical experience, that vicious actions (performed for example in the service of a party or for the preservation of the state) would prove necessarily advantageous. The instability of human emotions, the continuous change of circumstances, and the presence of a high level of risk meant that the possible impact of one's actions, especially in a complex political or strategic setting, would be very difficult to calculate.

If it was possible to find several examples of immoral and cruel actions proving beneficial to those who committed them, there were at least as many cases in which similar strategies misfired, so that, quite often, calculated betrayals and crimes turned against those who had committed them. Though one generally expected certain standard responses from people, anybody could act out of character, and sometimes men would go against their apparent interest, for reasons that were neither obvious nor rational. As to the impact of certain individual actions and initiatives upon political regimes, experience was even less helpful, as the factors involved were too complex and intricate to be assessed from the outside with any degree of accuracy.

Montaigne's discussion of the relation between the useful and the honest—developed in particular in Book III of the *Essais*—rested upon the premise that the distinction between public and private morality, implicit in current *raison d'état* arguments, had no real substance. All collective actions were ultimately the product of individual choices and carried an individual responsibility: it was true of broad popular movements, as it was true of the acts of regimes and institutions; even the indifference and inertia often displayed by the mass of the population (including the writer himself) in the face of the abuses committed by a minority were a form of complicity that carried a degree of personal responsibility:

> The corruption of the age is produced by the individual contribution of each one of us; some contribute treachery, others injustice, irreligion, tyranny,

avarice, cruelty, in accordance with their greater power; the weaker ones bring stupidity, vanity, idleness, and I am one of them.[27]

Men justified their evildoings by ascribing them to the service of the state or of some public cause, but in the end what suffered was their personal moral integrity and their reputation. In this respect the position of leaders and sovereigns was not different from that of ordinary people: what they risked by acting badly was a loss of the confidence others placed in them. No doubt the position of rulers was an especially difficult one, given the weight of their responsibility and the complexity of the situations they had to address: to those who had the care of government, the conflict between utility and honesty would often seem insoluble, and the temptation to break the rules would be, accordingly, very strong, especially in situations where much was at stake.

When confronted with a difficult moral dilemma, the prince may choose to bend to necessity, therefore deviating from his ordinary duties and from his faith. But this choice was by no means inevitable or obligatory; no one could blame him, if he should choose instead to remain faithful to his own principles:

> We cannot do everything. Do what we will, we must often commit the protection of our vessel, as to a sheet anchor, to the guidance of Heaven. For what juster necessity is he [the prince] reserving himself? What is less possible for him to do than what he cannot do except at the expense of his faith and his honor, things that perhaps should be dearer to him than his own safety, yes, and even than the safety of his people? When with folded arms he simply calls God to his aid, may he not hope that the divine goodness is not such as to refuse the favor of its extraordinary hand to a hand pure and just?[28]

The argument about the greater responsibility of princes cut both ways: precisely because they were responsible for others, rulers needed to act well, offering to their people an example of virtue. As public attention was constantly focused upon the high and mighty, and registered down to the most insignificant of their gestures, a wicked or base action committed by one of them, even in the interest of the state, would have a far greater impact upon public imagination than a similar one performed by an ordinary individual; similarly, a noble, generous action performed by a prince would have a major influence, and by his gesture he might set a virtuous trend others would be encouraged to imitate.

A king could hardly persuade his subjects to be tolerant and forgiving while himself offering examples of cruelty and revenge; he could hardly enjoy their confidence when he was observed practicing deceit and breaking his word. As to the suggestion that the sovereign might get away with the simple appearance of virtue, as opposed to its substance, Montaigne thought (again like Guicciardini in his analysis of *riputazione*) that this was just not good enough: sincerity was the very essence of virtue, and no durable bond of trust between a sovereign and his subjects could be built upon a lie that, sooner or later, would be unmasked. A ruler must place himself on a footing of moral equality with his subjects, proving his good faith, rather than engaging in a cynical manipulation of their opinion.

Montaigne's criticism of the logic of reason of state raises the question of his response to Machiavelli's work, an issue on which there is very little consensus among scholars: in fact, commentators have read Montaigne alternately as a follower and as an opponent of Machiavelli, and seem to disagree about the precise extent of the possible "borrowings" from the Florentine writer in the *Essais*. If the text of the *Essais* contains only two, rather anodyne references to Machiavelli's writings (one to the *Discorsi*, the other to the *Arte della guerra*), it is quite clear that Montaigne had a close knowledge of the whole of his oeuvre; he was also familiar with the debate that developed around it, though apparently he was not interested in joining the anti-Machiavellian crusade that united Huguenot and Catholic writers in the aftermath of the Saint Bartholomew's Day Massacre.[29]

There were in fact obvious analogies between the bleak vision of modern European society outlined by Montaigne in the *Essais*, and the one set forth half a century earlier by Machiavelli: the two writers had in common a skeptical, disenchanted understanding of political power and human motivations, a strong awareness of the role of chance in human affairs, and a profound admiration for the achievements of classical antiquity. Yet the analogies stopped at a rather superficial level, confined as they were to a set of common intellectual references and to some broad methodological insights. In particular, Machiavelli's influential redefinition of virtue was cast as the revival of classical republican values, with an insistence upon military and patriotic commitment, and the independence from foreign rule; Montaigne, on the other hand, pursued an emphatically unheroic, modern ideal of "ordinary" virtue, based upon the experience of common people in running their daily lives, where peace, security, and the satisfaction of material needs were the most relevant considerations. The writers were also separated by their different attitudes to Christian values, to which Montaigne, unlike Machiavelli, clearly subscribed; thus, if they produced equally powerful visions of the same dismal reality, their respective imaginative worlds had little in common.

All considered, the emphasis placed by some commentators upon the relation between Montaigne and Machiavelli seems mainly the product of modern intellectual preoccupations: as is often the case, we assume that the works of two major, near contemporary thinkers must be bound by some special critical relation. Yet Montaigne apparently read Machiavelli essentially as an inspiring historian of the Roman republic, rather than as a political theorist: his criticism of the doctrines of reason of state and of "utilitarian" attitudes to the exercise of power did not specifically address Machiavelli's own work, but denounced a broader and more diffuse contemporary mentality.

Ordinary Virtues

Like most of the classical sources it drew upon, the text of the *Essais* was not always consistent in the use of the term "virtue," which sometimes indicated a single general concept, and sometimes referred to the specific human qualities associated with it. In the essay "Of the Most Excellent of Men" (II, 36), Montaigne praised Epaminondas, claiming that he was superior to other great figures of the past because of his "conscience," the capacity to exercise one's moral judgment by distinguishing right from wrong: this was in fact the only quality that truly mattered, and it outweighed all others.[30] Elsewhere in the text the writer referred occasionally to one or other of the qualities traditionally associated with virtue, such as goodness, wisdom, justice, liberality, compassion, trust, and sincerity; but the essential attribute of the virtuous man was "innocence," the absence of moral blame, and this condition depended on the intention that guided the action, not on any properties of the agent (for example, a man capable of generosity or courage, who acted for the wrong motives, was not strictly speaking virtuous).[31]

As to the term "honest" (*honnête*), Montaigne employed it—together with other adjectives such as *bon, digne,* and *juste*—to signify moral probity, following the standard usage of *honestus* in classical Latin sources. On the other hand, the use of the word "honesty" (*honnesté*) to indicate simplicity of style appeared occasionally in the *Essais* in the opposition between sincere (honest) expression and scholastic artifice, but it did not carry the connotation of elegant sociability and aristocratic refinement, which it eventually acquired in seventeeth-century French literature.[32]

Not all people were virtuous in the same way: there were different paths to a good, blameless life, in accordance with the individual nature of human beings and with the circumstances in which each person was placed. Moreover the degree of moral effort required from each person in order to be good would very much depend on one's natural disposition: some people would find it very easy to refrain from certain vices, for which they felt a spontaneous abhorrence, while others would have to exercise a strenuous control over their own instincts to achieve the same result. The writer, for example, not being inclined by nature to strong impulses, did not consider that he had any special merit in refraining from violent or excessive actions, of which he was simply incapable. On the other hand, an individual prone by nature to violent passions would have to struggle to repress them, and deserved praise if he succeeded.[33]

The relation between intellectual and physical factors was also relevant: for example, a stupid man might perform some brave and heroic deed simply because he was unable to assess the risks involved; certain virtues, such as chastity, temperance, and sobriety, would prove easier to exercise for someone whose physical powers were somewhat diminished from illness or old age; states of mental exaltation or derangement would also enable some to endure hardship and sufferings beyond the capacity of normal persons. Finally, there were purely accidental circumstances that led some people to see their virtue put to the test, while others went through life without ever finding themselves in a similarly crucial position. Thus individuals were often praised for deeds that required no particular merit on their part, and even for actions that deserved blame.[34]

It is often difficult to distinguish, in Montaigne's moral arguments, the specific input of the classical philosophical traditions that influenced him, separating stoic, epicurean, skeptic, and cynic components, as well as their Christian reformulations: scholars have argued at length, for example, over the relative importance of stoic and epicurean "phases" in Montaigne's thought. Assessing which of these traditions carried the greatest weight is not, however, a very instructive exercise: out of this tangled philosophical heritage, there were essentially a few major themes that Montaigne was anxious to bring forward, recasting the original classical arguments to suit the context of contemporary debates.[35]

One of these themes was the preference for moderate sentiments, and the rejection of traditional heroic notions of virtue. Some ancient philosophers claimed that it was possible to talk of virtue only in the presence of a tension or struggle. Men who were naturally good might be innocent, but should not be called virtuous: nobody, for example, would describe God as "virtuous," since for Him being good would entail no effort. Montaigne acknowledged that this position was justified to some extent, but was reluctant to subscribe to the idea that virtue must be associated with suffering and intensity of emotion. Comparing the death of Cato with that of Socrates, he asked whether the moral exaltation, indeed, the voluptuous pleasure that Cato allegedly felt when ripping out his own entrails, was necessarily superior to the calm serenity displayed by Socrates when drinking the poison. His answer was a negative one: if Cato's death was more "dramatic," Socrates' was more "beautiful," since it revealed the harmony and peace of his spirit.[36]

The variety of human sensibilities and circumstances meant of course that it was impossible for human beings to judge the true moral value of individual actions (only God could do that). Yet in so far as one had to express a preference for the kind of virtuous behavior that would be most beneficial to society, Montaigne felt an obvious distrust of any excessive or strenuously heroic display of virtue, whether coming from some hero of antiquity or from a Christian saint; in fact he admitted that he could not readily associate some extreme examples of religious zeal, or certain rigorous ascetic practices, with the true spirit of Christianity.[37] Human beings should be capable of virtue not only in exceptional circumstances, but during the whole of their lives, in order to perform with conscience and dignity the duties of their everyday existence. Being able to live a perfectly ordinary life in a peaceful and honorable manner, without failing in the exercise of such simple virtues as honesty, sincerity, and kindness, was the most remarkable of human achievements:

> To win through a breach, to conduct an embassy, to govern a people, these are dazzling actions. To scold, to laugh, to sell, to pay, to love, to hate, and to deal pleasantly and justly with our household and with ourselves, not to let ourselves go, not to be false to ourselves, that is a rarer matter, more difficult and less noticeable.[38]

An important corollary of this preference for ordinary virtues was the belief that men could not be expected to prove equally happy and good regardless of the external conditions of their existence. The ideal of indifference to the world and self-sufficiency—which allowed the wise man to retain his integrity and equanimity whatever his circumstances—was central to stoic morality and occupied a similarly prominent place in Christian literature; yet Montaigne regarded it as very uninspiring, at least as far as ordinary people were concerned. Exceptional individuals may be able to focus entirely upon their inner life, but normal persons were inevitably affected by distressing experiences such as physical pain, need, or the suffering of people close to them. Thus one's moral attitude was not, as a rule, impervious to the material circumstances of one's life, to one's entourage and environment.

In the essay "Of the Inequality between Us" (I, 42) Montaigne addressed the classical theme of the contrast between real moral worth and false appearances. In complex, stratified societies such as modern France, men were not valued for their natural qualities and abilities, but were judged instead by their rank, their wealth, their clothing, and the other trappings of their status. Human beings were naturally equal, and the great distance that social conventions created between them was not founded upon any real worth, upon the properties of the "naked" creature, but on accidental factors such as birth, fortune, success, or popularity. As a result of this distorted perception of merit, men had lost all sense of dignity and independence; they had become "stupid, base, servile, unstable," and totally dependent on others for recognition and self-respect.[39]

This insecurity, which led modern men to seek constantly the judgment and approval of other people, meant that their moral performance would be deeply affected by their social status and by the current prejudices attached to it. For example, it was generally acknowledged by moralists that social privilege could become a serious obstacle in the pursuit of virtue: since the people of rank had much to lose, it would be very hard for them to endure with fortitude the loss of their advantages through misfortune and death. Moreover, their social status would deprive them of that sincere criticism which alone could forge human character, while the enjoyment of power would expose them to the corrupting influence of ambition.[40]

However, if wealth and power represented obvious obstacles in the pursuit of virtue, poverty did not seem to Montaigne a guarantee of moral excellence. A long tradition in both pagan and Christian moral teaching claimed that humble, simple people were generally more capable of virtue than the rich and mighty. This belief was justified by a variety of considerations: humble people were more virtuous because they lived in closer contact with basic natural realities, and were readier to obey nature's commands, for example by accepting with resignation suffering and death; a life of toil and need left little scope for those intellectual musings which tormented the idle and the educated; it also offered limited opportunities for vice and self-indulgence. In the Christian version, the ignorance and simplicity of the poor, together with the hardships they endured, brought them closer to God: to them in particular was promised salvation and a privileged place in the afterlife.

If he was prepared to accept that the life of humble people brought them closer to basic natural responses, Montaigne believed that a condition of need and material deprivation, far from making people virtuous, may encourage them to behave badly, for example by breaking the law in order to obtain, through theft or violence, those basic necessities they could not acquire by other means. This reaction was quite understandable and justified, since a man who was dying from hunger or cold was beyond the reach of civil law, and could not consider himself bound by it. If being virtuous meant living justly under the law, then the very poor could not afford virtue. When the Cannibals visited Rouen and observed the contrast between rich and poor inhabitants of the town, they failed to understand how those who were starving in the streets could refrain from attacking their rich neighbors:

> . . . they had noticed that there were among us men full and gorged with all sorts of good things, and that their other halves were beggars at their door, emaciated with hunger and poverty; and they thought it strange that these needy halves could endure such an injustice, and did not take the others by the throat, or set fire to their houses.[41]

In a similar spirit, Montaigne described his conversation, at Armagnac, with "*le Larron*," a former beggar who had become a notorious local brigand: after discussing with him the moral implications of taking other people's property, the writer confirmed that the *Larron* regarded theft as a dishonest deed, and deeply disliked practicing it, though unfortunately not as much as he disliked being poor.[42] Saints may live by choice in conditions of extreme poverty and hardship, turning their physical sufferings into moral assets: this however was no accessible path to salvation for ordinary people, who must have their basic material needs satisfied before the spiritual ones could be taken into consideration.

The "Étage Moyen"

What emerged from Montaigne's discussion of privilege and poverty was that the exercise of virtue would prove easier for those people—like the writer himself—who belonged to the *étage moyen*, the middling rank. Such people did not suffer from need and humiliations, nor were they driven by the ambition to rise in society, but were contented with their present condition; they were not exposed to those temptations that threaten the very poor or the very rich, and could achieve that moderation and equanimity which were essential to lead a good life. Above all, members of the middling ranks enjoyed the vital benefit of independence. Unlike the poor, they did not need to serve or to be the recipients of charity; unlike those who competed for social advancement, they did not need to enter in relations of patronage with those richer and more powerful than themselves, and were not compelled to pursue a career as courtiers, seeking the favor of kings.

This ideal of independence was vividly and proudly expressed in the last known letter that Montaigne addressed to Henry of Navarre, in September 1590, apparently in reply to the king's offer of some compensation for the expenses the writer had incurred in his service:

> Sire, may it please Your Majesty to do me the favor of believing that I will never begrudge my purse on the occasions for which I would not want to spare my life. I have never received any gift whatsoever from the liberality of kings, any more than I have asked it or deserved it; and I have received no payment for the steps I have taken in their service, of which Your Majesty has had partial knowledge. What I have done for your predecessors I will do still more willingly for you. I am, Sire, as rich as I wish to be.[43]

People of this standing in life could generally rely on their own resources; or, if they needed some service performed for them, they could simply pay for it, rather than entering into onerous bonds of obligation, regulated by honor and patronage. Their only dependence would be on the rules of civil association and on the law. All relations of domination and dependence were incompatible with virtue, since they distorted people's moral attitudes by placing considerations of honor and allegiance before the law, and by depriving them of the freedom to live as they choose:

> I have a distaste of mastery, both active and passive. Otanes, one of the seven who had some right to the throne of Persia, took a course that I would gladly have taken. He abandoned to his competitors his chances of attaining it either by election or by lot, provided that he and his family might live in that empire free of all subjection and mastery save that of the ancient laws, and have every freedom that would not be prejudicial to these, balking at either commanding or being commanded.[44]

Once again, in tracing the portrait of the honest man as someone who lived in modest independence without seeking wealth or favor, Montaigne echoed classical ideas about the virtuous life. But in the *Essais* the ancient notion of independence acquired a new substance: the ideal of the wise man keeping his distance from the undignified competition of those seeking favor evolved into the vision of an entire community of independent agents, living freely under the law, a peaceful society held together by the civil bonds of economic exchanges and by legal agreements.[45] Unlike other models of sociability that would take shape within French culture in later decades, the moral ideal evoked in the *Essais* was not reserved for persons of distinction, philosophers, or intellectuals forming a kind of select society within society, but was meant to be "popular" in the sense that it must be accessible, both in theory and practice, to the average member of the community.

In practice the project of following the common path in the pursuit of virtue meant promoting those qualities which could assist people in the performance of their daily duties, in the ordinary circumstances of their lives, rather than focusing upon the accomplishment of glorious deeds. Thus the human qualities that must be valued and encouraged, were those accessible to the large majority of members of a society. Some may object that this choice would lower the level of moral discourse: should the moral philosopher really address himself to manual laborers and artisans? Doing so would certainly force him to simplify his language and to adjust his rhetoric to less exalted standards; and yet in everyday life one was actually dealing most of the time with such humble persons. Possibly interacting with them was not as intellectually rewarding as conversing with poets and philosophers: but unless it was possible for all the members of a community to share a common language and common values, the whole notion of virtue within human society was meaningless.

In the essay "Of Physiognomy" (III, 12) this theme was illustrated

through the example of Socrates, who was described as a Christ-like figure, a spiritual master capable of making his soul move with the natural
motion of common people:

> His mouth is full of nothing but carters, joiners, cobblers and masons. His are
> inductions and smiles drawn from the commonest and best-known actions of
> men; everyone understands him.[46]

What was advisable for moral philosophers—that they must be able to
talk and act in tune with popular sentiment—was even more crucial for
political leaders and sovereigns. Unfortunately, rulers were generally disabled in the exercise of virtue, in the first instance (if they were born to the
highest rank), by their education, and then by their elevated position. Not
only would they acquire early in life all the vices associated with high social status: pride, ambition, selfishness, indifference toward people of lower
condition; they would also suffer from lack of discipline, self-criticism, and
any opportunities to compete with others on a footing of equality. These
disadvantages of education would then be accentuated by the corrupting
exercise of power and by the flattery to which they were constantly
exposed.

Mastery, the power of dominion over others, inevitably undermined the
quality of human relations; a ruler would always be to some extent at odds
with the interests of his subjects and would see things from a perspective
that was quite different from that of the common man. However, in so far
as the natural qualities of a leader or ruler were not entirely crushed by his
public persona, these qualities would be the same of those one would find
desirable in any human being. The highest moral achievement a king
could hope for was to experience the same difficulties and oppositions
normally encountered by ordinary people in the course of their lives.[47]

Montaigne's insistence on the priority of ordinary virtues has often been
interpreted as a choice to favor private over public values: following an established philosophical stereotype, in corrupt and troubled times the wise
man must preserve his integrity and independence by withdrawing into
the safe haven of his own domestic concerns. Yet the discussion outlined
in the *Essais* pointed well beyond this traditional stoic posture, suggesting
at the same time a radical redefinition of the relations between private individuals and political power. If the domain of politics often appeared as an
alien, separate sphere, the reason was that this domain, far from being
public, represented the exclusive field of action of minorities bent on promoting their own particular interests or on pursuing a sectarian cause.

In contrast with this appropriation of the *res publica* on the part of particular groups, the stability of political societies could not be secured without recognizing the needs and expectations of the larger community of
common people: such needs could not be systematically sacrificed or ig-

nored without creating a dangerously divided and unstable polity. Thus the project of restoring virtue in modern society was inseparable from the necessity of finding a common ground and common language accessible to the community at large: if this failed, virtue would indeed remain in people's minds as a nostalgic dream or a pious ideal with no relevance to contemporary circumstances.[48]

The discussion outlined in the *Essais* suggested that the eclipse of virtue in French society had long-term causes, upon which the religious conflict had acted as a catalyst, bringing out with dramatic force the devastating effects of the erosion of public ethos over centuries of oppression and corruption. Montaigne apparently believed that the acute crisis of the civil war, with morality at its lowest ebb, was just a passing phase, from which French society would eventually recover. But he was also convinced that that recovery could never take the form of a return to the past: the aristocratic and heroic ideals of virtue inherited from antiquity and from the feudal tradition were unsuited to the circumstances of modern European society, which must face up to the broader social and political implications of Christian universalism.

Chapter 3

FREEDOM OF CONSCIENCE

THE POLITICS OF TOLERATION

THE ESSAY "Of Freedom of Conscience" (II, 19) occupies a special place within the *Essais*, and not just in the sense that it is strategically—some claim even symbolically—set at the center of the text, in the middle of Book II.[1] Although the issue of religious dissent and toleration was a recurrent theme in his work, this is the place where Montaigne addressed the subject more fully and systematically. In contrast with the usual practice of presenting a variety of historical examples, the entire essay was constructed around a single historical figure, the Roman emperor Julian, known as "the Apostate" for his attempt to restore paganism in the empire. If the choice of title is intriguing (the phrase "freedom of conscience" does not in fact appear anywhere within the essay itself), the vindication of Julian was developed in an unusually bold and provocative style, turning this traditional enemy of Christianity into a classical hero and a great tragic figure.

The date of the essay also significant: the first draft was written around 1578, in the aftermath of the proclamation of the Edict of Beaulieu in May 1576, the first serious attempt made by the French monarchy to revert to a policy of religious compromise, after the calamitous events of the Saint Bartholomew's Day Massacre. In the early months of 1576, the youngest of the Valois princes and heir apparent to the crown, the Duke of Alençon, taking advantage of a moment of military weakness and considerable financial difficulty of the monarchy, formed an alliance with the Protestant princes, against his own brother Henry III. The result was a temporary peace agreement (known as *paix de Monsieur*), settled on terms generally advantageous to the Huguenots; the agreement was completed by an edict of toleration, issued at Beaulieu on the 6th of May, 1576, which anticipated in its main provisions both the Edict of Nantes of 1598, and the legislation adopted in 1787 by the declining Bourbon monarchy to acknowledge the civil rights of the Protestant minority.[2]

A Divided State: The Early Debate on Toleration (1561–62)

Sixteen years before Montaigne wrote his essay on freedom of conscience, the viability of a policy of religious toleration had been extensively discussed in response to the Edict of Saint Germain (generally known as the *édit de janvier*) issued by Chancellor Michel de l'Hospital in January 1562, in what soon proved to be the last attempt made by the French crown to prevent the impending war. Like the chancellor's other initiatives aiming at the reform of French institutions, the *édit de janvier* saw the light in circumstances that appeared initially favorable to a new political course. Between 1560 and 1561, a series of royal decrees had already marked a change in the policy of repression of heresy pursued until then by the Valois monarchs. In particular the Edict of Romorantin (May 1560) had restored the legal competence in matters of heresy to the ecclesiastical courts—which could not resort to torture or inflict death penalties—dissolving the special court attached to the *parlement* of Paris (the infamous "*Chambre ardente*") created by Henry II in 1547 to prosecute religious dissenters. The Edict of Saint-Germain of July 1561 had proclaimed a general amnesty (the first of a long series) for all those accused of heresy and related crimes. The *édit de janvier* completed these measures of clemency with a settlement that allowed Protestants to practice their religion without being molested, provided their worship took place in private spaces and outside the precincts of the towns.[3]

The conditions dictated by the edict were in fact quite restrictive: Protestants had to vacate all the buildings previously used for Catholic worship that they had previously occupied, and refrain from any act of vandalism such as the destruction of images or reliquaries; they must inform the king's officials of the schedule of meetings and prayers and allow them to be present if they wished; they were also bound to observe the current legislation ("*garder les lois politiques*") that regulated public holidays, processions, and other ceremonies of the Catholic Church. In exchange, the king committed himself to punish anyone who interfered with or disrupted Protestant worship. Even so, the measures adopted were sufficiently "liberal" to require an additional royal declaration concerning the interpretation of the edict, which was issued on 14 February 1562, stating:

> we never intended or intend by this edict to approve the existence of two religions in this kingdom, but only one, that of the Holy Church.[4]

A variety of circumstances had contributed to this change of policy: the death of the king Francis II after only a year of reign, and the minority of his successor Charles IX, had considerably weakened the monarchy, forcing the Regent, the queen dowager Catherine de Médicis, to seek an equilibrium between the influence of the Catholic clan of the Guises and the Protestant affinity of the Bourbon-Condés. The appointment of Antoine of Bourbon, king of Navarre, to the governorship of Guyenne and Poitou in 1559, and then, in 1560, to the position of "lieutenant general" (commander in chief of the king's army), was part of this design of broadening allegiances. The Regent herself, possibly influenced by her Florentine background, and in contrast with her deceased husband, seems to have been personally favorable to a policy of religious compromise.[5] But the most decisive factor of all was the fact that the presence of the Huguenots on French territory, and their influence over a part of the great nobility, especially in the South, had become too significant to be kept in check through repressive measures by a diminished and shaky royal authority.

Like all later documents of the same kind, the edict assumed that the division between Catholics and Protestants was a temporary state of affairs, a phase of uncertainty and confusion (possibly a divine punishment for the sins of the Church), which God, in His mercy, would sooner or later bring to an end. Some believed that the conflict would be resolved by the return of the heretics to the true church; for others the prospect was the creation of a new, ecumenical Christian church, built upon those features which were common to both confessions (such as baptism, the belief in salvation, and the observance of the Commandments). In any case the legislation regulating religious dissent should be regarded as an interim, a set of temporary measures designed to cope with exceptional circumstances; its final purpose was not the establishment of a bi-confessional state, but the achievement of *concordia*, civil peace among dissenting Christians.

With the new edict l'Hospital took the view that it was not within the competence of secular power to settle issues that were essentially doctrinal and that depended on the beliefs and sentiments of the religious communities and their leaders. In particular, it was inappropriate for the king to employ the repressive force of the state to eradicate heresy: at best the monarchy could give its contribution from the outside, promoting initiatives such as the convocation of a council of the Christian churches of France, in order to attempt, at a national level, that reconciliation which the Council of Trent had failed to achieve on a wider scale.

A few months before the proclamation of the edict, in September 1561, representatives of the two churches had been summoned at Poissy, in the presence of the king and the assembled court, for a *colloque* of prayer and discussion of the controversial issues that divided them (the term initially employed of *concile national* was abandoned, for fear of a negative reaction on the part of the Roman authorities). In spite of the considerable pomp and publicity lavished on this event, the discussions with the Protestant delegation, led by Théodore de Bèze, failed to reach any kind of agreement, and could only confirm that the breach between Catholics and Huguenots was beyond repair; however, by shifting the responsibility to an ecclesiastical assembly and to the religious communities, the monarchy signified its intention to step aside.[6]

When arguing in favor of this new course, the chancellor made appeal to the traditional Christian arguments against the practice of persecution and forced conversion. Resorting to punishment, even death, against heretics was contrary to the Christian sentiments of charity and forgiveness: patience, humility, wise doctrines, and exemplary works were the only weapons suitable to be employed for the salvation of those who had fallen into error. Moreover, the imposition of faith on the part of the magistrate was a self-defeating exercise, since faith was, by definition, a spontaneous disposition of the soul, which could not be simply willed into existence, nor imposed by the law.

In addition to the Christian principles and sentiments expressed by the chancellor, some of the supporters of the new legislation offered more prosaic considerations of expediency: persecution had a negative impact upon popular opinion, because the sacrifice of people ready to die a horrible death for their faith convinced the impressionable public of the validity of their beliefs. Besides, repression often missed its target: many of those who were tried and executed for heresy were too ignorant to have any real understanding of the dogmatic issues at stake, even less of their implications; they followed their masters or social superiors out of deference, or from a mistaken sense of loyalty, and frequently became the victims of unscrupulous demagogues, who manipulated them for their own political purposes (all arguments that Montaigne would also endorse).[7]

Yet the most cogent practical argument against persecution was the dismaying awareness that the number of those who had converted to the new faith had became far too large to allow either their removal to another country or their physical elimination. Earlier on, when the spreading of heresy had just begun, such drastic solutions might have been feasible; but now such a significant mass of people, with solid roots in various regions of France, fully armed, would not submit to repression without resisting their persecutors. The project of forcing them into exile was equally unrealistic, since the loss of the economic resources represented by the Protestant population could not be sustained without causing the ruin of the entire nation.

The central argument underlying the edict was that the preservation of civil peace at all cost was an absolute priority, since only by keeping peace could the monarch justify his authority. If the king failed to provide safety and ensure the concord of his subjects, his power was void, and disobedience was the inevitable consequence. In a pamphlet entitled *Discours sur la pacification des troubles,* signed by some unnamed "*Grand personnage*" (probably emanating from l'Hospital's entourage, if not written by the chancellor himself), the climate of "disorder" and "barbarism" prevailing in France was imputed to a growing sense of fear.

A justified fear for their lives, and fear alone, had led the Huguenots to rebel: once their safety was assured, they would have no motive for resisting the king's authority. The chancellor's policy toward religious dissent was thus built around the distinction between heresy and sedition: the king need not concern himself with religious dissent, but only with acts of disobedience and insubordination; in the eyes of the monarch there were no Catholics or Huguenots, but only loyal subjects and rebels. As l'Hospital explained in his speech pronounced at Saint-Germain on the 3rd of January, 1562:

> The King does not wish you to discuss which opinion is best, since the question here is not *de constitutenda religione*, but *de constitutenda respublica*: and many can be *cives* without being Christians: even those who have been excommunicated do not cease thereby to be citizens. And it is quite possible to live in peace with those who hold different opinions.[8]

Unfortunately, in the context of the 1560s, this clear articulation of the distinction between citizenship and religious affiliation could not be translated into policy, nor put into practice, without running into a maze of legal ambiguities. The obvious criterion for establishing which actions did constitute sedition, and which were the legitimate expression of religious faith, was their conformity to the laws of the realm: but since French law dictated extensively in matters of worship, the distinction between actions that could be regarded as legitimate or indifferent, and actions that were illegal, became blurred.

Wherever local communities fought over the control of religious buildings, disputed the expenses for their upkeep, contested the protocol of public holidays, weddings and funerals—that is to say, in the great majority of controversial cases—private worship and general policing became hopelessly entangled. The confusion was increased by the fact that, at a local level, both the judiciary (the local *parlements* and the other related courts) and the executive (the king's lieutenant and his officials in the region) had jurisdiction over matters of public order and could command the intervention of public force: naturally each institution regarded itself as better suited to handle the sensitive matter of religious dissent, and their directives were often in conflict with one another.

Moreover, French magistrates and public officials were required to deal with religious affairs and to perform acts of religious significance (like formulating oaths or prayers) as part of their public duties. In 1562, for example, the *parlement* of Bordeaux required from its members a public oath of allegiance to the Catholic faith: this old practice, which existed in the statutes but had been ignored for decades, suddenly acquired great importance. Montaigne had no difficulty in complying with the request (on 12 June 1562 he presented himself in front of the *parlement* of Paris *"pour être reçu à faire profession de foi"*); but he was well aware of the fact that others had been put in an impossible position. In the *Essais* he described his embarrassment in learning, years later, that one of his fellow councillors had been prepared to conceal his religious affiliation, rather than resigning his post: a behavior that he judged feeble and cowardly, but still indicative of a state of "indigestible conflict" that had been created within the courts.[9]

In fact magistrates were accused by both sides of adjudicating cases taking into account the religious affiliation of the parties concerned. How could judges, who had taken an oath of fidelity to the Catholic Church, rule impartially in those cases where Catholic and Protestant interests were opposed? Why should Protestants submit to the judgment of tribunals that might be biased against them? What was the legal position of Catholic subjects in those regions where a local *seigneur* had converted to the new religion and imposed it on his vassals? Who could arbitrate whenever mixed marriages or conversions led to family disputes over property and inheritance? In the absence of independent authorities and of clear procedures of arbitration, the list of dubious or contested cases was potentially unlimited; if, at a local level, solutions of compromise were often successfully found, these hardly added up to a coherent policy.

Two publications, both emanating from parliamentary milieus, and both written by moderate Catholics, illustrate the difficulties raised by the edict. The first was a pamphlet, published in 1561 under the title *Exhortation aux Princes et Seigneurs du Conseil Privé du Roi*, written by Estienne Pasquier, at the time *avocat au barreau* at the *parlement* of Paris (the text appeared without the author's signature, but carried his recognizable initials).[10] A personal friend of Montaigne, Pasquier was destined to a long and successful political career as chancellor of France under Henry III and Henry IV. The *Exhortation* defended the view that it was possible to enforce a policy of religious concord, acknowledging bi-confessionalism, without any negative consequences for royal authority, and without any alteration in the scope of government (*police*).

Disorder and unrest were not caused by the permissiveness of legislation, but by the partiality of magistrates; it was not the law itself that was at fault, but those who failed to apply it properly. A magistrate or public official who sided with one or other confession was abusing his position, since instead of enforcing the king's justice, he was favoring the seditious activities of one faction, using his own religious faith as a pretext to justify conspiracy and intrigue. Only by maintaining a rigorous neutrality might the civil authorities hope to preserve peace. It was by proving to be above the parties involved that the king could impose his will, "holding his naked sword in the middle, without inclining it on one or the other side, except to strike whoever should initiate tumults and revolts."[11]

Pasquier rejected the suggestion that, by proving tolerant, the king would encourage the Huguenots to increase their demands; on the contrary, he argued that, like all good subjects, the Protestants accepted the principle that the sovereign must punish rebellion and criminal disobedience. What had alienated their fidelity to the crown was the king's determination to force their conscience, and to interfere with their most intimate beliefs. By showing respect for their faith, the monarch would immediately regain their trust and secure their loyalty.

When he stressed that the king and his officials must remain impartial between religious factions, Pasquier did not of course mean that France should become a non-confessional state, a notion that would have been unthinkable in that particular context. Like l'Hospital, Pasquier believed that the monarchy should promote a broader, more ecumenical understanding of the Christian faith, one that might be acceptable to both Catholics and Protestants, while their differences remained unresolved. This result could be achieved by setting aside controversial dogmatic issues, focusing instead upon those beliefs and practices that were accepted by all good Christians of both confessions. This common Christian heritage should be more than sufficient to ensure that the subjects of the king would "fear God" and therefore submit to the sovereign's authority and obey his laws.

In contrast with Pasquier's spirited defense, the government's new policy came under severe scrutiny in a report drafted for the *parlement* of Bordeaux (probably toward the end of 1561 or early in 1562) by one of its *conseillers*: this text, known as *Mémoire sur la pacification des troubles*, has been attributed to a young magistrate from Sarlat, Estienne de La Boétie, Montaigne's colleague and intimate friend. During the months of September and October 1561 La Boétie had accompanied Charles de Coucys, sire of Burie, lieutenant of the king of Navarre in the Guyenne, in a tour of inspection of the region of Agen, where various incidents between Catholics and Huguenots (especially acts of vandalism or contested occupations of religious buildings) had been reported to the authorities. Burie's instructions were to work out some kind of agreement between the two religious communities that might satisfy at the same time the directives of the chancellor and the suspicions toward the new religious policy manifested by the *parlement*.

Although a large ultra-Catholic constituency, both within the parliament of Bordeaux and among the local nobility, demanded harsher measures against the Huguenots, the situation of the region, very close to the areas controlled by the Protestants, and under the governorship of the king of Navarre, called instead for a strategy of prudence and compromise. The mission was apparently successful in reaching a settlement between the two parties, thanks in particular to the initiative of allocating to the Huguenots the use of some religious buildings—a measure that went beyond the directives of the edict. However, on his return, La Boétie expressed a series of reservations, which would soon be confirmed by the rapid breaking down of the agreements; if he was a personal admirer of the chancellor (in the posthumous edition of La Boétie's works, Montaigne dedicated his late friend's Latin poetry to l'Hospital), the young magistrate remained unconvinced of the efficacy of his religious policy.[12]

The central argument set forth in the *Mémoire* was that the acceptance of two religious confessions within the kingdom would inevitably lead to a "duplication of police," that is to say to the division of France in two separate sub-states. Such policy would inevitably "break the union of the body of this monarchy and divide the king's subjects in two separate groups." In support of his claim the author stressed that the religious conflict was characterized by the lack of an attainable object: in appearance the parties fought over a particular issue, such as the possession of a building, or the right to perform some ceremony; but as soon as this demand was satisfied, the pressure shifted to a new request. This dynamics, which kept the conflict alive in spite of repeated concessions and compromises, could be understood, if one considered that the real object of the struggle, the affirmation of the true faith against a rival, supposedly erring sect, was a global one, and did not admit any partial solutions:

> "But they will live more peacefully knowing that the king has allowed everyone to live according to his doctrine." Those who think this are wrong . . . It is a vain fantasy, and truly a dream, to hope for concord and friendship between those who have so recently become opposed and divided over this dispute, so that each side regards the other as infidel and idolatrous.[13]

Thus the author gave voice to the frustration experienced by those who attempted to defuse the conflict and to prevent a civil war. On the whole French public institutions, not least the *parlements*, had plenty of experience in negotiating conflicts: mediation was one of their main functions, and they generally performed it very effectively. Yet the sort of confrontations they were used to had a finite object: in disputes over taxes, competence, privilege, or status it was generally possible to find a middle ground; the dispute could be settled more or less durably and advantageously, but some solution was always within reach. Here, however, the real object was elusive, and the price demanded—in the last instance France itself—could not be extracted without the destruction of the other party.

In particular the *Mémoire* claimed that the king could not, as it was demanded by some, remain *super partes* in a conflict of religion. In so far as the king was a professed Catholic, he could not be truly impartial toward those subjects who, in his eyes, had fallen into heresy, nor remain indifferent to their errors. As a sovereign, his concern was naturally for the peace of the kingdom: but as a Christian, he was bound "by his conscience and his honor" to guide his subjects on the path to salvation. A conduct of "dissimulation," in which the king should conceal his beliefs for reasons of political opportunity, would undermine his credibility and ultimately lose him the trust of his people. The often cited example of the emperor of Germany and of the Augsburg *interim* of 1555, as well as the customary references to the Roman and Ottoman empires, were ill-chosen and did not apply to the French case. The ruler of an empire, who governed alien nations, with different customs and traditions, rather than his own "natural people," was not morally obliged to impose religious uniformity—a task which in any case would prove beyond his powers. The status of the king of France was different, because he ruled over his own "natural" subjects, of whom he was "fully and absolutely master and lord." There was, in other words, a direct relation between the form of rule and the sovereign's spiritual obligations; in particular, the sovereignty of a particular nation imposed stricter obligations than a wider imperial dominion.

The report also argued that the position of the king would be politically easier if, rather than trying to keep his distance between two competing confessions, he were to create a new church, imposing by a single stroke (*tout à un coup*) the same doctrine and rituals equally to all his subjects. This new national church (apparently modeled on the Anglican experience, though the text did not discuss the English example) should be directly subjected to the king, who would control the ecclesiastical hierarchy as well as church revenues; the king should choose bishops of proved fidelity; the *dîme* should be paid directly to the crown, who would then provide, out of it, what was necessary to keep the French clergy in suitable style. The new church should engage in a revision of rituals, prayers, and sacramental practices, so as to reconcile Protestant and Catholic sensibilities. The author assumed that only a small minority of believers understood the dogmatic issues at stake, while the large majority would be satisfied with some adjustments to the exterior aspects of worship, and would be prepared to endorse whatever interpretation the authorities chose to provide for them; this is why it would be advisable to avoid any inquisition into people's beliefs, confining the intervention of magistrates to the punishment of acts of insubordination and vandalism.

As to the various historical examples of religious coexistence, it was claimed that, as a rule, toleration proved easier between alien religions than between contiguous ones. One reason was that there was little scope for dogmatic disputes between, say, Christians and pagans; but a more important reason was that a tolerated religious minority (like the Jews in Rome, or the Christian subjects of the Ottoman empire) would form a self-contained community, with no political claims toward the state that tolerated their presence. The problem with French Protestants was that they belonged fully and prominently to the body of the nation, and could not simply be excluded from it, or live within an enclave like some alien tribe. The solution envisaged by the edict, of allowing Protestant worship within private places, while forbidding it in public spaces and buildings, would create an asymmetry that could not be sustained in the long run.[14]

The report clearly suggested that what was really happening in France, as a result of the permissive compromise made by the monarchy, was the formation of a separate Protestant state within the state. This claim was probably less farfetched than it may sound, if one considers that, already in 1562, the Protestant communities of the Languedoc and of the Guyenne had established a hierarchy of independent authorities responsible for all aspects of collective life—not only religious activities but also the administration of justice, the collection of taxes, and military defense.[15] The provisions of the edict led toward a state of affairs that would inevitably result in the division of French national territory in two separate principalities, or in a federation as in the German case. The *Mémoire* stressed the dangerous international consequences of such a fragmentation, which might open the path to foreign intervention and ultimately cause the decline of France as a great European power.

Both these pamphlets represented, in different ways, the opinions of a minority. Pasquier's terse defense of the chancellor's policy went against the sentiments that prevailed equally in the *parlement* of Paris and in the provincial parliaments, where the large majority of *conseillers* were hostile to any concessions made to the Huguenots. In fact, l'Hospital's difficult relations with judicial institutions, and especially with the *parlement* of Paris, of which he had been a member, were an important factor in the failure of his policy of toleration as much as in the defeat of his other initiatives of reform.

If La Boétie's reservations about the new policy were shared by many, as was his vision of a Gallican Church, placed directly under royal control, his suggestion of creating a "new" religion and of "adjusting" sacraments and rituals to suit the sensibilities of both confessions would have shocked Catholics and Protestants alike. In any case, the solution he proposed to the religious conflict, which combined Gallican loyalties with the classical republican ideal of a civic religion, had no place in the strongly polarized religious debate of the time; by 1562 it was probably already too late to risk the royal "coup" that the writer was advocating, and the opportunity for the French state to regain effective control over ecclesiastical practices and institutions would not present itself again until 1789.

There is little retrospective evidence to tell us what Montaigne himself thought, at the time, of his friend's assessment of the crisis.[16] He certainly shared La Boétie's belief that very few people did in fact understand the doctrinal issues that divided Catholics and Protestants; but unlike his friend, he was convinced that appearances (gestures and symbols) formed an essential part of people's religious experience, more important perhaps than dogmatic truths; this attachment to the exterior dimension of worship was of course an indication of the imperfect grasp that the majority of human beings had over spiritual matters, but it remained nevertheless crucial to their rapport with the divinity.[17]

Thus in the *Essais*, he criticized the project of "correcting" Catholic dogmas and practices to make them more acceptable to Protestants, describing it as an imprudent, and probably useless, exercise; he also expressed the view that, if the Christian religion was reduced to the scale of a national church, it would inevitably be exposed to all sorts of political pressures and changes: witness the case of England, where the nation had kept changing religion following the personal preference of her different sovereigns.[18] It is unsurprising, in the circumstances, that the *Mémoire* should be left unpublished on its author's death in 1563 (it is not even clear that it was ever submitted to the *parlement* of Bordeaux), and that Montaigne should decide against including it in the posthumous edition of La Boétie's works he edited in 1571, in the tense political climate that preceded the Saint Bartholomew's Day Massacre.

If they expressed minority views, destined to remain unheeded at the time, the *Exhortation* and the *Mémoire* set forth in very clear terms the options open to the French crown if it was to pursue a peaceful solution to the conflict. They denounced the ruinous inefficacy of repression and war, but also the considerable practical difficulties that a policy of toleration would inevitably encounter, and in particular the impossibility of enforcing such a policy without the active (and impartial) cooperation of the courts. On the whole the debate raised by the *édit de janvier* fixed the points around which all subsequent discussions of religious toleration would continue to revolve: the notion of an *interim* solution in preference to any permanent settlement; the vague expectation of a national council or some other ecumenical initiative to smooth over religious differences; the difficulty involved in the project of "tolerating" Protestants as a minority with diminished civil and political rights;[19] the stern rejection of any solution to the crisis that might involve the transformation of the French kingdom into a confederation of separate states.

An Ungodly War: From Beaulieu to Blois

In many respects the peace settlement precariously established at the time of the Edict of Beaulieu can be regarded as an overdetermined result. After Charles IX' s death in 1574, the new king, Henry III, on his return to France following his disappointing experience as king of Poland, was confronted with a volatile political situation marked by a series of conspiracies at the French court and by tangled international intrigues, all centered around his younger brother and heir, the Duke of Alençon. Henry of Navarre—a virtual prisoner at the court since the Saint Bartholomew's Day Massacre—gave a vivid rendering of the prevailing atmosphere during those months when he related to a correspondent:

> We are ready nearly all the time to cut each other's throat; we go around wearing daggers and coats of mail, sometimes even a light cuirass under the cloak.[20]

By the early months of 1576 Henry III was also facing a concerted military mobilization on the part of the Huguenots: the prince of Condé, having secured substantial support from the Elector Palatinate Frederick III, was ready to cross the Rhine with German and Swiss troops, while Navarre, having finally made his escape from the court, regained the Béarn and resumed his leadership of the Protestants in the south of France. When Alençon—who had also fled from the court—announced his decision to join forces with the Protestant princes, the king had no choice but to negotiate terms. The fact that Alençon was next in the line of succession to the crown lent considerable political weight to his move: for the first time the division of France into Catholic and Protestant principalities (following the German model of the Augsburg *interim*) appeared as an impending outcome of the conflict, an outcome that the leaders on both sides were determined to avoid at all cost.[21]

The Edict of Beaulieu of 6 May 1576 satisfied most of the Protestants' requests, extending to a considerable degree the concessions made to the Huguenots before the Saint Bartholomew's Day Massacre by the *édit de janvier* in 1562, and by that of Amboise in 1563. While in those edicts Protestant worship was allowed only outside urban areas, and on the lands of Protestant *seigneurs* with the right of high justice, it was now permitted anywhere in the towns and across the country, wherever a Huguenot community was in existence; if necessary, where there was a shortage of adequate buildings, the construction of new temples was also permitted. The only area that remained out of bounds was Paris, but there too the Protestant-free zone was reduced from ten to two *ligues* around the capital. Protestants were also allocated reserved areas for burial, while provisions to permit and regulate mixed marriages and the marriage of priests were introduced.

Public officials were no longer required to make a public profession of fidelity to the Catholic Church, and a neutral, non-confessional formula was to be adopted for public oaths at trials. Prudently, the edict did not include, on the other hand, the measure advocated by the Huguenots, of outlawing non-Christian religions.[22] As in the previous edicts of toleration, Beaulieu imposed a complete oblivion (*oubliance*) of past offences, and offered a general amnesty for all crimes associated with the conduct of the war (criminal acts committed outside military operations, by individual initiative, were supposedly excluded from the amnesty). Abjurations obtained under duress were declared invalid (though in fact they would be automatically invalid in terms of the canon law): following the massacre both Condé and Navarre had been forced to abjure, and had subsequently denounced the circumstances of their forced conversion, returning to the reformed faith. Though no sanctions were proclaimed against the authors of the Saint Bartholomew's Day Massacre (an unlikely initiative given the personal participation of Henry III in the killings) for the first time since 1572 the massacre was described as "disorder and excess," and all celebrations of the event, such as those promoted by Charles IX during his reign, were forbidden. The murdered Admiral Coligny was rehabilitated and his inheritance restored to his family.[23]

A crucial measure introduced by the edict was the institution of bipartisan courts (*chambres mi-parties*) attached to the eight *parlements*, tribunals composed of equal numbers of Catholic and Protestant magistrates, which were entrusted with the arbitration of all controversial matters connected with the application of the edict and with confessional coexistence. After 1576 these courts were subjected to various changes, and were repeatedly reformed, suspended, or abolished by a series of ephemeral legislative measures. The Edict of Nantes retained three of them (at Toulouse, Grenoble, and Bordeaux), plus the so-called *chambre de l'édit*, attached to the *parlement* of Paris, which included only a minority of Protestant councillors: though incoherently organized these courts were to prove essential to the enforcement of religious coexistence during Henry IV's reign.[24]

In addition to these general provisions, Alençon obtained the title of duke of Anjou (Henry III had been duke of Anjou before becoming king), adding considerable lands and revenues to his other entitlements. For their part the Protestant princes were confirmed in the tenure of the *gouvernements* to which they had hereditary claims: Condé in Picardy and Navarre in Guyenne, as well as their Catholic ally Montmorency-Damville in Languedoc. The Huguenots also gained eight fortified towns (*villes de sécurité*) instead of the four allocated by previous agreements, plus some financial settlements, which did not figure in the official documents, to sustain the defense of these cities in the eventuality of a Catholic assault: another concession that would be renewed in a set of secret clauses by the Edict of Nantes.

One of the requests repeatedly set forth by the Protestants had been the convocation of a meeting of the Estates, to address the catastrophic administrative and financial situation created by the civil war. This time the request was accepted, and the Estates were duly summoned at Blois in December 1576. Meanwhile, however, the concessions made by the king to the Huguenots had set off a popular mobilization of the so-called Catholic League (the *Saincte Union*) determined to prevent the enforcement of religious toleration and to continue the struggle against heresy; the movement began in Picardy (the *gouvernement* assigned to Condé) and rapidly extended to other regions. The king himself, on the strength of this new wave of popular support, rapidly shifted his strategy from reconciliation to war.[25]

For the nobility of Guyenne and the authorities of Bordeaux—as ever, torn between their Catholic allegiances and their traditional ties to the king of Navarre—the situation must have been very tense. Navarre himself related in his correspondence how, on his way to Cognac to meet Henry III and the Duke of Alençon in October 1576, he was met by a delegation of the *jurade* (the town council) of Bordeaux, led by the president of the *parlement,* Lagebaston (a moderate who, in 1572, had attempted to prevent the execution some three hundred Protestants in custody in the city); the delegation begged him to avoid making an entrance into the town, since his presence might be interpreted as the prelude to an occupation, causing panic and disturbances among the population. The fact that Navarre agreed with reasonably good grace to change his itinerary suggests that the fears of the local *notables* were probably well founded.[26]

Thus the elections to the Estates took place in what was already a climate of military mobilization: the Huguenot leadership deserted the electoral meetings, claiming that the voting procedures had been rigged; only one Protestant representative was returned for the nobility, M. de Mirambeau (for Saintonge), while Navarre's friend and advisor Philippe Duplessis-Mornay, who could have counted on the support of both Protestants and Catholics, declined the mandate. Even in the virtual absence of any Protestant deputies, the discussion at the Estates registered the presence of significant dissent. Opposition to the resumption of the war came from a number of deputies of the Third Estate—such as Jean Bodin—but also from a significant proportion (about a fourth) of the representatives of the Second. All those who spoke against the war stressed the dramatic condition of poverty created by years of conflict, and some, like Louis of Bourbon, duke of Montpensier, actually described to the assembly, in vivid terms, the misery and suffering of the peasantry they had witnessed on they journey to Blois.[27]

This awareness of the terrible impact of the war upon the population weighed heavily upon the Christian conscience of some of the deputies: while professing their fidelity to the Catholic Church, their abhorrence of heresy, and their loyalty to the king, the dissenting speakers claimed that to pursue a civil war, even in defense of the true faith, was against God's will, since it destroyed all the foundations of a Christian community: peace, security, obedience to the law, charity, and mercy. In the words of

Pierre de Blancheford, whoever desired a civil war was ungodly, and it would be more appropriate to pray for his soul than to follow his advice.[28] If the king's desire to take arms in defense of the true faith was commendable, the king himself was subject to God's will, and must bend to the obligation of protecting his kingdom from ruin. To give up fighting did not mean to renounce the struggle against heresy, but to pursue it by less destructive means, such as preaching, dispensing religious instruction and the like.

In a pamphlet entitled *Remontrance aux états*—presented as the work of an anonymous Catholic writer—the Protestant author, Philippe Duplessis-Mornay, neatly exemplified this combination of political and Christian arguments, describing peace both as a political necessity and as a moral imperative. Without peace, the Estates were a useless instrument, since any requests that might be put to the king by the three orders could not be satisfied: because of the war, the nobility would be drained of their resources as well as of their blood; the Church would see her properties pillaged and confiscated; the Third Estate would suffer most of all, since farmers and peasants would be left without assistance, commerce would decline, and the king would no longer be in the position of either reducing taxes or of correcting the abuses of justice.[29]

The moral consequences of the war would also be disastrous, since the conflict turned Christians against each other, bringing them in the end to despise all religion and ignore all moral principles. The state, the author observed, was formed by two religions; if both were allowed to express themselves freely, war would be the inevitable consequence; but if the state chose to promote war, it would be destroyed and both rival churches with it. Thus the civil war appeared as a self-defeating exercise, in which each side tried to preserve its religion, through the destruction of all that religion stood for in terms of private and public values.

The debate around the Edict of Beaulieu showed that by 1576, only four years after the Saint Bartholomew's Day Massacre, the idea of a biconfessional French society under a Catholic monarchy had acquired clearer contours; the new approach to religious coexistence did not simply allow the reformed religion a measure of toleration, but actually accorded to the Protestant minority recognition and entitlements nearly equal to those of the Catholic population. As was later the case with the Edict of Nantes, this result was not pursued through the acknowledgment of a general right to religious freedom, but through a careful partition of zones of influence and resources between the two confessions across the kingdom—religious diversity adding itself to a number of other divisions and asymmetries that characterized sixteenth-century government.

In practice, however, in 1576 the French monarchy did not possess the means necessary to enforce a policy of religious coexistence across the kingdom, any more than it had the power to enforce religious conformity by crushing or expelling the Protestants: after fourteen years of almost continuous war, and in spite of the pogroms of 1572, the situation was very much the same as in the early 1560s—the only difference being that the resources to feed the military effort on both sides were gradually running out, with parties increasingly forced to rely upon foreign support. It is impossible to tell what things might have been like had the Valois monarchs pursued a consistent strategy throughout, rather than swinging between bouts of aggression and half-baked attempts at reconciliation; predictably, their incapacity to decide on a coherent line of action and abide by it had disastrous effects, as Montaigne repeatedly observed in the *Essais,* when he remarked on the disconcerting instability of French legislation during the wars.[30]

But was there any type of political action that, consistently followed, might have proved effective in mastering religious dissent and the civil conflict generated by it? In so far as the civil war presented the familiar characteristics of a princely *fronde,* the conflict did lend itself to a settlement: existing alliances might shift, new distributions of power and territory might be negotiated, agreements reached: a good example was offered by the duke of Alençon, who soon lost all interest in the cause of the French Protestants, transferring his personal ambitions to the Protectorate of the Low Countries.[31] Yet even when the leaders' personal aspirations were satisfied, the broader issues at the heart of the conflict remained intractable and it was unclear if, and to what extent, they might form the object of negotiation and compromise, within the parliaments and the Estates as well as in the country at large.

Montaigne and the "Politiques"

The short-lived peace of 1576 saw the resurgence of bipartisan opposition to the war: moderate Catholics and Protestants, who had been reduced to silence by the tragic events of the Saint Bartholomew's Day Massacre, and who were now prepared to accept some form of confessional coexistence, rather than enduring a continuation of the conflict. Unsurprisingly, in a climate where partisan passions remained very strong, these moderates were accused by both parties of betraying their faith, or even of being unbelievers and atheists. The contemptuous terms of *moyenneurs* and *politiques* used to describe anyone who spoke out against the war were indicative of these feelings of suspicion and resentment; in a similar spirit, the great aristocrats around the duke of Alençon were called *malcontents.* Thus in 1576 an anonymous pamphlet claimed that the *politiques* were "more wicked and dangerous than the heretics themselves,"[32] while the

Protestant Pierre Viret maintained that seeking a religious compromise was equivalent to bargaining (*moyenner*) "between God and his Adversary, and between Christ and the Anti-Christ."[33]

Like other labels attributed by a militant group to its political opponents, the term *politiques* did not correspond to an actual party, not even to a well-defined movement of opinion or to a specific ideology.[34] Possibly by the late 1580s, when in Paris the *Ligue* arrested hundreds of people suspected of disaffection toward the Catholic cause, the party of compromise acquired, at least in that particular urban setting, a clearer profile: professional men, magistrates, and public officials, broadly united by Gallicanism, national sentiments, and loyalty to the crown.[35] But all along, during the protracted period of the war, the cause of peace united all sort of people and motives: dissatisfied opportunists like the Duke of Alençon; devout Christians of both confessions, who regarded peace and the preservation of life as the supreme good; landowners sensitive to the plight of their tenants and peasants; public officials concerned with the preservation of public order; men whose livelihood and social status were threatened by the economic crisis caused by the war; individuals caught up in a conflict of loyalties between their religious affiliation and their place within the social hierarchy; members of either church confused about their beliefs and ill at ease in a polarized dogmatic confrontation; possibly, also, disaffected intellectuals and religious skeptics. For many of these, the pursuit of a compromise was justified at the same time by reasons of principle and by prudential and utilitarian considerations.

Though in many ways an empty shell to which it is difficult to attribute a specific ideological or historical content, the term *politique* has survived and continues to indicate a policy without principles, driven by necessity and tinted with opportunism, a skeptical, pragmatic response to the ravages of partisan struggle. Montaigne's discussion of toleration—which concluded with the deadly remark that, in endorsing it, the French kings, "having been unable to do what they would, pretended to will what they could"[36]—seems a natural candidate for the role of manifesto of this pragmatic approach, its bleak realism set against the rigid principles of the men of faith.

On the whole, modern commentators, even sympathetic ones, have responded to the essay on freedom of conscience with a certain caution, if not with suspicion.[37] The essay was unquestionably a vivid and passionate plea for toleration, and yet it was formulated in terms that may prove confusing, and even disappointing, for the modern reader. In his discussion the writer showed no appreciation for confessional pluralism, and clearly stigmatized religious dissent as a destructive force within French society, an unwelcome addition to the country's many political and social divisions.[38]

In particular, he did not endorse the distinction between "heresy" and "sedition" that characterized the position of moderates such as Pasquier and l'Hospital in the 1560s: for him, as for La Boétie, militant religious dissent and rebellion were bound to become inextricably confused, as they resulted in a similar violation of the existing laws and of social order, even if the original motivations of the rebels were different in the two cases. In some sense both militant heretics and their persecutors seemed to have lost touch with reality: the former wanted to assert their beliefs by altering the policy of the state; the latter wanted to punish religious dissenters for their beliefs rather than for their actions.

Toleration itself was presented in the essay at best as the result of the impotence and ineptitude of the political power (as in the case of France), at worst as a malignant strategy aiming at the destruction of all religious confessions (as in the example provided by the emperor Julian). Thus the main objection to intolerance and repression set forth was the fierce condemnation of the excessive violence (both public and private) employed for this task, and the cruel punishments inflicted on heretics. This condemnation was not, however, specific to a situation in which the victims were religious dissenters, but would apply to all circumstances in which some individuals, or some groups within the community, were persecuted or treated brutally and cruelly by the political authorities; indeed the same arguments, advocating moderation and clemency, could be applied to the treatment of ordinary criminals.[39]

The additional difficulty, in the legal pursuit of heretics, was the fact that their "crimes" (in so far as these consisted of religious acts and religious beliefs) could not be judged effectively and objectively by the ordinary instruments at the disposal of the law, since they belonged to a supernatural dimension of human experience. In the essay "Of Cripples" (III, 11) Montaigne returned to this issue in discussing the treatment by the law of people who stood accused of witchcraft, stating bluntly:

> To kill men, we should have sharp and luminous evidence; and our life is too real and essential to vouch for these supernatural and fantastic accidents . . . In those other extravagant accusations, I should be inclined to say that it is quite enough that a man, whatever recommendation he may have, should be believed about what is human.[40]

Rational certainty was as impossible to achieve when dealing with religious beliefs as when addressing any miraculous or supernatural phenomena: people who claimed they could perform miracles, or believed they were in touch with ghosts and apparitions, may be dishonest, deluded, or mentally deranged; they may also be genuine saints and prophets. Whether one believed them or not, the repressive instruments of justice were unsuited to dealing with spiritual, invisible forces; human justice could only grasp effectively real actions committed in the real world.

Having thus set a clear limit on what political authority may legitimately inflict on its subjects—a limit dictated by justice and humanity—Montaigne's approach was rigorously pragmatic: he did not raise questions of principle, but focused exclusively upon what could be done in practice by ordinary political means. Thus the central question addressed in the essay on "freedom of conscience" was not whether an attitude of toleration was in principle just and desirable, but whether toleration, when introduced in the context of a fierce struggle between competing sects, could actually grant durable peace.

By stressing the dimension of political viability, Montaigne rejected at the same time two possible approaches to the question of toleration, which he apparently judged equally inconclusive: the first one was the defense of the principle of freedom of conscience taken apart from the material context in which such freedom may, or may not, be exercised, from its immediate consequences and human costs.[41] The second was the pursuit of a political compromise that might reform institutional and social practices while ignoring the real motives and forces behind the conflict. A compromise might be a good thing in itself, in so far as it indicated the willingness to discuss and negotiate: but it would not prove effective unless the real object of the controversy was clear.

What was the religious conflict really about? Was it about faith, about opinion, about interest, or perhaps about all of those things together? To what extent were these different dimensions of the conflict that divided France actually within the scope of action of political power, and within reach of legislative intervention? Inevitably, by trying to address these questions, Montaigne's text dramatically shifted the focus of the analysis, from the pros and cons of toleration to a new range of even more intricate questions concerning the nature of human beliefs, religious or otherwise, and the shaping and governance of public opinion.

Chapter 4

FREEDOM OF CONSCIENCE

GOVERNING OPINION

MONTAIGNE'S CHOICE of Julian the Apostate as the protagonist of the essay on freedom of conscience (II, 19) was not in itself especially novel: for over a century the Roman emperor had exercised a considerable attraction on European Renaissance writers; he featured in fact not just in religious works like Erasmus's *Apophtegmata* (1531), but also in dramatic ones such as Lorenzo de Medici's *Rappresentazione di San Giovanni e Paolo* (1489) and Hans Sachs's *Der arg Kaiser Julianus* (1553). In France in particular, Julian had been for some time at the center of an intellectual revival: the fact that he had lived in the province of Gaul and expressed a great appreciation for the town of Paris (*Lutetia Parisiorum*) in his *Misopogon* had helped to promote him to the status of French humanist *ante litteram*. His writings were reedited, and scholars attempted as far as possible to reestablish the historical truth about his personality and his career, beyond the traditional stereotype of the renegade enemy of Christianity.[1]

Naturally the emperor could not be altogether absolved of his attempt to restore paganism: but his intellectual qualities and moral virtues were recognized, together with his political achievements and his capacity to exploit religious diversity to the advantage of the empire. Thus in Jean Bodin's influential *Methodus*—the work on historical methodology that Montaigne discussed in Book II of the *Essais*—Julian's case was presented as an illustration of the errors of judgment into which historians might be led, if they failed to verify their sources.[2] In a pamphlet published in 1563, during the debate over the Edict of Amboise, *Remontrances du parlement de Bourgogne*, the Catholic Jean Bégat cited Julian as an example of how people who held different religious beliefs could be made to cooperate harmoniously within the same polity, a model the kings of France would be well advised to follow.[3]

Protestant pamphleteers were generally more severe with Julian than Catholic ones, and even moderates, like Innocent Gentillet and Philippe Duplessis-Mornay, endorsed the traditional image of the emperor persecuting Christians, practicing black magic, and celebrating human sacrifices; yet one of the editors of Julian's works, Pierre Martini, was a *protégé* of Henry of Navarre who had been appointed in 1572 to the chair of Hebrew at the Protestant college of La Rochelle.[4] The French myth of Julian did not in fact die out with the end of the religious wars: it was revived in the late seventeenth century by the revocation of the Edict of Nantes, while the figure of the "apostate" emperor continued to appear in Enlightenment debates over religious toleration.[5]

If Montaigne's fascination with Julian was part of a broader intellectual trend, well established within French culture, the writer went surprisingly far in portraying his subject as a truly heroic figure. As it has often been pointed out, Julian was the only historical character to have a whole essay dedicated to him; from the start Montaigne described him as a monument to ancient virtue, in terms very similar to those he employed to celebrate the qualities of that other "soul of the old stamp," his much regretted friend Estienne de La Boétie.[6] "Très grand homme et rare," Julian was a man guided by philosophical principles, a wise legislator, a brave and gifted military commander, a just and merciful ruler whose habits, in spite of his youth, were austere and chaste: a reborn Alexander the Great without the Macedonian's drinking habits. At the same time Julian's grandeur bore the mark of heroic defeat, since his sentiments and actions went against the tide of overwhelming historical forces, which dictated the decline of those classical values he stood for. Like La Boétie, the emperor represented a dying breed, a species now extinct, the incarnation of a classical ideal that had sadly disappeared from the modern world.

"Thou Hast Conquered, Nazarene"

Setting aside the nostalgic attraction of Julian's personality and his political and military achievements, the aspect of his life that the sixteenth-century reader would have found most sympathetic was his position as the protagonist of a major conflict of conscience: Julian appeared above all as an individual torn between his public responsibilities and his private religious convictions. In his discussion of Julian's career, Montaigne dismissed the view that the emperor was an apostate who had abandoned the true faith, by suggesting that probably he had never been a Christian in the first place; in spite of his Christian education, he had always remained a pagan at heart, but had concealed his attachment to the old religion, until changing circumstances made it possible for him to express openly his beliefs. Thus, during the earlier part of his life, until the death of his co-ruler Constantius, Julian had experienced a situation of secrecy and concealment, which spoke to the imagination of those of Montaigne's contemporaries who had been forced into the same position by persecution and sectarian struggle.

A great admirer of classical antiquity, Montaigne made it clear that his admiration did not extend to pagan worship: he regarded Julian's massive sacrifices of animals and his obsession with prophecies and oracles as both ridiculous and distasteful, stigmatizing these beliefs and practices as a serious flaw in his otherwise admirable character. But if he disapproved of the young emperor's paganism, the writer felt obviously sympathetic toward his plight; a climate of intolerance and sectarian fanaticism, such as the one experienced by the empire after Constantine's conversion, would inevitably result in the corruption of religious sensibilities, generating confusion and skepticism in the minds of many, and encouraging superstition. The comparison with contemporary circumstances was only too obvious:

> It is ordinary to see good intentions, if they are carried out without moderation, push men into very vicious acts. In this controversy on whose account France is at present agitated by civil wars, the best and soundest side is undoubtedly that which maintains both the old religion and the old government of the country. However, among the good men who follow that side, . . . we see many whom passion drives outside the bounds of reason, and makes them sometimes adopt unjust, violent and even reckless courses.[7]

Persecution was not very good for one's morale: saints and obstinate individuals might see their faith strengthened by it, but for many ordinary people, too timid to resist pressure, there would be a desire to conform, accompanied by a humiliating sense of inadequacy and guilt.

As it appeared from his comments about the fellow *conseiller* who had concealed for years his religious affiliation, Montaigne regarded the position of those individuals who chose to hide their beliefs with a sense of embarrassment mixed with compassion. In the essay "Of Conscience" (II, 5) he related how, during the wars, he had once traveled in the company of his own brother and an unknown gentleman, through an area under Catholic control. The stranger wore crosses sewn on his clothing, a sign of recognition used by Catholics; it was only when he noticed the man's uneasiness every time they went through a town, or met with loyalist troops, that Montaigne realized the unknown traveler must be a Protestant in disguise; as to the agitation he observed in the stranger "through his mask and the crosses on his cassock," the writer thought it was due less to his fear of discovery than to a feeling of shame.[8]

Set against these examples of modern cowardice and duplicity, Julian's individual challenge to the empire through the restoration of paganism acquired considerable grandeur and dignity. His attempt to reverse the historical process that saw the triumph of Christianity was of course doomed to failure, and yet Montaigne felt respect for his courage and integrity. In the only passage of the essay added to the 1588 edition, he recalled the anecdote according to which the emperor, fatally wounded on the battlefield during a campaign against the Parthians, cried out: "Thou hast conquered,

Nazarene!" This, he claimed, was just a legend, but it was possible that, before dying, Julian had been visited by some ghost or vision of doom, similar to those experienced by Marcus Brutus in Gaul and, later, in Persia before his final defeat: a comparison that established a symbolic parallel between the emperor and the last defender of republican liberty.[9]

If the idea of clandestine belief spoke to modern sensibility, it was above all the notion of apostasy, so intimately associated with Julian's name, that featured prominently in modern debates. The cases of "political" abjurations extracted under duress, such as those of Navarre and Condé in 1572, after the massacre of the Saint Bartholomew's Day, were only the tip of the iceberg of a much wider phenomenon that touched Catholics and Protestants alike. Where many chose to hide their true faith from fear of losing their status, or in order to avoid a conflict with their friends and family, there was also a small crowd of proclaimed "converts" whose position was less than transparent. A significant number of Christians whose beliefs concerning particular practices or religious dogmas were not in full conformity with those of the church to which they belonged were subjected to such pressures by their community, that sometimes they ended up defecting to the rival confession.

These conversions, which predictably attracted considerable publicity, often proved traumatic for the converts, without really offering a solution to their doubts and hesitations. In normal circumstances such persons would probably have continued to worship undisturbed, keeping their skepticism and erratic beliefs to themselves; but in the new climate of inquisition and scrutiny, as the boundaries of orthodoxy became more rigid, they were forced into the uneasy role of protagonists of some miraculous conversion they had never truly experienced.[10]

"Forsworn on Mere Necessity": Navarre's Conversion

A few years after the publication of the first edition of the *Essais*, the issue of apostasy acquired a new, politically crucial significance, adding a new dimension to the symbolic implications of Julian's figure. In 1584, following the death of the Duke of Anjou (previously of Alençon), Henry of Navarre became the heir apparent to the French crown, and the question of his religious affiliation turned into a matter of paramount importance for the future of the monarchy. The problem was, in the first instance, one of legitimacy. Navarre's hereditary claims, based upon the Salic law of succession, appeared solid enough, and were not generally disputed; but how could a heretic prince become king of France, when the first commitment of the French crown was to the defense of the true faith and the struggle against heresy?

Catholic opinion hostile to Navarre resorted to the same line of argument used by the Huguenots, after the Saint Bartholomew's Day Massacre, to question the legitimacy of the Valois monarchy: a prince who placed himself outside the law of God—in this case through heresy—could not rule; his position became automatically that of a usurper and a tyrant, and the subjects were under no obligation to obey him. On the other hand, those who supported Navarre's claims—Huguenots as well as loyalist Catholics—did so on the ground of the traditional Gallican doctrine: the king of France was no vassal to the pope, and was not subject, directly or indirectly, to the authority of the Church; as he derived his power directly from God, he could not be dictated to by anyone in matters of orthodoxy.[11] The natural way out of this conflict was for Navarre to abjure once again; Henry III himself strongly advocated this solution: fatally wounded by a Catholic fanatic in 1589, from his deathbed he acknowledged Navarre as his legitimate successor, while exhorting him to convert to secure the peace of the kingdom.[12]

While for Julian promotion to the imperial crown had meant the opportunity to express his religious views freely, Navarre was placed in exactly the opposite situation: he could only become king by renouncing his true beliefs. Yet apostasy, far from proving an easy option, also had problematic implications. To begin with, the king's conscience could not be forced any more than that of any ordinary individual, and the same arguments about the spontaneous character of a person's religious faith applied to the prince as to the lowliest of his subjects. Thus a conversion undertaken for reasons of political opportunity, even to secure the peace and unity of the kingdom, would still be invalid and defeat its own purpose, if it did not correspond to the sovereign's real sentiments. If he chose to recant in order to take up his crown, the king was exposed to the risk of becoming "a state Catholic," while an opportunistic conversion would turn him into an atheist, with no particular attachment to any religion.[13]

As Navarre himself piously claimed in a letter addressed to his cousin Charles of Bourbon:

> religion . . . cannot be taken off like a shirt; it is written in the heart, and— thanks be to God—it is so deeply impressed into mine, that it is not in my power to part from it, as it was not in the first instance in my power to enter it.[14]

At the same time the possibilities of altering the king's beliefs through persuasion and religious instruction were more limited than in the case of ordinary persons: the sovereign's inner thoughts were in fact protected by the veil of the *archana imperii,* and could not be disclosed and openly discussed like common opinions; because of his exalted status, his views deserved special consideration and respect, which precluded to some extent the process of conversion.

Unable to assess the possible political impact of his conversion upon both religious parties, Navarre postponed it until 1593, when he was finally satisfied that changing confession would gain him the approval of the Catholic majority, without losing him altogether the support of Protestants, in France as well as abroad.[15] After protracted negotiations—conducted with loyalist exponents of the French clergy, rather than with the Roman authorities—the terms on which his abjuration was orchestrated were such as to undermine the traditional significance of apostasy as rejection of heresy and as submission to the authority of the Church.

In his public profession—pronounced in the abbey of Saint Denis, which had been reconquered by loyalist troops in 1590—the king altered the traditional formula by avoiding any derogatory reference to the Reformed religion as heresy. He also blurred in his statement some aspects of the Catholic doctrine he found especially unconvincing, such as the cult of saints and the existence of purgatory. On these as well as on other controversial matters of dogma, he emphasized his willingness to submit to the opinion of a majority, following the views of learned members of the clergy and of theologians of recognized wisdom, without actually pretending to be convinced by their arguments.

Thus, rather than making a profession of faith, Navarre formulated his abjuration in terms that privileged the dimension of opinion and consensus. Becoming a Catholic in this new context meant submitting not to superior dogmatic evidence, but to the strength of a dominant human opinion: it being impossible to establish the truth, the king, as a peace-seeking Christian, was ready to suspend his judgment on controversial matters, siding with the majority in order to promote *concordia* and unity of sentiments among his subjects. In fact on this occasion, as in a number of other public speeches, Navarre used the term *catholique* in its original sense of "universal," rather than in the current one that identified Catholicism with the Church of Rome; he also frequently spoke of *christianisme*, without reference to any particular confession.[16]

Politically speaking, Navarre's conversion was undoubtedly a success: it allowed him to rally the support of loyalist Catholics and of moderates in general, moving toward the much desired final reconciliation of the country. However, the ecumenical content he had attempted to confer on his gesture was lost upon contemporary opinion: supporters and opponents alike were ready to see his decision as essentially opportunistic, even if they differed in their assessment of the validity of his motives.

Significantly, the king's first public declaration of his intentions to convert, issued on 4 April 1592, went under the name of "*l'expédient.*"[17] In a letter addressed to Navarre in July 1593, Elizabeth I of England expressed her dismay at his decision, by deploring the French king's plan of using evil means even toward a good end (a concept that seems to come straight out of the pages of the *Essais*).[18] In a similar, if opposed, perspective, the Protestant Maximilien de Béthune (the future duke of Sully)—Navarre's long-term friend and supporter—described the king's conversion as the "quickest and easiest means" to undermine the position of his enemies, breaking the Catholic "monopoly" over the kingdom; thus, just like the indignant English queen, he also endorsed the view that Navarre's motives must necessarily be instrumental.[19]

The ambiguity of the conversion was not confined to Navarre's individual position, but extended to his entourage and to the public image of the court. In her *Memoirs*, Henry's wife Marguerite of Valois provided an idyllic picture of her husband's court at Nérac—where she rejoined him in 1579—as a place where people of different religions could associate freely and live in good harmony:

> Nobody—she wrote—commented about our difference of religion, as the King my husband, with the Princess his sister [Catherine de Bourbon], went their own way to the sermon, while I, with my attendants, went the other way to mass in a chapel located in the park. Afterwards we met and walked together . . .[20]

From the queen's account, Nérac emerged as a place of libertinage and license, both in the original sense of derogation from religious orthodoxy, and in the more current one of sexual promiscuity (after the ecumenical walks in the park, the king and queen gave an additional proof of their tolerance by pursuing amiably their separate love affairs). Yet Marguerite's narrative conferred to this license a positive meaning, turning it into a literary ideal that combined concord, harmony, intellectual pleasure, and the Neo-Platonic practice of "honest" love. It was at Nérac, sometime in 1579 or 1580, that Montaigne met the queen and became part of her literary circle; the suggestion that the "Apology for Raymond Sebond" was inspired by Marguerite (though in fact she was not explicitly named in the text) suggests that the literary and philosophic ideals of Nérac did play some role in the elaboration of the writer's work.[21]

In his play *Love's Labour's Lost*, written in the aftermath of Navarre's conversion, William Shakespeare described how the king of Navarre and his attendants—after making the solemn promise of forsaking all women in order to pursue their studies without frivolous distractions—were only too eager to break their vows at the earliest opportunity. Thus the author subscribed to the literary ideal of the court of Nérac as a "court of love," where real sentiments and emotions finally triumphed over pedantry and the sterile pursuit of academic learning. At the same time he voiced the English disapproval of Navarre's betrayal of the Protestant cause: in his ironical representation the court of Nérac became a place of deceit and opportunism, were words and vows were uttered in vain, where promises were void and loyalties changed according to whatever was perceived as the "necessity" of the moment.[22]

Bordeaux acknowledged Navarre as king of France on 2 January 1590, five months after Henry III's death, thus becoming the first French town to accept the new sovereign. This result was achieved through considerable pressures exercised by Navarre's supporters upon the town authorities and especially upon the *parlement,* where the majority of councillors was generally hostile to the idea of a Protestant monarch. Montaigne, who had been mayor of Bordeaux until 1588, cooperated actively with his successor, the marshal of Matignon, to bring about this result. His commitment to Navarre's cause is well documented by his correspondence, though unfortunately little is known about the content of the more confidential diplomatic missions he undertook at the time on the king's behalf.[23]

Montaigne was also among those who believed that Navarre's religious commitment—like that of other leaders of the war—was dictated largely, if not exclusively, by reasons of political opportunity. In his *Memoirs* the jurist Jacques-Auguste de Thou, one of his friends, recalling a meeting with the writer at the Estates of Blois in 1588, reported the latter's views on the subject in the following terms:

> The religion which the two of them [Navarre and the Duke of Guise] publicly exhibit is simply a façade to secure the support of their factions. The fear of being deserted by the Protestants is what is preventing the King of Navarre from returning to the religion of his ancestors, and the Duke would be firmly committed to the confession of Augsburg [the German model of bi-confessional coexistence] . . . if he could follow it without compromising his interests.[24]

There is no reason to doubt, if not the precise wording, at least the substance of Montaigne's judgment. Writing to Navarre on 18 January 1589 (a year before their hard-won success with the Bordeaux authorities), the writer had playfully reminded the king that he had been his supporter, even when he had to seek absolution from his confessor for his loyalty:

> From the first I have considered you as destined for the rank you now occupy, and you may remember that even when I had to confess it to my curate I did not fail to look upon your successes with a distinctly favourable eye. At present, with more reason and freedom, I embrace them with my full affection.[25]

At the time Navarre was still a Protestant, yet the letter clearly implied that, since he had finally been acknowledged as the legitimate sovereign (and thanks to his military and political victories), one was now free to show loyalty to him without being accused of a sin. Thus Montaigne recognized—more readily and explicitly than his new king—a clear-cut discontinuity between the dimension of individual faith on the one hand, and the political use made of religion by the different factions, on the other. Opinion, rather than faith, was the real winner in the battle for the king's soul, and it was on that ground alone that the question of religious coexistence must be addressed.

The Ambiguities of Toleration

It has been suggested that Montaigne's admiration for Julian revealed how by 1578-80, when he wrote the essay on freedom of conscience, the writer had lost his Christian faith, a fact made obvious in the text of the "Apology for Raymond Sebond" (II, 12), completed roughly during the same period.[26] This inference seems rather far-fetched, since Montaigne's involvement with skeptical philosophy was not incompatible with enduring religious sentiments on his part, nor with his general attachment to Christian values; thus in discussing Julian's policies the writer was not comparing the respective merits of paganism and Christianity as religious doctrines (he had no doubts as to the superiority of the latter); he was simply assessing the strategies adopted by the Roman emperor on the one hand, and by the French monarchs on the other, to control religious dissent.

The common element was that both Julian and the Valois kings had resorted to a policy of toleration to free the state from the plague of a war between religious sects. However, their respective motivations, and the path through which they had come to choose such a policy, were quite different. Julian had adopted toleration as soon as he had gained full control over the empire; the Valois monarchs, on the other hand, had resigned themselves to a compromise with the Protestants only after failing in their repeated efforts to crush and exterminate them. For the emperor, toleration was a deliberate choice, therefore an act of power; for the French kings, it was a sign of weakness and defeat.

Moreover, in Montaigne's eyes Julian had the immense merit of having consistently avoided the use of violence and cruelty in dealing with his religious enemies; true, he had been hostile to the Christian clergy, forbidding their public teaching and limiting their influence, but always "*sans toucher au sang*," without shedding blood.[27] This moderation on the part of a pagan stood in damning contrast with the unimaginable atrocities committed by Christians of all denominations, before and during the religious wars, atrocities for which the French monarchs obviously carried a heavy responsibility. Thus Julian's essentially principled and moderate conduct was a measure of the extent to which Christians had debased themselves, sinking into fanaticism and violence: while a man whose idea of worship consisted in slaughtering farm animals was capable of mercy and toleration, his Christian counterparts gave evidence for the belief that "there is no beast in the world so much to be feared by man as man."[28] At the same time Julian's liberality and love of learning were set against those Christian zealots, whose assault against pagan books had caused more damage to European culture than "all the bonfires of barbarians."[29]

The difference between Julian's religious policy and that of the Valois was not confined to the means they employed. The French monarchs had resigned themselves to toleration as a last resort, after all aggressive solutions had failed; they had embraced it reluctantly, in the vague hope of gaining time, without any clear expectation as to the future prospects of religious coexistence in the kingdom. For his part, Julian had permitted religious freedom with the specific design of breaking the strength of the sects, convinced as he was that this line of action would finally lead to the decline of a divided Christianity. His hope was that, without the restraints exercised until then by imperial power, the rival Christian groups would simply continue to fight each other until their mutual destruction.

Both the Roman emperor and the Valois had failed in their intent: by the time of Julian's premature death, the struggle among the sects had not resulted in the expected dissolution of Christianity, while in France the measures of toleration introduced during the *paix de Monsieur* had been set aside before they could bring any detectable results, let alone a durable settlement; in both cases the experience had been one of short duration, thus leaving open the question of the possible impact of toleration over longer periods of time. On the whole, the essay "On Freedom of Conscience" presented toleration as an exercise in the limitation of damage, both in the moral and in the practical dimensions. By pursuing a policy of permissiveness and clemency, the sovereign at least refrained from committing acts of cruelty, which were repugnant to Christian conscience, and which could only result in the moral degradation and corruption of the community. At the same time, toleration was potentially less disruptive of civil relations than any active struggle against heresy or religious dissent, since the state would engage its strength and authority only in the minimal task of the external control of public order.

If Montaigne's analysis confirmed that there were compelling reasons for preferring toleration to repression, it still left open the issue of the efficacy of toleration itself, raising a series of puzzling questions that focused upon the alternative means at the disposal of the state to shape and control people's beliefs. In their writings, moderates made frequent appeals to dialogue, instruction, and preaching as desirable ways of resolving the religious conflict: but to what extent could this practice of gentle persuasion actually work as a means to grant civil peace, and how long would it take for it to become effective? What sorts of forces led to the growth or decline of religious sects?

To questions such as these, Montaigne offered no final answers:

It may be said, on the one hand, that to give factions a loose rein to entertain their own opinions is to scatter and sow divisions; it is almost lending a hand to augment it, there being no barrier or coercion of the laws to check or hinder its course. But on the other hand, one could also say that to give factions a loose rein to entertain their own opinions is to soften and relax them through facility and ease, and to dull the point, which is sharpened by rarity, novelty and difficulty.[30]

By leaving the choice between these two alternatives unresolved in the concluding paragraphs of his text, the writer showed that the discussion of toleration as one of a number of political options could only lead to uncertain results, since in any given historical context the outcome of such a policy would depend on a number of circumstantial factors, and probably vary through time. The avoidance of violence remained an obligatory choice for any ruler, who was not prepared to violate grossly the basic principles of humanity; but in order to talk with any degree of confidence about the control of religious doctrines and sects, one would need a far better understanding of the mechanisms that governed the formation and spreading of human opinions.

Faith and Belief

In the *Essais* Montaigne returned over and over again to the puzzling nature of belief, which he analyzed both as a feature of individual psychology and as a dimension of collective behavior. In particular, the question of religious faith was extensively discussed in the "Apology for Raymond Sebond" (II, 12). There Montaigne established a clear distinction between the position of those happy few who experienced a vivid faith (*foy vive*), which they had acquired through an "extraordinary infusion" of God's grace, and the large mass of believers, who had not been similarly touched by the "ray of divinity," and simply tried to follow the precepts and rituals of their religion as they had absorbed them from their environment. The purpose of this distinction was in the first instance epistemological: Montaigne introduced it to show that faith could not be acquired by means of human reasons and discourses—that is to say through rational argument—as Sebond had assumed, but had irrational, ultimately superhuman motivations.

At a different level, the same distinction was used to stress the qualitative difference between the behavior of these superior "true believers" and that of "ordinary" worshippers, a difference that had become apparent in the context of the religious wars. Those really and deeply touched by faith would never turn religion into an excuse for fighting, for engaging in rebellion or attacking their neighbors; in fact even a relatively superficial understanding of their own doctrine should show Christians that such manifestations of religious zeal were simply incompatible with Christian teaching. Unfortunately, while even pagans were generally capable of acting in a manner coherent with the doctrines they professed (see the example of the philosophers of classical antiquity), Christians were prepared to ignore them altogether, or to twist them beyond recognition to suit their own partisan purposes.[31]

Montaigne did not explicitly discuss the position of the believer who finds himself the victim of persecution; possibly the closest he came to the subject was in the illustration of the character of Socrates, who is described in Book III of the *Essais* as a prophetical, Christ-like figure: his example makes it clear that the virtuous man at odds with political authority, notwithstanding his outward conformity to the laws of his country, would naturally choose to suffer unjustly rather than engaging in rebellion; if this was true of men who had not benefited from the Christian revelation, the same argument would apply a fortiori to the virtuous man who was also a Christian.[32] However, when he imagined himself as the victim of persecution by the state of which he was a subject, for whatever motives, religious or otherwise, Montaigne's response was less self-sacrificing: if he did not consider engaging in rebellion, he would unhesitatingly choose emigration, and this even in circumstances where the threat to his person and his liberty was a minimal one.[33]

The example of Socrates suggested that, in exacting obedience from the subjects, the state should be satisfied with their loyalty to the law, while claiming no jurisdiction over their private thoughts and beliefs. This should apply not just to those who kept their faith to themselves, but also to those who engaged in peaceful preaching. Julian had banned Christians from public teaching in the empire; but only a ferocious regime would actively persecute unarmed saints and prophets. In any case, the strong faith that moved such individuals would place them well beyond the reach of any human influence and authority, making them impervious to any pressure or intimidation.

Montaigne assumed that those individuals who were touched by genuine religious faith would never, under any circumstances, represent a political problem, because they would never do anything to harm other human beings or to disrupt their own community.[34] Such pious people would only engage in prayer, meditation, preaching, and charitable activities, without concerning themselves with political matters. Moreover, the number of persons who answered that particular description was obviously so small, that they could hardly represent a threat to public order. Equally negligible was the number of individuals who were sufficiently intelligent and learned to understand in full those obscure theological issues that were at the heart of the disagreement between Catholics and Protestants: you could hardly fill a room with them, let alone start a civil war.[35]

The arguments about the detachment of true religious faith from any secular matter, and about the relative obscurity of the doctrinal matters at the heart of the conflict, show that Montaigne did not attribute to the war between Catholics and Protestants a specifically religious significance. This is a very important point, possibly the single most important aspect of the writer's understanding of the conflict. To claim that the actors of the wars were not motivated by truly religious considerations did not of course mean that they were all in bad faith, that they consistently used religion as a pretext to fight over political issues or to defend their material interests; it rather stressed the difficulty, for most people, of separating specifically religious issues from all those other opinions and prejudices that shaped their lives.

The writer was quite prepared to acknowledge that many of the participants in the conflict were sincere, and that their attachment to whatever religious beliefs they happened to hold was genuine enough. However, these beliefs belonged to a level of human experience untouched by divine inspiration, and that remained firmly grounded within secular preoccupations. Thus, unsurprisingly, the unfolding of the conflict followed purely human, ordinary patterns:

> And we think it strange if, in the wars that at this moment are oppressing our state, we see events fluctuating and varying in a common ordinary manner. That is because we contribute nothing to them that is not in ourselves. The justice that is in one of the parties is there only as an ornament and a covering; . . . God owes his extraordinary help to faith and religion, not to our passions. Men are the leaders here, and make use of religion; it ought to be quite the contrary.[36]

In its imperfect human (rather than superhuman) dimension, religion was only part of a package of myths, norms, and practices that defined a specific culture, and was therefore combined with prejudices, interests and expectations of a purely mundane nature. Religion in this sense was absorbed by the individual from the community to which he belonged, like any other cultural feature: one was a Christian in the same way in which one happened to be German or from Perigord, by an accident of birth. At this inferior level of religious experience, Christianity lost its transcendental superiority and became like any other mythology, cult, or set of rituals practiced by mankind in its long history anywhere on earth.[37]

It was precisely in this anthropological dimension, in which Christianity was just like any other religion, and religious creed was indistinguishable from any other kind of opinion, that the policing of belief became relevant. If true faith remained untouched by secular considerations and material constraints, religious opinion, like all other types of opinion (Montaigne used *opinion* and *croyance* as synonymous), formed an essential part of the fabric of society, and stood in a relation of close interaction with social and political power. To ask how, by what means, political authority could hope to control religious dissent was equivalent to asking if, and how, it was possible to govern opinion.

That in principle opinion could be influenced, if not directly controlled, by political power, was self-evident, but in practice the exercise of influencing public views was a very difficult one, since people's beliefs represented an especially opaque and intractable aspect of human experience. But what made opinion so ungovernable? In Montaigne's analysis men's opinions were essentially dictated by their passions and shaped by their imagination. Rationality played a very marginal role in the process, so that the content of opinion was generally arbitrary, and opinions themselves were often only distantly related to the real circumstances and interests of the people who held them.

The immense power of human imagination meant that people were capable of believing practically anything, even in the face of the most overwhelming evidence to the contrary; the same combination of passion and fantasy could make them fiercely attached to their beliefs so that, once taken to heart, any opinion was powerful enough for someone to espouse it even at the cost of his own life. At the same time the instability of human passions, the ever-changing flow of our mental states and emotions, meant that beliefs, once enthusiastically embraced, could be all of a sudden capriciously rejected or abandoned. It was sometimes difficult for the individual to understand why he himself reacted in such a way: a fortiori other people's motives and collective responses would often remain unfathomable.[38]

At a social level, habit played an important role in conferring to human opinions a degree of stability and continuity. Most people were inclined to accept uncritically the prejudices of their own culture and social milieu, and this natural tendency of humans to conform meant that communities could be organized, even for very long periods of time, around shared precepts and practices. However, the fact that some opinions were shared by entire communities did not prove that they were reasonable, dictated by public utility, or even by common sense: experience showed that the same collective endorsement was often given to destructive and socially pernicious beliefs, resulting in aberrant practices such as, for example, human sacrifices or collective suicides.[39]

Moreover, while the "softer minds" of common people made them fall easy prey to superstitious doctrines, many examples indicated that the higher ranks of society were by no means immune to vulgar credulity and to the most fantastic opinions.[40] Thus the apparently plausible view, that opinion would always be transmitted from the top of the social scale down to the common people, was misleading, since it ignored the extent to which belief remained ultimately a highly individual experience. No individual was so humble or uneducated as to lack a singular, original relation to belief—a reality amply illustrated by a whole crowd of lunatics, visionaries, mystics, makers or beneficiaries of miracles, people whose uncommon powers to project their own individual vision had very little to do with social rank or education. The relations between individual and collective beliefs, between educated and popular opinion, were intricate: vanity, opportunism, superstition, fantasy—all contributed to their complexity.

In the essay "Of Cripples" (III, 11), written around 1585–88, several years after the one on the freedom of conscience, the writer illustrated this complexity by looking at the growth and dissemination of popular beliefs about witchcraft and miracles. The reputation of extraordinary and totally fantastic events spread because single individuals and whole communities influenced each other in their eagerness to impress or to have a story to tell; educated people and leaders of communities often encouraged and endorsed the most vulgar superstitions, in order to gain popular favor and to enhance their own reputation:

> The private error first creates the public error, and afterward in turn the public error creates the private error. Thus this whole structure goes on building itself up and shaping itself from hand to hand; so that the remotest witness is better instructed about it than the nearest, and the last informed more convinced of it than the first. It is a natural progression.[41]

Precisely because popular credulity was such an irresistible force, the means traditionally employed to control opinion—deception and repression—were not guaranteed to prove effective in the long run: they might perhaps achieve some immediate result, but since they only addressed the surface of opaque and unstable social and psychological forces, they could easily provoke unforeseen reactions, generating disruption instead of order. Public opinion could not be dictated to: when arguing, the more aggressively someone tried to impose his own views, the more he revealed the intrinsic weakness of his position.[42] As to the art of rhetoric, that stock in trade of politicians and demagogues, its corrupting effects upon communities were so unpredictable, and so potentially pernicious, that both Sparta and Athens had introduced severe measures to limit its usage.[43]

In discussing the subject, Montaigne frequently employed illustrations and metaphors borrowed from medical experience: people who developed a fanatical attachment to a particular opinion were similar to those patients who suffered from imaginary diseases or conditions, from which they refused to be cured; a society torn by civil war was like a body attacked by some infection and that could not expel from the system the poisonous "humors" that had accumulated inside it. Sometimes the de-luded patients could be cured of their imaginary complaints by an equally fictitious medicine, or by a "diversion" that engaged their emotions else-where; a diseased community could be relieved by its internal tensions by the emigration of a part of the population, or by a foreign war that of-fered an alternative outlet to its destructive energies (though the latter remedy could hardly be regarded as an acceptable solution). As a rule, however, because societies were organisms composed of living individu-als, they could not be cured by any external remedies mechanically ap-plied, but must be left to heal in their own time and through their own resources: sometimes the patient would die, more often it would surprise the doctors with its resilience and unexpected capacity for recovery, di-recting its energies toward a new object.[44]

This way of looking at the dynamic of opinion presented toleration in a less than favorable light, as a form of "treatment" in which patients were left to their own devices, while the disease affecting them ran its own course, a declaration of impotence on the part of incompetent or indiffer-ent doctors. The problem was that the only effective "cure" for a "dis-eased"—that is to say turbulent and fanatical—opinion was not immedi-ately accessible to political power, since it involved a long-term process of reeducation of society as a whole, the radical renewal of collective values and attitudes.

Educating Opinion

Was political authority totally powerless in the face of the vagaries of opin-ion, and was toleration simply the prudent acknowledgment of this impo-tence? In his discussion of Julian's case, Montaigne claimed that the prac-tice of controlling opinion through intimidation and repression was both immoral and ineffective. It was immoral not because personal beliefs en-joyed a special status as a privileged sphere of freedom, but simply because rulers were never justified in using arbitrary violence, let alone cruelty, against unarmed subjects, whatever the motive: in this respect Socrates, the person who held heretical views, or the mad woman who thought she was a witch, had the same right to be protected by the law and to be treated with mercy.[45] Repression was also ineffective because it only rein-forced the beliefs of the most obstinate and fanatical, while terrorizing and confusing everybody else.

Hints scattered throughout the *Essais* suggest that the writer was espe-cially disturbed by the experience of martyrdom, a phenomenon that had acquired growing symbolic importance in the context of the wars. If orig-inally Protestants had condemned the cult of martyrs and of their relics traditionally practiced by Catholics, the experience of persecution had led them to develop a parallel cult of their own, leading to a sort of competition between the two confessions in the particular field of self-immolation.[46] In particular, Montaigne pointed out that the cult of martyrs, far from being a specifically Christian phenomenon, featured in many other religions: it was in fact an instance of those inferior, earthly forms of worship that Christianity shared with other doctrines and confessions.[47]

In his view, Christianity had already accumulated a sufficient number of martyrs and did not need to add to an already impressive score. The account he provided in the text of the motivations of those who were ready to suffer torments and to die on religious grounds suggested that their choice was often the result of rather idiosyncratic individual sensibilities or the product of pressure exercised by others; moreover, the example of ordinary individuals recklessly sacrificing their lives and braving horrible torments contributed to create among the people at large an attitude of indifference to suffering and to the value of human life.[48]

If he was very clear about the negative impact of repression, his views on the possibility of controlling opinion by nonviolent means were more nuanced. No doubt "peoples let their belief and hope be led and manipulated in whatever way has pleased and served their leaders." However, this kind of docile response would stop at a rather superficial level, ready to change back as soon as another emotional cord was struck. Manipulating people by playing upon their emotions might prove useful in given circumstances; yet, as many historical examples showed, it was a risky exercise, and often a futile one. People should not be "assisted with fraud": it was only by establishing durable bonds of trust with the community that sovereigns could hope to have a lasting impact upon collective beliefs.[49]

In the end, the only effective way in which regimes could hope to stabilize opinion was by altering the circumstances of people's lives, by modifying the conditions within which their beliefs took shape. This meant in the first instance satisfying some basic collective needs: securing peace, granting the stability of the law, protecting the poor from destitution, and so on. The writer's insistence upon the irrational character of belief did not exclude the view that the disorder brought into French society by religious dissent was to a large extent the result of a failure in governance, which had led to the growth of evils such as poverty, corruption, and the abuse of authority.[50]

At a different level, opinion could be significantly influenced by the long-term improvement of civic and religious education. In the *Essais* Montaigne discussed at length the subject of the education of children; the eldest son of an affectionate father with a genuine passion for literature, the writer had received a somewhat unconventional education at home, and later had become a pupil at the newly established Collège de

Guyenne, where he had benefited from the teaching of personalities such as Andreas Guveanus, Elie Vinet, Marc-Antoine Muret, and George Buchanan. Even at boarding school, the vigilant care of his father (who took pains to watch closely over matters such as school dinners and punishments) had spared him the kinds of hardship and deprivation to which pupils were frequently subjected. Aware of the privileged character of his own upbringing, he was very sensitive to the shortcomings of the education currently imparted to the children of the French aristocracy and the professional classes.[51]

In the essays "Of Pedantry" (I, 25) and "Of the Education of Children" (I, 26), as well as in other sections of the text, he developed an extensive criticism of current pedagogical practices. Among the main points of his own vision of education were the superior importance of the formation of character and the moral awareness of children, as opposed to the mere acquisition of notions; a profound contempt for the type of schooling designed to produce "donkeys" burdened with ill-digested erudition, and more generally a rejection of any form of knowledge imposed by authority and uncritically accepted by the pupil. He also set forth a passionate condemnation of the brutal physical punishments to which children were currently subjected both at home and at school, stressing in particular the fact that French law failed to protect minors from their parents and guardians, that is to say in those circumstances where they were most likely to become victims of abusive practices.[52]

Recalling his own experiences of amateur theatricals at the Collège de Guyenne, Montaigne insisted also on the civic dimension of education, arguing that games, drama, and other forms of collective entertainment, far from offending Christian morality as some claimed, were an ideal medium for promoting a sense of "community and good will" among the public. Magistrates and sovereigns would be well advised to resort to these emotionally rewarding forms of collective education, which could improve public ethos in an open and pleasing manner.[53]

There was an obvious convergence between Montaigne's belief in the necessity of reforming the education of French elites, and some major pedagogical projects associated with the Counter-Reformation, such as the institution of Jesuit colleges; the writer's personal association with some leading Jesuits, such as the Castilian Juan Maldonado—one of the pioneers of the new model of schooling inaugurated by the Society of Jesus—may have led to an exchange of views on the subject of pedagogical practices.[54] However, Montaigne's main concern was not the reform of institutions, civic or religious, as much as the necessity for a radical change in individual attitudes, leading to a more respectful, more affectionate treatment of children, to the condemnation of violence, and to an essentially modern, antiauthoritarian conception of the acquisition of knowledge.

There were on the whole many ways in which political regimes could create the conditions for a "healthier"—that is to say less fanatical, divided and prejudiced—opinion, in the same way in which they could corrupt public ethos by their abuses: these where, however, long-term trends that depended on a wide variety of historical factors. Whatever the specific circumstances, the control governments exercised over individual belief was bound to prove inadequate, since public opinion, as an aggregate, did not exhaust the resilience of individual views, nor the vitality of spontaneous collective experiences. If the exercise of toleration was seen as a loss of political power, it was at the same time an acknowledgment of the limits on political action set by the very nature of human convictions. Thus the problem of that elusive "freedom of conscience" evoked in the text was less a moral than a cognitive one: whatever the pressure of power and of institutionalized belief, individual conscience was able to resist it through its opaque and inscrutable singularity, which God alone could penetrate.

Chapter 5

TURNING THE TIDE

TRUST AND LEGITIMACY

Trouble in Bordeaux

On the 17th of August, 1548, the lieutenant Tristan de Moneins, sent by king Henry II to Bordeaux to deal with an outburst of riots against the *gabelle* (the salt tax), was killed and torn to pieces by the crowd together with some tax collectors.[1] Montaigne recalled the episode, which he claimed to have witnessed "in his childhood" (he was fifteen at the time), discussing the reasons that had brought the unfortunate envoy to his death. Moneins had been safely under armed guard inside one of Bordeaux's forts, the Château-Trompette, when he had injudiciously agreed to go to the town hall (*mairerie*) in rue des Ayres, thus exposing himself to an attack by the protesters.[2]

The current view—Montaigne explained—was that he was killed because he took a foolish risk; yet this was not quite true: his real mistake was not the choice of confronting the people in person, but the attitude he adopted in doing so, first surrounding himself with armed soldiers—showing his mistrust and will to intimidate—then revealing his fear and his anxiety to win over the angry crowd. What was required instead to confront "the frenzied populace" was an attitude of "gracious severity . . . security and confidence," which alone might have gained their respect.

The episode was presented in Book I in the essay "Various Outcomes of the Same Plan" (I, 24), which illustrated how the same line of conduct might lead to opposite results. Constructed in the rather loose descriptive fashion typical of the early drafts of the *Essais*, the text related a string of historical anecdotes taken from Montaigne's favorite sources, from Plutarch to Amyot. The Bordeaux story, however, was added to the 1588 edition (B text) and had an obvious contemporary ring to it, since Montaigne connected the *gabelle* killings with an incident of which he had himself been protagonist in the same town several years later, in the spring of 1585.

At the time the writer was serving his second term as mayor of Bordeaux, a post to which he had been appointed in 1581. The political climate in the city was especially tense, since the majority of parliament, under the new presidency of Jean de Louppes de Villeneuve, as well as some of the king's officials in town, supported the Catholic League, and were hostile to the group of moderate loyalists to which Montaigne himself belonged. In particular, it was feared that two of the commanders of the royal troops stationed in the city, Jean Gourdon de Genouillac de Vaillac and Jacques d'Escar de Merville (the latter had stood unsuccessfully against Montaigne on his reelection to the *mairie* in 1583), might attempt a military coup.[3]

The traditional occasion of a review of the troops gave special cause for alarm, since it seemed the perfect opportunity for a military takeover, and some members of the town council argued that it would be more prudent to cancel the parade altogether, or at least to disarm the companies suspected of disloyalty. Montaigne for his part took the view that such precautions would prove useless in the face of a determined attack, and that it was best to show the soldiers that they were trusted, by standing among them "head high and countenance open," and by allowing them to perform the customary artillery display. This strategy, he concluded, proved successful, inaugurating a climate of advantageous "mutual confidence" between the town authorities and the troops.[4]

The two Bordeaux episodes, like many other historical examples presented in the *Essais*, showed how the outcome of difficult human confrontations often depended on the individual attitude of the agents: a word, an impression, a gesture, the fleeting emotion of a single moment, could reverse the situation in one's favor or turn it into a disaster. At first Montaigne used these cases to illustrate the uncertainty of human affairs, always exposed to the whims of Fortune, and to stress the difficulty of predicting historical outcomes with any degree of accuracy. He also echoed the conclusions that classical stoic morality derived from this condition of uncertainty: because, however one decided to act, one could not be sure of the outcome, it was best to behave consistently with honor and magnanimity. There was in fact no guarantee that dishonorable actions would succeed better than honorable ones: on the contrary, history offered plenty of examples of men who had hoped in vain to triumph through infamy. Montaigne would also have been familiar with the particular twist given by Machiavelli to this type of argument, when he suggested that virtue (in the distinctive sense of courage and daring) would "attract" success, since Fortune favored those who challenged her.[5]

As his reflection progressed, however, Montaigne moved away from these classical exempla and from the question of how the virtuous individual (or, in Machiavelli's perspective, the aspiring leader and conqueror) should behave in the face of life's hazards. What interested him instead was the precise nature of the feeling that led human beings, sometimes impulsively, to replace an instinctive response of fear and distrust with one of acceptance and cooperation. Thus his concern shifted from the conventional definition of an ideal moral posture, to that decisive interaction between real people that so often determined the twists and turns of historical events. In the *Essais* this positive response to another human agent was identified as *fidelité, confiance,* and *fiance* (in English: fidelity, confidence, and trust) and gradually came to occupy a prominent place in Montaigne's analysis.[6]

Authorities on Credit

One important dimension of human experience in which trust clearly played an essential role was the shaping of men's beliefs and opinions. Most of what human beings knew, or thought they knew, about this world and the next, they learned not from direct experience, but from the experience, recollections, and beliefs of other people. This process of learning from the authority of others applied both to one's immediate environment (as in the case of a child learning from her parents) and to more organized forms of knowledge such as history, geography, science, or theology. Historical facts, like geographical accounts or scientific doctrines, were acquired through the testimony of other people, most of the time people who had been dead for a long time, whose narratives, statements, and observations had been transmitted by oral tradition or recorded in writing. Religious dogmas were of course a privileged area of authority, since they were supposed to reveal God's own truth: yet even in this particular area one should distinguish between faith—which was directly inspired by God—and the teachings of Revelation, which were transmitted through the intermediary, and therefore the authority, of human agents.

Montaigne suggested that establishing the truth about any claim based upon authority was a process similar to that of judging the reliability of witnesses at a judicial inquiry. Experience had taught him how the exercise of assessing testimony was on the whole a risky one, partly because people were naturally given to telling lies, partly because even honest witnesses would often prove mistaken or confused. Inevitably, complex historical events were far more difficult to reconstruct than isolated incidents, since witnesses, even when they were reliable and well-informed, would have a partial or distorted perception of the wider context: a military commander on the battlefield, for example, though in theory an ideal witness, in practice would see the battle from a particular perspective and miss out on lots of things that went on all around him at the same time.[7]

Taking into account the uncertainty of individual perceptions, Montaigne believed that, as a rule, the reputation and credibility of witnesses carried more weight than the plausibility of the information they imparted. Jean Bodin, for example, was wrong when he questioned Plutarch's account of the self-sacrificing spirit of the Spartans: his judgment was based upon the fact that certain forms of heroic behavior seemed excessive and impossible to the modern mind; yet on this point he should have trusted Plutarch, who had a far better understanding of the mentality of ancient peoples than any contemporary author.[8] Another example was provided by the experience of supernatural events. As a rule it was reasonable to be suspicious of any reports of ghostly apparitions, monsters, and miracles: such phenomena, when they were not a deliberate hoax, were often the creation of diseased minds or fictions of popular imagination. However, if an authoritative Christian writer like Saint Augustine described a miraculous event—a blind child whose sight was restored through the intercession of a holy relic—supporting his narrative with the testimony of two learned bishops, one should perhaps suspend one's judgment before dismissing the whole story as simply incredible.[9]

Clearly there was a significant degree of arbitrariness in what humans chose to believe or disbelieve, as well as in the assumptions that were made about the truth of testimony. Very often people's judgment about such matters was very poor indeed, and many who should have known better ended up giving credit to the most absurd and fantastic claims. And yet the recourse to authority was inevitable, since it would be impossible for anyone to verify the foundations of all received knowledge.

A similar practice of taking authority "on credit," in Montaigne's own phrase,[10] helped to legitimate the power of political regimes. The instability of human behavior meant that it would be impossible for men to live together within society without placing their trust in each other's willingness to submit to common rules. Sovereigns and political institutions alike derived their authority not from the sheer exercise of force, but from the trust people placed in their entitlement and ability to govern. Predictably, however, in this as in other domains of authority, the allocation of trust to rulers was based upon judgments that often proved irrational, injudicious, or confused.

In some cases people displayed toward their leaders and social superiors a fierce loyalty that was hardly justified by the circumstances: Montaigne cited the case of the servant from Toulouse who chose to be executed with his master—a young scholar who stood accused of heresy—simply because he could not admit that the latter might be wrong about anything. Just like trust, mistrust of those in power could be carried to the extreme consequences; thus the citizens of Arras were understandably hostile to king Louis XI when he occupied their town (until then under Flemish rule): yet the choice of many of them, who preferred to be executed rather than shouting "long live the king!," went against common sense.[11]

It was reasonable to assume that people who operated in immediate personal contact—neighbors, associates, relatives, patrons and clients—could develop a relationship of confidence, since their expectations in relation to each other were quite specific and could be easily put to the test. But if one looked at the link that normally existed between a sovereign and his subjects, it was far less clear that such a remote connection could be properly described as a bond of trust. Most of the time people obeyed a bad prince and a good one in the same way, submitting indifferently to tyrannical regimes and to just and legitimate rulers. Montaigne illustrated this point with an episode from the life of one of his favorite historical characters, the emperor Julian: to his courtiers, who praised his sense of justice, Julian objected that he might have felt proud, had they been ready to recognize in the same way any injustice committed by him. The problem with monarchy was that the crushing power that the sovereign held over his subjects placed him beyond the reach of any genuine appraisal or criticism; because the king did not answer to anyone for his actions, it was difficult to say whether he was or was not trustworthy.[12]

In countries where monarchy was the traditional form of government, if the subjects were freed by some upheaval from the domination of their king, they would eagerly rush into servitude to a new master; in the same way, those nations that had been accustomed to republican institutions would remain faithful to them, resisting any attempt to replace them by some other form of regime. At a different level, people attributed to their sovereigns imaginary virtues and vices, and loved them or hated them with very little reference to any real circumstances. Clearly, in the relations between rulers and subjects, habit on the one hand, and imagination on the other, played a far more significant role than any well-considered assessment of the reliability of the rulers themselves.[13]

If this was true, what was the role of trust in political societies? No doubt trust played a crucial role in establishing relations of sociability and cooperation among men; however, its relevance to the cohesion and stability of large political communities of long standing could be questioned. Machiavelli for one had forcefully argued that the legitimacy of political regimes rested upon factors other than the existence of any bonds of fidelity between rulers and subjects. The fact that the French state had not actually collapsed, in spite of the detestable climate of hatred and fear generated by the civil war, seemed to confirm the truth of this claim about the irrelevance of trust: a dismal conclusion that Montaigne found himself compelled to put to the test.

Life without Trust

As the reflection of the *Essais* progressed, and especially in Book III, Montaigne focused increasingly on the question of the specific role of trust. The loss of confidence and the antagonistic passions experienced by contemporary French society offered a privileged insight into this issue, since

they brought out tensions and contradictions that in a more stable historical setting would remain undetected. Montaigne subscribed wholeheart-
edly to the classical Ciceronian view that a well-ordered political regime
was one in which people were subjected to impartial rules and procedures,
not the arbitrary will of persons. Thus in a good polity people placed their
trust in the law and in public offices, rather than in the benevolence of particular individuals. In this respect the civil war marked a dramatic regres-
sion of French society, since the loss of confidence in public institutions
pushed people back into relations of personal dependence and subjection:
abandoned by the state and by its laws, a disoriented, frightened population turned for safety to the protection of powerful individuals, of warlords, factions, and clans.

Private relations of fidelity replaced those bonds of trust, which should
unite the people and the state. The writer was painfully aware of this reality, which he experienced as an intolerable loss of personal freedom: well-
connected and well-liked by high-placed men and women in both parties,
he deeply resented the feeling that he owed his safety to their influence,
rather than the protection of the law. In the essay "Of Vanity" (III, 9) he
contrasted the heavy burden represented by the exchange of personal favors and loyalties with the lighter, far less demanding obligations created
by economic relations: where services were for sale, all one had to give in
exchange for them was money, while in bonds of personal obligation one
had to pay with one's whole person; relations based upon sentiments of
personal honor were far more taxing than those regulated by economic exchange and legal constraints.

> Now I hold that we should live by right and authority, not by reward or favor.
> How many gallant men have chosen rather to lose their lives than to owe
> them! I avoid subjecting myself to any sort of obligation, but especially any
> that binds me by a debt of honor. I find nothing so expensive as that which is
> given me and for which my will remains mortgaged by the claim of gratitude,
> and I more willingly accept services that are for sale. Rightly so, I think: for
> the latter I give only money, for the others I give myself. The tie that binds
> me by the law of honesty seems to me much tighter and more oppressive than
> is that of legal constraint.[14]

The dismaying experience of living in a society that had reverted to ar-
chaic forms of personal dependence offered the first part of answer to the
question of whether trust was necessary to the preservation of political systems. The French case showed that polities could indeed survive to the decline of trust, and continue to function, even when the population had lost
all faith in their rulers, and when the citizens lived in dread of their neighbors. A society of criminals, such as the colony created by Philip the Macedonian by gathering a collection of especially wicked and depraved men,

could be perfectly functional. The habit of belonging together within the same political space, and the residual existence of some basic common interests, meant that people were able to adjust to the absence of order and justice, in the same way in which a collection of objects, thrown together at random, may settle into an untidy heap. The problem was that life on the heap was very unpleasant: while the privileged members of society suffered a significant loss of security, and therefore of freedom, the poor were exposed, without defense, to the ravages of depredation and violence. Even future generations were affected: they were in fact deprived both of material resources, since the economy of the country was wrecked by civil conflict, and of moral ones, through the destruction of stability and peace; they were in fact "pillaged" of everything they had, even of hope.[15]

Experience showed that a polity without trust was viable, but that it was not really fit for humans to live in. For any regime, a generalized loss of confidence was not a normal state of affairs, but a pathological condition: those contemporary writers who set forth a model of political power sustained by infamy, and legitimated by deceit, had lost sight of what human communities were for. Montaigne was ready to admit that the factors leading to the decline or the regeneration of states were rather obscure: in the text he employed a variety of medical metaphors, comparing political societies to patients, who may succumb to a lingering illness, or recover from it, in ways that baffled the most experienced physicians. It would be pointless to establish a general pattern of decline and recovery, since, just like living organisms, nations were very different from each other, and because every particular historical setting was unique.[16]

Rather than proposing a general explanatory model, Montaigne concentrated upon one particular feature of public confidence: its ultimate dependence on the feelings and actions of single individuals. If in orderly, stable regimes, people placed their trust in public institutions, the institutions themselves could command confidence and respect, only in so far as the persons who represented them were individually worthy of trust. The mass of the people might remain unaware of the real qualities or vices of their rulers, and the considerable attention paid by the public to each gesture of princes generally produced a distorted image of their true character and of their actions. And yet the spreading of abuse and corruption, from the royal entourage down to magistrates and public officials, could not go unnoticed, and would sooner or later destroy whatever credit the state in question may have enjoyed in the past.

In France the collapse of trust in royal authority and the growing sentiments of fear and insecurity among the population had been a decisive factor in bringing about the civil war. As some observers had suggested in the early 1560s, fear alone had pushed the Huguenots to rebel against the crown: had the king reassured them and granted their safety, the conflict could have been avoided. Montaigne did apparently share this judgment, as well as the belief that a parallel sentiment of fear had motivated the Catholic pogroms of 1572.[17] The text of the *Essais* made no explicit reference to the Saint Bartholomew's Day Massacre; modern readers may find this omission surprising, forgetting that the Catholic literary establishment, including several personal friends of Montaigne, engaged in extensive celebrations and praises of this particular royal initiative, which had allegedly "saved" France from a Protestant conspiracy. On the other hand, the *Essais* contain several passages where the massacre of civilians, both in contemporary and in ancient times, in France as well as abroad, were strongly depicted and denounced. In one of the early essays—" Of Fear" (I, 18)—written shortly after the events of 1572, the writer sketched a tragic picture of some ancient town where people, struck by "panic terror," rushed against each other in a frenzy of violence, mistaking their neighbors for invading enemies. Thus in the streets of "Carthage":

> You heard nothing . . . but frightened cries and exclamations. You saw the inhabitants running out of their houses as at a call to arms, and charging, wounding, and killing each other, as if they were enemies coming to occupy their city.[18]

If this extreme feeling of mistrust, leading to rebellion and civil war, seemed exceptional to an external observer, it represented in fact only the last phase in a slow process of erosion of confidence within the community. Before people actually got to the stage where they feared for their lives, the practice of patronage and corruption—so often denounced by the partisans of judicial reform during the 1550s and 1560s—had created a climate of suspicion and disaffection toward public authority; the systematic violation of the law, ignored and tolerated by many, had gradually led to more serious transgressions and abuses.

Montaigne argued that the responsibility for the decline of public ethos was widespread: from the king and his court, down to the last negligent magistrate or corrupt official, everyone was to blame. A lesser degree of blame must be extended also to all those private individuals, like the writer himself, who had stood by as the rules of justice and civil coexistence were being trampled upon, rather than rushing to their defense. If the decline of trust had been caused primarily by the ambition, greed, and brutality of a few powerful actors, the indifference and cowardice of many bystanders had also significantly contributed to it. Thus the betrayal of trust appeared at the same time as a diffuse feeling that pervaded all levels of social interaction, and a very personal experience that engaged the moral conscience of each member of the community.[19]

The Corruption of Language

One particular dimension of trust relations that featured very prominently in the *Essais* was that of language; Montaigne's choice of placing speech and conversation at the center of human sociability is probably one of the best-known aspects of his work. But in the *Essais* conversation was not presented simply as a pleasure and a social and intellectual accomplishment: discourse and verbal exchanges were described as the vital bonds of human community; through them people were able to cooperate, to make agreements, and to settle their differences. Because the only alternative to verbal exchanges in human relations was the use of violence, whenever conversation stopped, brute force and war took over. Clearly, in Montaigne's analysis, language and trust were intimately connected, since it was essentially through language that humans could communicate their intentions, make promises, and win each other's support. Thus the deterioration of language in any society corresponded to a deterioration of public confidence, while the spreading of moral and political corruption was always associated with "the banishment of truth."[20]

Looking at contemporary French society, Montaigne denounced two especially pernicious ways in which the corruption of public discourse manifested itself. The first was represented by the fashionable contemporary political culture, which considered deceit and mendacity as suitable instruments of governance. The damage caused by such ideology (broadly associated with the Machiavellian tradition and the doctrines of reason of state) was enormous, since infamy and deceit, recommended as useful skills for rulers, became common, and indeed acceptable, within society at large, destroying any confidence people previously had in the institutions and in each other.[21]

One of the first precepts of a good education was that children must be taught not to cheat or lie; instead, modern men were "trained for infamy." Montaigne criticized in particular the view that the obligation of keeping one's word was a relative and flexible one: on the contrary, promises must always be kept, and only very special circumstances (such as the promise to commit some wicked action) could constitute an exception. Deceit was unacceptable even in dealing with criminals: Montaigne judged especially odious the artifice practiced by some magistrates, who extracted information from suspects by false promises of pardon.[22]

The second form of corruption of public discourse denounced in the *Essais* was the deterioration of the letter of the law. Before the civil war, the different bodies of French legislation were already suffering from a considerable lack of clarity and transparency in the formulation of their prescriptions, which often proved contradictory or redundant. Since the beginning of the war, this phenomenon had been accentuated by the growing instability of the new legislation introduced to deal with religious dissent, and by the constant shifting in terminology: criminal actions were now described as permissible, while previously innocent ones had been stigmatized as criminal.

The initial effect of these changes in the letter of the law had been to create puzzlement and confusion among the population; but in practice this confusion meant that public trust was being betrayed by the authorities and the magistracy, since the subjects now suffered punishment for committing actions that the law had previously described as licit: they were punished in fact because those responsible for making and enforcing the law had simply changed their minds. Through this process, which destroyed the credibility of the law, right and wrong became confused and perverted. Indeed, the worst possible misfortune a political community might experience was a state of affairs in which wickedness became lawful, acquiring the status of authority.[23]

It is important to stress that, for Montaigne, speaking honestly and sincerely did not mean simply "telling the truth," at least as one understood it, but also expressing oneself with simplicity and directness; it was not just the content of discourse that was important: the mode of address mattered as well. If speech was the vehicle of human relations, it was essential that the language used in all manner of communication and public discourse should be simple and focused upon essential matters. Once again the example to be followed was that of Socrates:

> Our world is formed only for ostentation; men inflate themselves only with wind, and go bouncing around like balls. This man did not propose to himself any idle fancies: his aim was to furnish us with things and precepts that serve life really and more closely: . . . There is nothing borrowed from art and the sciences; even the simplest can recognize in him their means and their strength.[24]

Thus the project of restoring language set forth in the *Essais* as a condition for re-creating confidence within the community had potentially very far-reaching implications, which went well beyond the scope of immediate political action: it required, in the first instance, placing people in a position where they might prefer to speak to each other, rather than to fight; it involved the moral reeducation of society as a whole to the values of honesty and sincerity; it also implied what can only be described as a democratization of public discourse—a task in which, in Montaigne's view, religious reformers had sadly failed, reproducing in their propaganda the elitism and arrogance of traditional authorities.

Trust and Royal Power

Throughout the text of the *Essais*, Montaigne's views on the prospects of a return to civil peace seem to point in two quite different directions: sometimes the French crisis was described, with a certain detachment, as a puzzling historical phenomenon, the outcome of which, like its causes, remained uncertain; elsewhere the writer adopted instead the perspective of the individual agent, calling for a more active contribution to civil reconciliation.

Thus on the one hand he presented those factors that determined the preservation or the ruin of political regimes as complex and obscure, arguing that they did not lend themselves to simple explanatory models, and could not be effectively guided by political intervention. Seen from this perspective, the current crisis appeared almost as a natural calamity (if a manmade one), in the face of which the only sensible response was to wait until the destructive forces that swept over the nation had finally exhausted their course. There was in fact no instant recipe, no master plan to generate a recovery, which rather must come in time from the hidden resources of French society itself, from the community's potential for self-regeneration.

On the other hand, since the decline of the state originated in a multitude of individual acts of abuse and betrayal, each person could contribute to the restoration of public confidence by the simple expedient of adopting an open, honest attitude. By proving worthy of trust, and by showing to others that they were trusted, each person could start a kind of virtuous cycle within his own, however limited, sphere of influence. Such display of individual goodwill might of course prove ineffective, but it did answer to the obligation of acting honestly and humanely toward others whatever the circumstances.[25]

The narrative of the *Essais* betrayed the author's fascination with the theme of the unarmed man or woman who, through the sheer force of persuasion, succeeded in turning the tide of events: stopped the hand of the executioner, confounded the traitor, placated the hostile crowd, touched the heart of the enemy. Some of the episodes related by Montaigne conveyed a sense of tragic grandeur: thus he described Alexander the Great drinking a potion prepared by his doctor and friend, Philip, after learning that the latter had been paid by Darius to poison him; turning to contemporary events, he provided a moving account of how the Catholic leader François de Guise confronted a member of his household, who was plotting his assassination.[26]

Other incidents, especially those taken from the writer's own experiences, were reported in a lighter, self-deprecating tone. He related with relish his adventure with a band of marauding soldiers, who had tried un-successfully to break into his house, as the chateau, by its owner's militant choice, was not protected by any special security. With similar irony he de-scribed his negotiations with a band of masked horsemen, who had cap-tured him while he was traveling in the thick of a forest, demanding a ran-som for his release. While there was nothing especially heroic about these encounters (break-ins and kidnappings were quite common during the wars), the writer was obviously proud of the fact that, in both cases, his as-sailants admitted they had given up their evil intentions because they were won over by his open manners and countenance, by his *franchise*. The im-portant point was not that he had behaved with special courage or dignity (he admitted he was in fact quite scared), but that he had succeeded in talking to them and in creating some kind of rapport. In a memorable *coup de theatre*, while his fellow-bandits hunted around to recover the pris-oner's scattered belongings, their chief had taken off his mask, introduc-ing himself to his victim and making him the gift of his liberty.[27]

What emerged from these different narratives was a picture of trust as a diverse reality, ranging from the exemplary gestures of great historical per-sonalities, to the ordinary incidents in the daily life of common people placed in difficult circumstances; at all levels one could choose between the way of communication and persuasion on the one hand, and that of fear and aggression on the other. Thus Montaigne's reflection on trust de-veloped as a detailed anthropological analysis, which took into account a variety of agents and circumstances—all of them relevant to the cohesion of a political community.

This complex account of human interaction stood in sharp contrast with the argument that dominated most contemporary writings on the subject: derived from traditional theories of royal absolutism, this argument placed the burden of the restoration of public ethos upon a single privileged actor, the monarch. Since the beginning of the religious wars, those intel-lectuals who gravitated toward the two rival courts—the glamorous en-tourage of the Valois in Paris and the somewhat more rustic establishment of the king of Navarre at Nérac—indicated royal authority as the only pos-sible agent of civil reconciliation. Catherine de Médicis, Charles IX, Henry III, the duke of Alençon, and Henry of Navarre were all subsequently cast in this role of monarch-savior, restorer of peace and justice, a theme that featured prominently in court pageantry during the decades of the war, and that Henry IV would later exploit to celebrate the advent of his new dynasty. The claim that the king alone possessed the quasi-divine author-ity necessary to restore public confidence was set forth by writers belong-ing to Henry III's prestigious Académie du Palais, such as Pierre de Ron-sard, Antoine de Baif, Guy du Faur de Pibrac, Giordano Bruno, and Jean Bodin, but also by Protestant authors like Agrippa D'Aubigné. In spite of the recurring tensions between the Valois and the king of Navarre, there were in fact ongoing contacts between the two royal entourages, and Montaigne's position of having access to both was far from unusual.[28]

If the royal protagonists and the language changed to some extent, all these formulations of the role of the king agreed in attributing to the monarch both the prerogative of legitimate sovereignty, and a superior moral and religious authority derived directly from God. Thus the king alone could arbitrate between rival factions, using severity or clemency at his discretion, as the exclusive dispenser of justice. He was at the same time the privileged mediator between the people and God: whether the solution of the religious crisis was identified with the suppression of heresy, the reform of the Church, or the establishment of religious coexistence, only the king could be the interpreter and agent of God's design.

This vision of the role of the monarch left little room for the issue of trust as such: the king did not need to win back the confidence of his people through some gradual process of persuasion and public reconciliation. Whatever the reasons that had originally led to the eclipse of royal power (be they heresy, rebellion, or divine punishment) the same power would be instantly restored, at some unspecified time, through some kind of sudden, blinding recognition. Throughout the long decades of the wars, countless poems, ballets, masques, and celebrations continued to illustrate this expectation of a royal epiphany by resorting to classical myths of rebirth, or to astral allegories. In this context fidelity (*fidélité*) to the king was an act of unconditional obedience and acknowledgment of his authority; it did not imply a specific bond of personal confidence, but simply the acceptance of an established order of subjection and allegiance.[29] It was only after the assassination of Henry III in 1589, when Navarre was finally in the position of claiming the crown, that the issue of public confidence acquired new relevance. Confronted with the slow and difficult task of making his authority accepted across France by a range of different constituencies, the new king resorted to a policy of agreements and to the language of trust, as a means of persuading his audiences of the legitimacy of his claims and of his genuine commitment to civil concord.[30]

In the *Essais* the only concession made to the current view of the monarch as superior agent is the acknowledgment of the influence rulers exercised through their example. Because people were overattentive to the attitudes and doings of princes, any display of virtue, moderation, or clemency on their part was more likely to strike public imagination than a similar example provided by ordinary persons—though in practice the public might be easily misled as to the true nature of such exemplary actions. This superior visibility of princes, and the influence they exercised, was not, however, a proof of their moral superiority, only a consequence of the role that the people liked to attribute to them.[31]

Throughout the text the position of monarchs is consistently presented as morally disabling. Those princes who were born to reign were deprived from early infancy of the essential components of a good moral education: the sincere appraisal of their conduct and the confrontation, on a ground of equality, with the abilities and views of others. Even those who had come to royalty later in life saw their moral character rapidly corrupted by the excess of power, by the fear they inspired, and by the flattery they attracted. Because in France many high-ranking individuals lived like petty monarchs in their domains (Caesar had already described Gallic warlords as "little kings"), the negative effects of the "disadvantage" (*incommodité*) of rank extended to a substantial portion of the privileged class.[32]

For Montaigne, the fact that the moral character of princes was crippled and corrupted by their exalted rank (a disability widely acknowledged by classical moralists) was only part of the problem; the most serious limitation in the position of kings was that they were deprived, for most of their lives, of any ordinary intercourse with other human beings. Unable to form bonds of communication, exchange, understanding, and confidence on a ground of parity with other men, they were in fact excluded from what the writer regarded as the very essence of human community: to him the image of monarchs "sitting alone at their tables" besieged by a crowd of gazers, or prisoners within the frontiers of their own kingdom, "unable to go freely about their travels," was a poignant illustration of their humanly deprived condition.[33]

It was unsurprising, in the circumstances, that the merits and demerits of sovereigns and of monarchical regimes should prove impossible to assess with any degree of objectivity. To illustrate this fact, Montaigne cited "two Scottish books" in which royalty was either vilified on principle or excessively exalted and treated as "superior to God": though he omitted the titles, he was referring to the work by his former tutor at the Collège de Guyenne, George Buchanan, *De jure regni apud Scotos* (1579), and to the answer by his opponent Adam Blackwood, *Adversum Georgi Buchani dialogum, De iure regni apud Scotos, pro regibus Apologia* (1581). Since superior and inferior ranks, the role of ruler and that of subject, were opposed "by natural rivalry and competition," no intermediate approach seemed possible.[34]

Once again, in discussing the role of royal authority in the process of civil reconciliation, Montaigne set forth a double perspective on the way in which power could be made legitimate. One way of looking at the issue was that legitimacy would eventually be restored through some obscure healing process, of the kind human societies were subject to, thus reestablishing the credit of a monarch who, for his part, would play only a symbolic role. In this way the instant result that royal apologists expected from the quasi-divine quality of the king would be achieved instead thanks to the willingness of the people to place themselves once again under the dominion of a master, without really questioning his trustworthiness. In other words, legitimacy would not come from any clear expectation in relation to the king, but the need to see order reestablished would bring about the almost mechanical reassertion of traditional bonds of subjection.

However, in the reflections on the subject he developed after the death of the duke of Anjou in 1584, when Navarre became heir apparent to the crown, the writer left some scope to the initiative of a determined and well-intentioned sovereign. While an established monarchical regime could subsist without a fresh input of trust, the instability and void of legitimacy experienced by the French state gave the opportunity to all men of good will to bring back into public life values such as honesty, sincerity, and moderation. The king himself could be part of this collective effort toward the restoration of public ethos by giving his enemies "as much occasion to love him as his friends," rather than treating them like a monarch exacting his due from his subjects.

Montaigne raised the point in more concrete terms in a letter to Henry of Navarre (the same in which he reminded him of his past loyalty): commenting on the line of action followed by Navarre's troops in the attempted siege of Paris in 1589, he admitted that the circumstances of a king besieging his own capital in the hands of rebels were "uncommon" and that perhaps they justified using unorthodox means; he still deplored, however, the episodes of pillaging and violence against civilians that had been reported:

> I would have wished, to be sure, that the individual profit of the soldiers in your army and the need to content them had not robbed you, especially in that principal city, of the fine recommendation of having treated your mutinous subjects, in the height of victory, with more solace than do their protectors; and that you had shown that they were yours, not by a passing and usurped claim, but by a paternal and truly royal affection.[35]

Just as ordinary people might prefer to show human decency, looking beyond the divides created by resentment and partisan opposition, similarly the king could choose to act with sincerity and humanity over promoting his cause by deception and those base means that expediency dictated, whatever the cost. Clearly the ruler's choice of rejecting crudely instrumental solutions required a superior degree of moral determination: the chief example Montaigne produced of such conduct, that of the Greek commander Epaminondas, only emphasized the exceptional and near-heroic character of such an achievement. The outstanding moral qualities of Epaminondas had already been celebrated in the essay "Of the Most Outstanding Men" (II, 36): there the Theban general was compared exclusively to other famous leaders from antiquity, but elsewhere in the text Montaigne admitted that modern instances of virtue could not compete with ancient ones.[36]

Contemporary France could still be said to breed virtuous men, but only "*selon nous*," that is to say, according to modern, somewhat diminished standards. However, one could not escape from one's own times; the universe within which French kings operated in the age of the religious wars was very distant not just from classical republican glory, but also from the "shining" heritage of ancient monarchical grandeur.[37] In these circumstances the virtuous path open to Navarre was a narrow one: since he was operating in a difficult practical context, nobody could expect from him exceptional and miraculous gestures; good will and ordinary decency on his part would already represent a significant result, and distinguish his attitude from the dismal performance of his predecessors.

A King in Trust

I did not call you, as my predecessors did, to make you approve their will; I gathered you to receive your counsels, to believe them, to follow them, in short to place myself in trust into your hands.[38]

This particular statement, part of a speech addressed by king Henry IV to an assembly of notables in Rouen, on 4 November 1596, shocked some of those present at the meeting, including the king's own mistress, Gabrielle d'Estrées, who was following the proceedings discreetly hidden behind a tapestry. Henry IV's performance also left a durable impression upon posterity: in her retrospective assessment of the revolution of 1789, *Considérations sur la Révolution française*, Germaine de Staël referred to it as to a landmark in French history, and claimed that "everyone" knew his words "by heart." Her historical sketch of the events leading up to the convocation of the Estates General in 1789 presented the Rouen speech as the perfect expression of those values upon which French constitutional monarchy should rest. Set against Henry IV's bold and generous address to the assembly, the half-hearted, unconvincing performance of his descendant Louis XVI, in his speech at the opening of the Estates, revealed the decadence and inadequacy of a monarchy that had betrayed its original principles.[39]

If the Rouen speech carried the image of a sovereign seeking his people's trust to rhetorical extremities, this kind of language was not infrequent in Navarre's public statements during this period. On other occasions the new king stressed the difference of his own attitude from that of his predecessors by pointing at the informality of his attire. On 7 February

1599, pleading with the *parlement* of Paris in favor of the ratification of the Edict of Nantes, he claimed:

> I do not come to speak to you wearing, like my predecessors, my royal robes, nor carrying my sword and cloak; neither do I come like a prince who meets some foreign ambassadors, but just like a father of the family, in my doublet. . . .[40]

Recent studies on the process of reconciliation after the religious wars have suggested that, for the first decade of his reign, the new king's relations with the different constituencies in the kingdom—the nobility, the towns, and the *parlements*—were constructed around specific agreements, and were therefore the expression of a form of royal power based upon contract.[41] This "contractualist" phase in Navarre's career allegedly began in the days following Henry III's murder, in August 1589, when he issued various public statements to reassure the French nobility and the towns of his intentions to respect the Catholic religion and the subjects' traditional privileges; it continued after his conversion to Catholicism in 1593, with a series of agreements he subscribed with the Protestant communities and with the rebel towns still controlled by the League, to secure their loyalty (at least about fifty such documents were signed in 1594); it extended to his protracted negotiations with the *parlements* to obtain the ratification of the Edict of Nantes.[42]

Once religious peace and the future of the Bourbon dynasty finally seemed secure, this language of contract disappeared from the king's rhetoric, to be replaced by a more conventional assertion of authority. The same studies point out that Navarre—an old hand at dealing with Protestant assemblies, where deliberations were often manipulated and elections rigged—was obviously familiar with monarchomach literature and language; in particular they recall that the king's closest advisor and speech writer for that period was the Protestant Philippe Duplessis-Mornay, generally recognized as the author, in the late 1570s, of the influential monarchomach pamphlet *Vindiciae contra tyrannos*.[43]

The suggestion that, by signing a set of particular agreements with his subjects, Henry IV directly transformed the nature of the French monarchy, seems rather far-fetched: the practice of making specific concessions to various constituencies in the kingdom at moments of national crisis was neither unprecedented nor incompatible with monarchical absolutism, though it might be an indication of weakness on the part of the crown. On the other hand, the claim that his language changed in his appeals to his subjects during the 1590s, in particular the "contamination" of royal rhetoric by monarchomach concepts, is well supported by textual evidence, no matter if the change was opportunistic and short-lived.

Set against this background, Montaigne's discussion of trust in Book III suggests that the notion of a new approach to royal power, one based upon a bond of confidence between king and subjects, was not confined to Protestant monarchomach literature, but was shared by some of Navarre's supporters in both religious camps. If Montaigne had few illusions about Henry IV's true motivations in his pursuit of legitimacy, he apparently believed him at least capable of performing convincingly enough in this novel role of monarch ruling by popular consent.

In the same letter to Navarre cited above, he predicted the new king's imminent success, by claiming that the people would turn away from his enemies, once they had become aware of the falsity of their "great promises." He then returned to one of his favorite images—the tide—by arguing that popular inclinations went "in waves": now that the people's mood had begun to flow in the king's favor, the same impulse would carry them all the way on the same course. Tactfully, the letter remained vague as to the actual sentiments and expectations that had caused such reversal of direction in the tide of opinion.[44] The painstaking analysis developed in the *Essais* showed clearly enough that the frontier separating fidelity from subjection and community from domination would always remain visible, even through the murky waters of Realpolitik, to those who cared to recognize it.

Chapter 6

LEARNING FROM EXPERIENCE

POLITICS AS PRACTICE

The Mayor and Montaigne

Montaigne was elected mayor of Bordeaux on the first of August, 1581: the news reached him at the beginning of September at Villa dei Bagni, near Lucca, one of several spa resorts he had been visiting, hoping to find a cure for his kidney stones. The official letters of appointment were waiting for him in Rome when he reached the city at the beginning of October, before starting his journey back to France. He had not canvassed to obtain the post (he had been traveling abroad since June of the previous year), and his first instinct was to decline the unsolicited honor, ignoring the town council's appeal to his "*amour de la patrie.*"[1]

In fact, by his own admission, a desire to escape from the deplorable political atmosphere in France had been one of the motives behind the writer's long journey.[2] However, on his return to Montaigne on 30 November, he was reached by a letter from Henry III, who congratulated him on his election, praising his "*zellée devotion à mon service*" and "*fidellité*" in terms that could only be interpreted as a royal command; the letter, and possibly additional pressure from his friends and patrons, finally persuaded him to accept.[3] It has been suggested that Montaigne's nomination was stipulated by the duke of Anjou (as representative of his brother Henry III) and Henry of Navarre during the negotiations of the peace of Fleix in November 1580, together with other local appointments: the strategic importance of Bordeaux, the sensitive nature of the post, and the fact that the writer was *persona grata* to both religious parties, are all elements that seem to support this interpretation.[4] On the other hand, it is impossible to tell whether the publication of the first edition of the *Essais*—a copy of which had been offered by the author to Henry III before leaving for his journey—had played any significant role in enhancing his reputation and recommending him to his patrons.[5]

In the essay "Of Husbanding Your Will" (III, 10), in a few, apparently sketchy paragraphs, Montaigne provided his own account of the context of his election, as well as a retrospective assessment of his performance in office. The main reason he had been chosen as mayor—he claimed—was the "honored memory" of his father Pierre de Montaigne, who had once occupied the same post and was still remembered for his good, charitable nature and his devotion to the people.[6] In fact his father's example had left upon the writer a rather discouraging impression of public service: as a child he remembered him as an old man "cruelly agitated by this public turmoil," tired and yet engaged in relentless activity, while he might have enjoyed in peace the comfort of his own domestic life—in short, a dutiful victim of the "*tracasserie publique*."

For his part, Montaigne had decided to be very open with those who had elected him about his own faults and limitations: the fact that he lacked some qualities undoubtedly useful in public life—memory, concentration, experience, drive—was compensated to some extent, in his view, by the absence from his character of other pernicious attributes common in those who governed, such as hatred, ambition, greed, and cruelty.[7] As mayor, he had consistently tried to do what his duty dictated, but had always remained aware of the fact that the office he occupied and his person—in his words, "the Mayor and Montaigne"—were two quite separate entities. Some of his fellow citizens had shown a sincere appreciation for his attitude, to the extent of supporting his reelection for a second mandate: a rare achievement of which he was rather proud. Predictably, however, his low-key performance had also attracted a certain amount of criticism: some thought he had failed to display the right degree of passion and zeal; others regretted that his administration should leave no noticeable mark. Montaigne himself was quite ready to agree with his critics, but he suggested that, in the circumstances, his moderate and unremarkable rule was not such a bad thing. The main point was that he had done as well as he could, given his temperament and his abilities; he had also been lucky, since none of the major disasters he feared for the town (such as a Protestant military occupation or a coup orchestrated by the supporters of the Catholic League) had actually occurred; all considered, he preferred to think that he owed his success to his good fortune (in other words, to God's grace), rather than to his own merits and efforts:

> In short, the occasions in my term of office were suited to my disposition, for which I am grateful to them. Is there anyone who wants to be sick in order to see his doctor at work, and shouldn't we whip any doctor who would wish us the plague in order to put his art into practice? I have not had that iniquitous and rather common disposition of wanting the trouble and sickness of the affairs of this town to exalt and honor my government; . . . Anyone who will not be grateful to me for the order, the gentle and mute tranquillity, that accompanied my administration, at least cannot deprive me of the share of it that belongs to me by right of my good fortune. And I am so made that I like as well to be lucky as wise, and to owe my successes purely to the grace of God as to the effect of my own action.[8]

Montaigne's subtly ironical, self-deprecating account of his experience in municipal office has generally been judged with severity by his commentators: in the past it was often read as an indication that the writer was not sufficiently committed to any public cause and that, all considered, he was not really serious about politics. More recently interpreters have focused upon the dualism implied in the distinction between the "Mayor" and "Montaigne" in the light of the stoic themes of the opposition between private and public morality and of the tension between individual integrity and public service.[9] It is certainly possible to recognize in Montaigne's narrative the echo of classical discussions on the respective obligations of the private citizen and the magistrate, and on the means by which the virtuous individual might preserve his independence from the demands of patrons and rulers. However, it seems unlikely that the main purpose of Montaigne's autobiographical account was that of revisiting these conventional philosophical topics, by setting forth an ideal standard of commitment to public life; it is even more difficult to believe that he meant to offer himself as an example to be followed by others. In the same essay the issue of public obligation was dismissed rather bluntly, by stating that nobody could lead his life in isolation from other people, and that one was therefore compelled by circumstances to participate in the affairs of the community to which one belonged. The narrative also showed how particular individuals (like Montaigne and his father) would respond differently to public responsibilities, according to their temperament and their particular circumstances, so that in practice the setting of fixed standards of evaluation made very little sense.

Written, like the rest of Book III, between 1585 and 1587, just after his four years in office at the *mairie*, the essay formed part of a broader reflection on the kind of knowledge that might offer practical guidance to people in running their lives as well as in the conduct of public affairs. The retrospective assessment of the writer's own political experience was in fact an essential component of his distinctive re-elaboration of skeptical methodology. The theoretical considerations on the inadequacy of human reason, outlined in the "Apology for Raymond Sebond" (II, 12)—generally regarded as the author's philosophical manifesto—were only an introduction to the central issue addressed in his work, that of the practical consequences, for human beings, of this epistemological failure. It was through the detailed analysis of the uncertainty and opacity of human agency, observed in the real context of everyday experience, that Montaigne's new brand of skepticism came into its own.

Imperfection and Chance

At the origin of the difficulties encountered in accounting for human agency, Montaigne recognized the imperfection of human nature. This imperfection—which Christian doctrine imputed to the stigma of original sin—had both moral and epistemic consequences: because men were unable to act consistently according to God's law, human societies and institutions could only provide inferior examples of order and justice; because men's beliefs and choices were shaped by irrational impulses, rather than by reason, human behavior proved opaque and unpredictable. It was on account of human imperfection that all those projects that outlined ideal political communities and institutions, proved dismally utopian—as utopian, in fact, as the attempts of encompassing the history of mankind within global explanatory schemes.[10]

Whenever he illustrated the imperfection of all things human—a frequent theme in the *Essais*—Montaigne never referred explicitly to the notion of original sin. This omission may be explained by the writer's determination to avoid in his work any explicit presentation or discussion of religious dogmas, the connection between imperfection and sin being in any case self-evident to a Christian audience.[11] Alternatively, it is possible that the omission betrayed a certain uneasiness on his part with some of the consequences that the Christian philosophical tradition derived from the axiom of man's sinful nature. His reservations about Augustine's vision of the progressive decline of human civilization have already been discussed in chapter 2 above. Another source of disagreement was the view that human sinfulness required the imposition of strong authority if social order was to be preserved: the *Essais* offered ample evidence to the effect that despotic and repressive political authority generated at least as much chaos and abuse as a state of anarchy. If the resort to violence was always deplorable at all levels of the social scale, its use on the part of rulers amplified its negative effects, corrupting the people rather than improving their moral standards. This point was poignantly illustrated by the comparison between the relatively innocent brutality that primitive tribes, such as the Cannibals, directed against their enemies, and the large-scale atrocities that Christian leaders deliberately inflicted upon innocent populations.[12]

If he avoided the issue of original sin, Montaigne was certainly prepared to admit that the imperfection of human societies was connected with the influence upon mankind of passions such as envy, greed, and cruelty: these common vices prevented human beings from recognizing justice and acting according to it, leading to bad practices and inadequate institutions. However, it cannot said in the same way that the author of the *Essais* attributed the failure of human reason to some kind of moral inadequacy on men's part. If men failed to be guided by reason, it was not because their sinful passions clouded their judgment: reason was just the wrong instrument to guide them through the intricate reality of practical life, which involved a wide range of unstable emotional factors. In other words, for Montaigne irrationality carried no moral stigma: in this respect his approach diverged sharply from Augustine's Platonic vision; a perfectly virtuous, saintly man could not be guided by reason alone any more than a vicious one, since it was faith, not reason, that led humans toward virtue and salvation.[13]

Obviously the imperfection of human nature was not the only source of uncertainty in practical life: other unknown factors were represented by natural events and accidents, and by all those material circumstances that affected men's lives while remaining outside their control. In the language of the *Essais*, all these sources of risk, human and nonhuman alike, were globally described as "chance" or "fortune" (*chance, fortune*), terms that the author used, perhaps improperly, as synonymous. Unlike other Christian writers, Montaigne was uninterested in establishing any association between "fortune" and "providence": objectively speaking, of course, anything men experienced was authorized by God, and, consequently, chance could be said to correspond to God's will; subjectively, however, since men had no knowledge or understanding of God's designs, they would experience it as a blind, random force. Once again, faith alone could transform, for those who possessed it, the random impact of chance into the manifestation of a benevolent divine intention and into the sign of God's grace.[14]

His insistence on the impact of chance upon human affairs is one of the themes that brought Montaigne's analysis very close to some of Machiavelli's insights: both writers shared an acute awareness of the highly risky and unstable character of human experience, regardless of whether this uncertainty might find some sort of explanation in a superhuman dimension. However, unlike Machiavelli, Montaigne avoided any classical personification of "*Fortuna*" as a force men could superstitiously hope to influence through their own qualities and attitudes. In Montaigne's more prosaic, unheroic reading, the only way in which humans could hope to master their own "fortunes" was by developing their ability to exercise some influence upon other people: in this perspective qualities such as honesty, trustworthiness, and the willingness to reconcile one's needs with those of others were more important than the kind of audacity and reckless daring that Machiavelli had regarded as indispensable to the success of his prince. But in the last instance, being aware of the weight of chance meant recognizing the distance that separated human projects from the inscrutable designs of the Divinity.[15]

Individual and Collective Agency

One particular methodological difficulty that dominated Montaigne's analysis of human agency was his insistence upon the essentially individual character of all human experiences. Whatever the shape of power structures and public institutions, their action depended in the last instance upon the character, interests, and beliefs of single persons. The choice of presenting an autobiographical account of the experience of public office helped to emphasize this point: Montaigne's performance was, in the end, the only one of which he was capable, given his nature and his personal history; it was also the only one he fully understood and could talk about. It was easy to imagine, for example, that some other man, appointed in his place at the *mairie*, might have acted differently—displaying greater commitment, keener ambition, or superior abilities—and yet such a person and the office he occupied would still remain clearly distinct, with a different individual character set against the constraints of his public function.[16]

The opacity and instability that characterized individual agency—to the extent that people were often unable to account for their own actions, let alone those of others—would not be significantly corrected by the fact of operating in a public capacity. Experience in office might teach men to disguise their true motives and sentiments; it could not change their character, nor confer greater coherence and rationality on their initiatives; indeed, in some cases the high position and the habit of power of rulers could make them less aware of their own limitations, and consequently more prone to commit errors than people of inferior condition; all considered, it was difficult to tell what sort of character and qualities were best suited to the task of government.[17] Montaigne recalled the case of one of his friends, who had "almost gone out of his mind from worry" in the service of a "prince" (Henry of Navarre). The same prince had confided to him that he only ever worried about things that appeared to be within his control; once he realized that there was nothing he could do about an impending evil or threat, he stopped thinking about it altogether: Montaigne himself had witnessed his surprising calm and detachment at moments of great crisis. Clearly the king of Navarre must have cared about his own success at least as much as the man who served him; the difference in their reactions was merely a function of their respective temperaments, and would still remain the same had their respective roles be reversed.[18]

Naturally there was a certain repetitiveness in men's attitudes, especially in those "waves" of popular sentiment that marked the fortunes of political regimes; whenever large numbers of people became involved in some mass movement, such as a rebellion or a civil war, they would display a tendency to conform to common patterns, for example by following their leaders, or imitating the behavior of the crowd. Yet this tendency did not exclude the possibility of highly individualized, and unforeseen, reactions. Human agency did not become any easier to understand and to control when it was deployed in a public setting: on the contrary, the involvement of large numbers of people, the interaction of different persons and groups, the disparity of their interests, the far-reaching consequences of most public initiatives, could only amplify the difficulty of the exercise. Thus individual and collective agency were placed by Montaigne in a continuum that left no qualitative difference between them, and no methodological barrier between the domain of personal choices and that of public action.[19] What changed was only the complexity of the factors, which had to be taken into account:

> Since the ethical laws, which concern the individual duty of each man in himself, are so hard to frame, as we see they are, it is no wonder if those who govern many individuals are more so.[20]

In this respect those interpretations that attribute to Montaigne the defense of a supposedly "private" sphere, against the interference of political power, seem both superficial and misleading. In Montaigne's intricate vision of human interaction, individuals could never successfully isolate themselves from the community to which they belonged; and, conversely, individual behavior would always have some sort of impact, however marginal, upon society as a whole, so that individuals would always carry a degree of personal responsibility for all collective initiatives developed around them.

Mediocrity and Moderation

Given Montaigne's insistence upon the individual character of agency, it is unsurprising that his reflection on practical conduct should focus upon the position of ordinary persons, without any special regard for rank or status. If in real life the author of the *Essais* found himself in the role of advisor to the prince, in his work he made few allowances for the special predicament of rulers, stressing instead the common qualities and common obligations they shared with their subjects. As it has already emerged from his reflections on virtue, Montaigne did not place at the center of human action the pursuit of grandeur and glory, either for the ambitious individual or for the conquering *res publica*. While expressing a passionate admiration for the grandeur of classical antiquity, he identified this grandeur with the display of selfless virtue and the devotion to civic values, rather than with the practice of domination and conquest. There was, in any case, an immense qualitative difference between the practice of conquest in the ancient world, and the conquests carried out by the moderns: in the first case, violence and enslavement were compensated, to some extent, by the civilizing vocation of societies that were committed to the pursuit of individual excellence, and to the spreading of their own remarkable cultural heritage; on the other hand, modern conquest—as shown by the tragic experience of the genocide of the Amerindian populations in Mexico—took the form of the most brutal, senseless destruction, unmitigated by any redeeming features.[21]

Thus the appropriate scope of all public action in the modern world must be the preservation of order and peace, both within and outside the community. Montaigne admitted that the awful experience of the religious wars in France made the project of a foreign conflict, undertaken as a "diversion" from domestic strife, almost attractive by comparison: this was, nevertheless, a wicked temptation, since war remained, in all circumstances, an evil, while aggression could never be justified by the convenience of a single nation.[22] The writer's commitment to the Christian values of peace and concord went together with a denunciation of the vanity of human glory: true glory belonged exclusively to God and his kingdom, while the fame that ambitious men hoped to attain, for example through their military exploits or the conquest of power, was uncertain and ephemeral. Thus mediocrity, rather than grandeur, was the moral ideal that seemed to emerge from the reflection of the *Essais*, an ideal wonderfully captured by the author's claim that he would rather be second, or even third, in Périgueux, than first in Paris (though, he admitted, third in Paris—his favorite place in the entire world—would also do very nicely).[23]

Various elements in the text seem to point in this direction. One leading theme is the insistence upon ordinary virtues and upon the necessity of sharing the preoccupations and sentiments of the majority of the people, conversing even with the most humble and uneducated, to form a bond of solidarity and understanding within the community. In the light of this obligation to be in tune with common views and needs, Montaigne claimed that the middling ranks represented—both subjectively and objectively—the most comfortable and desirable social condition: people who belonged to them (like the writer himself) had all the advantages of wealth and rank without any of the drawbacks. They were free from need, independent, well educated, respected within the community; yet at the same time they were not exposed to the corrupting influence of high rank, which so often resulted in arrogance, snobbery, excessive (and therefore crippling) ambition, indifference to the predicament of ordinary people. They occupied in fact an ideal middle ground in view of the preservation of sociability.[24]

Another significant indication of Montaigne's preference for mediocrity was the view that the good citizen should be ready to set aside his personal opinions (for example on political or religious reform), conforming instead to the position of the majority. Montaigne explained this submission to dominant opinion as an act of humility, by which the values of unity and concord were placed before the personal satisfaction of imposing one's particular reasons and beliefs on other people. In practice this choice would often result in the preservation of the status quo in social practices and institutions, and it is understandable that it is often interpreted as an indication of political conservatism on Montaigne's part. However, the writer's main concern was not the respect of tradition or authority (two things for which he felt little regard), but the preservation of consensus within the community and the protection of popular opinion from the manipulation of aggressive minorities. Moreover, the willingness to surrender one' s own convictions, accepting instead the views of others, or at least listening to them and taking them into account, was an essential condition for preserving social peace. In the context of the religious conflict, the obstinate, willful attachment to one's opinion (*opiniastreté*) seemed a most dangerous disposition.[25]

In the *Essais* the notion of mediocrity was thus intimately associated with that of moderation. In describing his own temperament, the writer presented his own incapacity for intense, single-minded dedication to any particular object, as an essentially fortunate circumstance; not exactly a source of pride, since it was largely involuntary, but a ground for relief. At the same time he expressed mistrust for all those agents who showed excessive zeal, or proved too passionate, in the defense of a cause, regardless of the intrinsic merits of the cause itself. Such intense feelings would often lead those who experienced them to justify any course of action in the pursuit of their object: they might be capable of acts of blind fanaticism—such as the destruction of pagan books denounced in the essay on the freedom of conscience (II, 19)—but also, if the opportunity presented itself, of the worst abuses and atrocities. The absence of measure did not seem desirable even when its object was the pursuit of a saintly life: thus Montaigne was suspicious of excessively severe ascetic practices and acts of self-immolation, which implied a rejection of common human standards.[26]

The Vanishing Middle Ground

If various elements in the *Essais* seem to point to a kind of ethics of mediocrity, the text does also bring to light a number of difficulties associated with this perspective. In the classical Aristotelian approach, finding the middle course between alternative attitudes or lines of action was possible by resorting to a process of induction: it was the rational assessment and comparison of past experiences that made it possible to identify a "just" and "moderate" middle ground. Montaigne's skeptical approach clearly precluded this procedure: the infinite differences that could be observed in comparing past and present events made it impossible to form any confident expectation about the future; Pyrronian questioning could help to identify opposed views and positions, but deliberately refrained from offering any synthesis between them.[27]

A recurrent theme in the *Essais* is the danger presented by excessive investment in philosophical speculation, especially for those who lacked superior intellectual powers: in most cases too much reasoning would lead to uncertainty and to the inability to act, instead of offering helpful guidance. Throughout his work Montaigne exposed the futility of the efforts invested by human beings in seemingly rational calculations, complicating things unnecessarily, and finally losing sight of those practical solutions that a more simple, instinctive response could reveal. This exercise was especially self-deceptive, since in most cases the decisions, apparently reached on the basis of elaborate reasoning, were in fact the product of mere chance.[28]

The classical skeptical answer to the inconclusiveness of rational calculation consisted in identifying a "middle course" of action, by conforming to common beliefs and customary practices, rather than by attempting to develop an original strategy. If Montaigne apparently endorsed this solution, he thought that the obvious advantages of submitting to popular opinion were seriously limited by at least two major considerations. The first consideration was a moral one: submission to the views of the community might occasionally dictate actions contrary to the common feelings of humanity. In such cases one was not bound to endorse grossly unjust or cruel actions simply in order to please one's fellow citizens or to serve the interests (however legitimate) of a particular party. The law of nature (the law of God) took precedence over the preservation of consensus within the community: if the laws and conventions of society had consequences that were humanly intolerable, one was justified in not conforming to them: this was true for magistrates and public officials as well as for ordinary people.[29]

The second consideration was a practical one: the project of following established conventions applied only to societies that were in a condition of relative stability. In circumstances such as those of contemporary France—where law and order were totally disrupted, and the community was divided among warring factions—there were no longer enough shared beliefs and practices to which one might conform. In some sense the two considerations were connected: a stable and well-ordered society might occasionally endorse objectionable practices, but would not engage in extensive and systematic abuses directed against its own members. The exceptional circumstances of the civil war precluded any definition of a "middle course" in terms of what was customary or "normal." Thus the skeptical rule of "conformity" revealed itself as a "fair weather" sort of ethics, valid only in especially favorable circumstances.[30]

While the pursuit of an ethics of mediocrity proved highly problematic, the ideal of moderation associated with it was also far less transparent and accessible than it initially appeared. In the essay "Of Husbanding Your

Will" (III, 10)—the same in which he assessed his own political career—
Montaigne acknowledged that the detachment and lack of passion that
characterized his own attitude toward the partisan struggles of his times
were inborn features, rather than the product of stoic self-discipline. But if
moderation was the product of a natural disposition that only some people would normally possess, rather than a moral achievement, how could
it be offered as an example to others or promoted throughout society at
large?

Whenever human passions were deployed in a public setting, the interaction between individual and collective responses was bound to prove
very intricate. While the writer, for example, approached partisan struggle
with the same lack of intensity he felt toward his own private goals, others
brought into the civic arena a range of violent emotions that in fact originated in other domains of their lives. Thus personal feelings of envy, hatred, and frustration, or simple considerations of interest, were transformed, in the context of the war, into partisan passions, easily exploited
by leaders and demagogues:

> I have in my time seen wonders in the undiscerning and prodigious ease
> with which peoples let their belief and hope be led and manipulated in what-
> ever way has pleased and served their leaders, passing over a hundred mis-
> takes one on top of the other, passing over phantasms and dreams. I am no
> longer amazed at those who are hoodwinked by the monkey tricks of Apol-
> lonius and Mahomet. Their sense and understanding is entirely smothered
> in their passion.[31]

However, the reverse was also true: many who did not feel very strongly
one way or another were carried away by the wave of current fanaticism,
because they were normally led to imitate the attitudes of their friends and
patrons, or could not face the disapproval of their social circle.

In circumstances where emotions were fierce, and where personal feelings and motives became confused with partisan passions, any pretense of
neutrality was simply hypocritical. In the context of a civil war, total impar-
tiality was practically impossible to achieve for anyone; even assuming it
was possible, such an attitude would prove insulting to friends and enemies alike, and could rightly be regarded as dishonorable. Yet throughout
the long decades of the wars, on the occasion of each truce, of each negotiation for peace, the people, like their leaders, affected the greatest indifference, as if their feelings had changed overnight, and all sense of outrage,
all desire for revenge, had suddenly disappeared from their hearts. This
false moderation, duly echoed in the official language of treatises and
agreements, was doubly dishonest, since those who affected it lied twice,
first to themselves and then to others. It was, moreover, an unhealthy sort
of fiction, potentially more dangerous than any frank acknowledgment of

feelings of hatred or resentment, since it made it impossible for French society to heal its wounds, and to make some sincere efforts toward reconciliation and forgiveness.[32]

Here Montaigne expressed an implicit criticism of the notion of *oubliance* (obliviousness) that featured very prominently in all peace agreements and edicts of toleration subscribed during the religious wars, and that would appear again—a few years after Montaigne's death—in the opening paragraphs of the Edict of Nantes.[33] In these documents the term *oubliance* meant in the first instance "general amnesty" for all the offenses and crimes committed during the wars. But its significance went beyond the strict legal meaning of immunity from prosecution: what the word intimated was that such offenses should actually be erased from collective memory, "like things that never took place." Montaigne's own understanding of moderation was more complex and problematic than this policy of obliviousness. If it was a good thing that people should distance themselves from the destructive passions and sufferings of the civil war, this distancing should come from a spontaneous process of regeneration of the community, not from the diktats of political authority; in particular the activity of forgetting (and forgiving) past offenses must begin with the mutual acknowledgment of past wrongs and grievances. Setting aside the specific issue of how former enemies might be reconciled, the whole project of acting according to the classical ideal of *mediocritas* was gradually dismantled in the course of Book III, leaving open once again the question of a possible alternative strategy.[34]

The Variety of Experience

At the beginning of the essay "Of Experience" (III, 13)—the last of Book III and the concluding section of the entire work—Montaigne surprised his readers by apparently reversing his previous judgments, offering a spirited apology of experience as a source of knowledge. No doubt, compared to reason, experience seemed a "weaker and less dignified" means of approaching the truth;[35] however, since knowledge was supremely desirable, where reason failed us, we must not despise any alternative source of instruction at our disposal. After this bold introduction, Montaigne went on to resume the arguments that he had already presented in the previous sections of Book III, in order to illustrate the difficulties associated with the project of learning from experience.

A first set of difficulties derived from the infinite variety of human experiences across space and time: there were in fact objective and significant differences in the conditions of human beings living in diverse historical and geographical settings. If the study of history and the writings of the ancients were understandably a source of inspiration for the moderns, in the end the experience of the great writers and leaders of the past was not really very useful in dealing with present circumstances; one could not readily model one's life upon Julius Caesar's, and understanding one's own predicament was more important than understanding Cicero's problems.[36] Distant cultural and geographical realities did also result in incomparable experiences; it was possible, for example, to imagine a well-ordered and highly sophisticated society that had nothing whatever in common with our history, traditions, and ways of thinking: Montaigne cited the case of China (brought to the attention of European readers by the publication of Jesuit sources), a vast empire successfully ruled by laws and customs totally unlike our own.[37]

Inequalities of social condition could also make people's experiences as remote from each other as if they inhabited different continents. Montaigne noted that his own lifestyle and that of the farm laborers working on his estates could not have been more dissimilar had the latter lived in some remote region of India. The poor inhabited a separate world of their own: thus his experiment of taking some beggar boys off the streets and placing them into his household had failed precisely because his and their respective views of what to expect from life were utterly incompatible.[38]

Differences in experience, however, were not confined to external circumstances; even among people of the same age and condition there would be variations in physical constitution and temperament. Imaginative persons saw things differently from prosaic ones; the experiences of men were unlike those of women; ill and disabled people perceived the world differently from the able-bodied. Age was also a relevant factor: humans developed different perceptions and responses to the events of their life as they grew older, so that the quality of their experience varied through time. Experiences were never perfectly identical and yet never totally unlike each other: their similarities encouraged all sorts of attempts to establish comparisons and regularities, while, at the same time, their diversity defeated classification. One constantly looked for rules, only to find instead an endless string of exceptions.

This paradox led to another set of considerations, one that focused upon the activity of interpretation rather than upon experience as such: no matter how large the variety of their experiences, men succeeded in producing an even larger variety of interpretations to explain them. Thus a reality that was already bewilderingly complex became even more obscure, when seen through the thick filter of an ever-growing mass of doctrines produced to explain it.[39] Here Montaigne returned to one of his favorite themes, the arrogance and futility of academic learning and bookish erudition, and the vertiginous escalation of derivative knowledge (commentaries of commentaries and interpretations of interpretations) that characterized modern intellectual life. He also revisited one last time the question of the deficiencies of legal systems.

The gap between the living reality of human experience and the attempts to master it through abstract schemes was never as poignant as in the case of the law. Engaged in Byzantine philological disputes over ancient codes, lost in the pursuit of universal categories, jurists ignored the destructive impact that their idle speculations had upon people's lives. The most elementary principles of justice were sacrificed to vain intellectual ambitions and to philosophical utopias. Thus the "imbecility" of justice came to symbolize men's inability to come to grips with their own experiences in a constructive way, using them to produce a better social order; it also exposed the grievous practical consequences of this epistemological debacle.[40]

The Exercise of Critical Judgment

If human experience was generally so difficult to apprehend, how did Montaigne support his claim that it was still possible to learn from it? A first tentative answer to this question was that being aware of the limits of experience was in itself an important step toward the pursuit of the truth. Nothing in fact kept men away from knowledge more effectively than the arrogant and misguided belief of being already in possession of it. A particular instance of this arrogance was exemplified by those arts that promised to guarantee the health of body and soul to those who committed themselves to their care; the example Montaigne discussed was that of medicine, though the same arguments could be applied to the teaching of moral and political philosophy: with all these disciplines, the pretension of possessing the secrets of physical or spiritual welfare was clearly unfounded.

Doctors, like other practitioners, claimed to be in possession of a special knowledge: but what did this knowledge consist of, when medical doctrines and prescriptions varied with time and place, and when each individual patient responded differently to treatment? No doubt extensive experience of a variety of medical cases might prove useful: but did that mean that in order, for example, to cure syphilis, a doctor should begin by acquiring the disease himself? Doing so—Montaigne maliciously suggested—might help; and yet what about all other complaints?[41] Naturally medicine, like other arts, was not entirely useless, and its practitioners could occasionally offer help to their patients. The problem was that, by arrogating themselves a superior status and authority, they concealed the real extent of their ignorance and impotence.

The recognition of one's ignorance was an essential component of the skeptical approach, which advocated the suspension of judgment on all acquired or pretended knowledge. Montaigne reformulated this classical philosophical *topos* in terms that stressed its interpersonal value. The suspension of judgment began as an individual discipline, to be exercised in the first instance upon one's own convictions and prejudices; however, the same critical attitude proved valuable in assessing other people's ideas and conduct. Obviously this critical exercise of judgment required a distinctive disposition, both on the part of the agent who applied the judgment, and on the part of whoever was on the receiving end of his criticism. Other people should be judged not just with intelligence and understanding, but also with a benevolent and disinterested disposition; on the other hand, only very few people were capable of accepting criticism without feeling hurt or offended, and even fewer managed to learn something from it. The point was that, whenever human relations were not open to this kind of critical exchange, people could hardly profit from each other's experience.

One particular category of persons for whom this critical activity seemed indispensable was represented by princes and men in power, individuals who led a "very public" life, and were consequently exposed to the opinion of so many observers. Whenever such persons acted without the benefit of criticism, they inevitably attracted the resentment, and even the hatred, of their subjects, while had they been well advised, they might easily have avoided this disapproval. Unfortunately, most of the time rulers and powerful men were surrounded by a crowd of opportunists and cowards, who chose to praise them and flatter them, carefully ignoring their errors. A good prince must be prepared to be judged: how could anyone believe that he had the courage to confront the enemy on the battlefield, when he was unable to face the judgment of a friend?[42]

Here Montaigne provided his own description of the role of advisor to the prince. Such role should be regarded as a sort of *office sans nom*, an unofficial and unrecognized position. It could not be exercised by the grandees who surrounded the prince, who had a stake in whatever decisions he made, not by his self-seeking favorites; at the same time it could not be left to all and sundry, since it was a task that required courage, subtlety, and discretion. The only type of man who could perform it was someone of middling condition (*moyenne fortune*), independent and satisfied with his own status. Such a man could "speak freely" to the prince, since he would have nothing to lose from telling the truth, and nothing to gain from concealing it; in addition, he would be in "communication" with ordinary people, therefore capable of interpreting their sentiments:

> I should have had enough fidelity, judgment and independence for that. It would be a nameless office; otherwise it would lose its effect and its grace. And it is a part that cannot be played indiscriminately by all.[43]

Whether the writer was expressing a personal ambition when he traced this portrait of the king's advisor, or just setting forth an ideal type, the temptation to give some biographical and sociological substance to the ideal figure of the free-speaking critic that emerges from the pages of the *Essais* has proved very strong. Thus scholars have described Montaigne as a "bourgeois gentleman," pointing out that he belonged to a new aristocracy, an emerging class of *nouveaux riches*, recently promoted to the lifestyle of the nobility, thanks to the rapid transformation of the French economy in the course of the sixteenth century. They have also highlighted Montaigne's affinity with a wide and loosely defined group of "political professionals," educated individuals who, all over Europe, gained access to public offices, chancelleries, and royal circles in virtue of their competences. Such insights help to bring into focus the tension between Montaigne's proud (and no doubt sincere) assertion of his independence on the one hand, and his position within a tight network of political and literary patronage on the other. Inevitably, however, they leave open the question of the broader significance of his appeal to the exercise of free judgment as a corrective to political action.[44]

Prudence

The view that rulers should be exposed to the critical judgment of others, if calamitous political mistakes were to be avoided, was an important example of how the awareness of one's deficiencies was the first step toward improving one's knowledge. On the whole, however, Montaigne thought that our capacity of learning from others remained very limited, and that in the end, for any man, the most instructive of experiences was his own: unless he could learn from it, he was unlikely to learn from anybody else's. But individual experience was, as we have seen, absolutely unique: this theme, which traversed the whole text of the *Essais*, was brought to a climax in the concluding pages of the book, by a review of the author's own physical peculiarities and favorite practices in matters of health and hygiene. In a kind of pyrotechnic finale, intimate details about his childhood ailments, his dietary and sleeping habits, his sexual routines, and his sufferings from gallstones, were lavished upon the reader, with the pretext that this was, at last, a subject on which he was supremely competent.

Thus for the last time the writer set forth his claim that the making of individual experience and the shaping of individual personality ultimately rested upon a multitude of accidental (and often apparently insignificant) details: only by manifesting its intrinsic diversity could a particular experience become truly exemplary. But if each individual experience was unlike any other, even assuming it was possible to learn from it, the learning could never be generalized, nor translated into common rules: the path toward the right sort of conduct would be different for each person.

Prudence—like mediocrity and moderation—had been one of the key classical concepts defining a wise and well-considered line of action; its value in guiding people in their daily life, and on the path to salvation, was also recognized by Christian doctrine, where prudence was classified as one of the four "cardinal" virtues. Yet on Montaigne's terms acting prudently, in the private as in the public domain, meant something quite different in each individual case, in such a way that the content of the virtue in question remained undetermined. For example, acting prudently did not necessarily mean acting carefully, assessing the different options and reflecting upon the possible consequences of one's actions: on the contrary, the prudent conduct might sometimes consist in acting impulsively, following one's spontaneous instincts.[45]

Montaigne described his own understanding of prudent conduct as "following nature." This meant, in the first instance, liberating the self from all rational misconceptions and artificial constructions, in the attempt to retrieve one's most basic needs and motivations. Thus he endorsed the view that humble, uneducated people were generally wiser in conducting their lives, since they had a simpler, more essential view of the human condition and of basic ethical values. However, even in the case of the humble folks praised by ancient moral philosophers and by the Gospel, human nature revealed itself as a complex and multilayered reality. Nobody on earth, not even the members of the most primitive communities, could actually be described as living according to the precepts of nature; at best their simplicity could offer an insight into a natural state that might have existed in a prehistorical past, but that was now lost forever. What humans called nature was in fact a compound of inborn features and artificial traits acquired through education and social training, in a context that they themselves had shaped and transformed. This is why habit was such an important dimension of human identity: it showed how the original personality had gradually crystallized around a particular set of attributes and practices.[46]

This appeal to nature as a supreme source of guidance should not be read in deterministic terms. It is true that the *Essais* placed great emphasis upon the physical makeup of personal identity and upon the irrational dimensions of the human mind. However, even the most basic of human impulses were to some extent a fabrication: by following his animal instincts and his passions man would not simply be submitting to some natural forces, but to a re-elaboration of those same forces for which he was to some extent responsible. At a different level "nature" described the whole range of physical and spiritual faculties that the individual had received from God, and which he must develop in full—whatever their limitations—in order to accomplish the scope of divine creation; discussing the combined powers of mind and body, Montaigne concluded:

> There is no part unworthy of our care in this gift which God has given us; we are accountable for it even to a single hair. And it is not a perfunctory charge to man to guide man according to his nature: it is express, simple and of prime importance, and the creator has given it to us seriously and sternly.[47]

The initial statement—that it is possible to learn from experience—developed into the view that the imperfect, tentative character of experience was inescapable, since such imperfection actually defined the human condition. To be reconciled with the limitations of one's experience was the necessary precondition for becoming truly human. In the concluding paragraph of the essay, Montaigne qualified this acceptance, the capacity to enjoy in full one's nature (*être*) as "*absolute perfection et comme divine.*" The adjective "*divine*" is often read metaphorically, as meaning simply "sublime," without implying any actual relation to the Divinity. In the last few lines of the text, Montaigne himself mitigated the rigor of his previous statement about our obligations toward the creator, by addressing his final prayer for health and wisdom not to the Christian God, but to Apollo, through a quotation from Horace.

Thus in his text, the human and superhuman dimensions were kept deftly apart, in a kind of precarious balance, the latter casting only a distant shadow (or distant light) upon the former, which gained contrast and definition through it. Half a century later, Montaigne's balancing act would fail to satisfy a devout reader like Pascal, who accused him of having altogether edited out of the *Essais* the presence of God and his Revelation.[48] Yet the whole argument about experience gained strength from the distance that was established between the imperfect world of men on the one hand, and the perfection of God one the other. By becoming aware of this distance, in other words by humbling himself and acknowledging his inadequacy, man surrendered to God's grace, thus acquiring the power of transcending his own limitations.

Politics and the Art of Government

What place did politics occupy within Montaigne's reflection on human experience? On the whole, the *Essais* did not place any special emphasis upon the specific domain of politics, to which it failed to confer any distinctive visibility, submerging it into the confusing background of its diverse historical and anthropological narrative; it also undermined the notion of a distinctive set of laws governing public actions and collective movements, favoring instead a more general vision of individual agency.

Thus in contrast with other contemporary writers, Montaigne implicitly exposed the very notion of "art of government" as little better than a sham: like other forms of professional knowledge that claimed to offer competent and informed practical guidance, such an art promised in fact far more than it could deliver, while the ambitious claims of its proponents fell far short of their actual results. At best it was an illusion of naïve intellectuals, who had spent too much time reading Roman classics, and liked to imagine themselves in the role of their favorite authors; at worse it was the expression of the arrogance and conceit of the men in power, or the brainchild of self-promoting charlatans.

In particular, Montaigne was ready to admit that rulers and political operators were often led by circumstances to act outside the constraints of ordinary morality and the limits set by the law of God; but he refused to attach to this dismal state of affairs any special dignity, as the imperative of some superior, esoteric skill: reason of state was simply an indication of the moral inadequacy and practical deficiency of most human agency, an unsuccessful attempt to disguise the lack of moral courage and compassion of those entrusted with the care of states. The point was that nobody was especially qualified to rule, except in the sense that all men had the capacity to interact—for better or for worse—with their fellow human beings. Thus if the *Essais* made few concessions to the notion of politics as a set of particular doctrines and techniques, the text conveyed a very vivid sense of politics as an everyday reality and practice. This undignified, artless kind of politics occupied the center of human experience; it was the murky ground where people's interests and aspirations, fears and delusions clashed, where they proved most vulnerable and dangerous; it was also, for many human beings, the battleground where the struggle for making life on earth just barely tolerable was fought every day, with uncertain outcomes.

CONCLUSION

Montaigne's Legacy

In conclusion: what was Montaigne's legacy to later reflections upon politics, more particularly to our own understanding of it? To a large extent the aim of this book has been to show that Montaigne's views on political issues should be taken seriously. No doubt the *Essais* were not written as a contribution to what we recognize today as political theory: a discipline of which, in its contemporary form of "art of government," Montaigne was inclined to question the credentials. Yet the fact that the author's insights on social and political practices came as the by-product of a broader reflection on a variety of philosophical questions does not make them less incisive or illuminating.

While Montaigne's contribution to politics should not be dismissed because of the form in which it is expressed, there is little to be learned from those interpretations which praise its affinity with a set of allegedly timeless but in fact essentially modern ideals. The celebration of Montaigne as the forerunner of the values of humanism and individualism—rights of man, individual liberty, toleration—is perhaps inevitable, given the status that the *Essais* enjoy as a major European classic; it does not help, however, to clarify the nature of the author's own intellectual project, nor to explain the content and the implications of the defense of such values in any specific historical context, whether his or our own.

Montaigne's work shows a stern attachment to basic Christian principles such as individual responsibility, freedom, charity, and mercy, an attachment that is indicative of the writer's moral disposition, even if it can tell us little about the precise nature of his religious beliefs. He remained faithful to these principles in a climate that saw the growing influence of utilitarian and opportunistic moral ideologies, and in circumstances where other Christian thinkers were increasingly ready to endorse strategies of exception and compromise. In this respect the condemnation of his work by the Catholic Church in the late seventeenth century, promoted by the party of the *dévots* in a climate of acrimonious ideological confrontation, has exercised a distorting influence upon later interpretations, blurring the significance and obscuring the colors of the writer's original project.

Like any educated person of his times, Montaigne approached ethical issues through the filter of Hellenistic philosophy and literature; but if the *Essais* reveal a tangled web of stoic, epicurean, and skeptical influences, they also establish a sharp dividing line between pagan and Christian morality and especially between the existential experience of the ancients and that of the moderns. Montaigne was ready to recognize the moral excellence of the ancients in some particular domains, such as for example their superior sense of personal honor and in their capacity for civic duty; he was also prepared to denounce the moral failings of contemporary Christian societies, which he depicted as torn by violent dissensions, brutal and corrupt; but he never cultivated the ideal of a return to the past, a return made impossible, in his view, by the double constraint of Christian revelation and irresistible historical change.

Montaigne's fidelity to Christian principles did not take the form of a conservative attachment to mainstream, traditional views, but carried with it some radical, novel insights. He was not especially concerned with the dogmatic aspects of Christianity, which he regarded as essentially inaccessible to human reason (his lack of interest in dogmatic issues explains to some extent why he failed to be attracted to the ideas of the Reformation and largely ignored contemporary religious disputes). His own perception of Christian principles focused essentially upon ethical and practical questions. It betrayed the influence of Franciscan theology: a religious current that had developed in opposition to Aquinas's Aristotelian revival, and that was characterized by its insistence upon human emotions, its skeptical undertones, and its strong commitment to social issues. It also showed some affinities with the ethos and intellectual preoccupations of the newly established Society of Jesus, in particular a marked interest in exotic cultures, a tendency to religious syncretism, and a strong universalistic bias.

However, what was truly original about Montaigne's contribution was not his defense of Christian values (or possibly of some unorthodox version of these), but the tension the *Essais* masterfully established between the values themselves, and their practical enforcement in the context of existing human societies. To begin with, the project of acting according to Christian principles within any real community runs into some major epistemological difficulties. The *Essais* gradually but effectively dismantled the view that the legislation of human societies had its foundation in natural law; they also utterly destroyed the credibility of the claim that Christian states, and Christian rulers, were the guardians and enforcers of a divine order on earth.

Montaigne did not deny the existence of a law of nature, originally inscribed in God's creation; he thought, however, that human societies had developed too far away from their original natural condition to retain any effective grasp over such law. If he firmly believed in the existence of a law of God and in divine justice, he also doubted that men could ever agree upon its prescriptions. Thus what went under the name of natural law or law of God in human legislation was just an artifice, a fabrication designed to serve mundane purposes. In this respect Christian communities were no different from, and enjoyed no superiority over, non-Christian ones.

The only dimension in which men had access to God's law was the intimate forum of their conscience: but the essentially individual character of this recognition meant that individuals might frequently experience a conflict between their own convictions and the rules established by the society they happened to live in.

A second cluster of difficulties were essentially practical: even assuming people were able to recognize some basic moral principles, they would still have overwhelming reasons (though admittedly bad as well as good ones) for departing from them. In fact in many cases behaving well would be just a matter of luck, of finding oneself in favorable, unproblematic circumstances. It was easy for Montaigne to see why many of his contemporaries thought that the effort of upholding Christian values (or indeed any kind of morally exacting values) was a self-defeating exercise, to be abandoned, at the earliest opportunity, in favor of more utilitarian, "realistic" rules of behavior. Yet what he also saw, and conveyed powerfully in his work, were the appalling consequences of giving in to the appeal of such instrumental models of conduct. Admittedly, political societies could survive, and even thrive, without the benefit of principles protecting human integrity; but the cost in terms of suffering and degradation would be appalling. Indeed, the prospect of such an inhuman, godless world was so unbearable that it justified the feeble, stumbling efforts of those men and women of good will who struggled to keep it at bay.

Unlike other Christian writers—such as for example John Locke—Montaigne failed to evoke in the *Essais* the prospect of God's punishment as an ultimate check against the evildoings of men. It is impossible to tell whether the reason for this omission was that he did not believe in the existence of such punishment, or whether he simply doubted the practical efficacy of any ultra-terrestrial threats. What he did appeal to instead was the assistance of God's grace, as the only force that could sustain human beings in their discouraging predicament. In his work damnation appeared very much as a feature of this world, rather than of the next: much of the human race was described as already living on earth in some hell of their own making, the product of senseless brutality, cruelty, or self-destruction; against these manmade hells, the exercise of mercy toward others (the prefiguration of God's own mercy toward us) offered itself as the only viable instrument of salvation.

With or without God's help, Montaigne did not believe that the defense of the safety and freedom of human beings could be dependably expected from political institutions, nor secured by purely political means. Naturally he recognized that some political systems were more promising in this respect—or at least had a better historical record—than others: they proved more stable, equitable, and effective at granting the protection of their own subjects. And yet no regime, not even the most just and egalitarian (such as a popular republic), was immune from the dangers of the arbitrary exercise of power: anywhere, at any time, just laws could be perverted to produce unjust verdicts, equitable institutions could be corrupted through the vices of those who run them; even those states that were able to enforce effective rules for the protection of their own subjects felt no restraint in dealing brutally with other human groups.

While the *Essais* show little interest in the shape of political institutions, and dismiss the notion of an ideal political regime as the most fanciful of utopias, they set forth a rich and diversified picture of the possible forms of community. In human interaction, between the two extreme conditions of enslavement on the one hand and equal freedom on the other, one discovered varying degrees of subjection and cooperation; many different factors—such as convention, economic need, fear, loyalty, deference, habit—dictated these uneven forms of dependence, which were only tangentially related to political systems and institutions.

In particular, Montaigne was interested in a phenomenon famously described by the *Discourse* attributed to his friend La Boétie: voluntary servitude, the persistence in human societies of forms of domination that were not imposed by force, but willingly accepted, often without apparent necessity, by large numbers of people. Yet where the *Discourse* focused upon the corruption of the monarchical state in contemporary France, the *Essais* explored voluntary servitude as a broader anthropological reality: a phenomenon as varied as the many reasons, good and bad, that men gave themselves to renounce their freedom. The result of this exploration was a poignant picture of the human community as a shifting frontier, where the inhabitable spaces of cooperation and peaceful exchange had to be reconquered inch by inch, over and over again, against their natural tendency to crumble and disintegrate under the pressure of oppressive forces. Thus the formula of "liberalism of fear" sometimes applied to Montaigne's political vision describes quite accurately the nature of much of his political activities (which were indeed a protracted exercise in the limitation of damage), but fails to capture the radical implications and the moral tension that shaped his work.

In Montaigne's analysis the issue of domination was inextricably connected with that of authority. It is possible to read the *Essais* as an extensive critique of the principle of authority, in all its different dimensions: epistemic, religious, scientific, historical, as well as political and social. Thus a society such as contemporary France, apparently ruled by force and social hierarchy, was ultimately held together by a tangled web of belief: opinion, rather than violence, was the basis of all durable bonds of subjection, as well as being the source of all relations of sociability. The *Essais* offered a sophisticated and essentially novel view of the role of opinion. In contemporary literature opinion had been described as the unsteady expression of popular prejudice, and set in opposition to the stable truths that characterized religious dogma, philosophy, and science; opinion was generally presented as an amorphous, passive force, ready to be molded by rulers or manipulated by demagogues. Montaigne's analysis began much along the same lines, but by questioning the foundations of dogmatic truth, his approach inevitably blurred the difference between truth and opinion, presenting all human knowledge in the shape of unstable, shifting beliefs.

As to public opinion, the *Essais* showed that popular belief on the one hand, and the views of the educated elites on the other, interacted in complex and unpredictable ways: in particular, the beliefs of the mass of the people were often more resilient and creative, and far less easy to control, than it was generally assumed by their social superiors. The question of authority and the critical role of opinion represent important elements of continuity, indeed the most obvious link, between the *Essais* and the intellectual universe of the Enlightenment. It would be heartening to imagine, as some commentators have done, that this continuity resided in the ongoing, epochal struggle between free judgment and repressive political power, independent thought and *ancien regime* obscurantism.

In fact Montaigne was especially perceptive in anticipating the ambiguous role that public opinion would play in modern societies, fluctuating between the roles of engine of emancipation on the one hand and passive resistance on the other, a catalyst of popular opposition to power, but also at the same time the quicksand into which the ambitions of reforming governments could sink without trace. What the *Essais* showed, what they still show us, is that in practice the defense of the basic rights of human beings would prove a far more intractable and elusive task than classical theories of the state and civil society had originally suggested; moreover, if the struggle to preserve human freedom was going to be fought on many different battlegrounds—social, political, economic, ideological—of all these, the individual conscience would still remain the most crucial.

NOTES

All references to Montaigne's *Essais* indicate the page numbers in the edition by Pierre Villey: Michel de Montaigne, *Les essais, édition conforme au texte de l'exemplaire de Bordeaux* (Paris, PUF, 1924), revised edition Quadrige, 1988, 3 vols.; they are followed by references to the English translation by Donald M. Frame: Michel de Montaigne, *The Complete Works, Essays, Travel Journals, Letters*, London, Everyman's Library, 2003; quotations (in English in the body of the text, in French in the notes) are also taken from the Villey and Frame editions. I have occasionally used the annotation of the English translation by M. A. Screech, Michel de Montaigne, *The Complete Essays*, Harmondsworth, Penguin Books, 1987. It is important to keep in mind that the subdivision of the *Essais* in separate numbered essays, though helpful to identify the different sections of the text, is a modern convention. For this reason the numbering itself is not always consistent and may vary from one edition to another. The numbering I have adopted is the one used by the main French critical editions as well as by the two current English translations by Frame and Screech. Unless stated otherwise, all translations from French sources other than Montaigne's writings are my own.

INTRODUCTION

1. Olivier Millet, *La première réception des "Essais" de Montaigne (1580–1640)*, Paris, Honoré Champion, 1995; see also Paul Bonnefon, *Montaigne et ses amis: La Boétie, Charron, Mlle de Gournay*, Paris, Armand Colin, 1898.

2. Rousseau's judgment appears in the "*préambule*" to the Neuchâtel manuscript of the *Confessions*: "Je mets Montaigne à la tête de ces faux sincères qui veulent tromper en disant vrai. Il se montre avec des défauts, mais il ne s'en donne que d'aimables; il n'y a point d'homme qui n'en ait d'odieux. Montaigne se peint ressemblant mais de profil. Qui sait si quelque balafre à la joue ou un œil crevé du côté qu'il nous a caché, n'eût pas totalement changé sa physionomie." Jean-Jacques Rousseau, *Les confessions*, ed. Alain Grosrichard, Paris, Garnier-Flammarion, 2002, vol. 2, p. 433. See also Colette Fleuret, *Rousseau et Montaigne*, Paris, Nizet, 1980.

3. George Hoffmann, *Montaigne's Career*, Oxford, Oxford University Press, 1998; Warren Boutcher, "Montaigne's Legacy," in Ullrich Langer, ed., *The Cambridge Companion to Montaigne*, Cambridge, Cambridge University Press, 2005, pp. 27–52. In recent years the importance of Montaigne's contribution to modern philosophy has been persuasively shown by works such as Frédéric Brahami, *Le scepticisme de Montaigne*, Paris, PUF,1997, and *Le travail du scepticisme, Montaigne, Bayle, Hume*, Paris, PUF, 2001; Ann Hartle, *Michel de Montaigne, Accidental Philosopher*, Cambridge, Cambridge University Press, 2003.

4. Pierre Villey, *Montaigne devant la posterité*, Paris, Boivin, 1935; Alan M. Boase, *The Fortunes of Montaigne: A History of the Essays in France, 1580–1669*, London, Methuen, 1935; Donald M. Frame, *Montaigne in France: 1812–1852*,

New York, Columbia University Press, 1940; Maturin Dréano, *La renommée de Montaigne en France au XVIIIème siècle (1677–1802)*, Angers, Editions de l'Ouest, 1952; Dudley M. Marchi, *Montaigne among the Moderns: Reception of the "Essays,"* Providence and Oxford, Berghahn Books, 1994.

5. Cited in Alan Boase, *The Fortunes of Montaigne*, p. 295; see also Mme de Sévigné's description of Montaigne as "bonne compagnie," in Marie de Rabutin-Chantal de Sévigné, *Correspondance*, ed. Roger Duchêne, Paris, Gallimard, 1972, vol. 2, p. 697 (Letter to Mme de Grignan, 6 Oct. 1679).

6. Blaise Pascal, "Entretien de Pascal avec M. de Sacy sur Epictète et Montaigne," in *Œuvres complètes*, ed. Michel Le Guern, Paris, Gallimard, 2000, vol. 1, pp. 82–98; on Montaigne and Pascal, see Léon Brunschvicg, *Descartes et Pascal lecteurs de Montaigne* (1942–45), Paris, Presses Pocket, 1995; Bernard Croquette, *Pascal et Montaigne: étude des réminescences des "Essais" dans l'oeuvre de Pascal*, Geneva, Droz, 1974; Charles-Augustin Sainte-Beuve, *Port Royal*, ed. Maxime Leroy, Paris, Gallimard, vol. 1, chs. 2 and 3, pp. 811–71; Marc Fumaroli, Preface to Blaise Pascal, *"L'art de persuader," précédé de "L'art de conférer" de Montaigne*, Paris, Rivages, 2001. On Montaigne and seventeenth-century moralists, see also René Bady, *L'homme et son "institution" de Montaigne à Berulle: 1580–1625*, Paris, Les Belles Lettres, 1964; Henri Busson, *Littérature et théologie: Montaigne, Bossuet, La Fontaine, Prévost*, Paris, PUF, 1962.

7. See Malcolm Smith, *Montaigne and the Roman Censors*, Geneva, Droz, 1981.

8. As examples of the contrasting views expressed on Montaigne's attitude toward religion, see Maturin Dréano, *La pensée religieuse de Montaigne*, Paris, G. Beauchesne, 1936; Clément Sclafert, *L'âme religieuse de Montaigne*, Paris, Nouvelles Editions Latines, 1951, part II, "La Morale chrétienne de Montaigne"; Jacques de Feytaud, "L'Eglise catholique face aux *Essais*," in Jacques Lemaire, ed., *Montaigne et la révolution philosophique du XVIème siècle*, Brussels, Editions de l'Université de Bruxelles, 1992, pp. 105–22; Don Cameron Allen, *Doubt's Boundless Sea: Skepticism and Faith in the Renaissance*, Baltimore, Johns Hopkins Press, 1964, pp. 75–110; Max Gauna, *The Dissident Montaigne*, New York, Peter Lang, 1989, pp. 73–154 and 166–70. See also Henri Busson, *Le rationalisme dans la littérature française de la Renaissance, 1533–1601*, Paris, Vrin, 1971.

9. André Gide, *Les pages immortelles de Montaigne, choisies et expliquées par André Gide*, Paris, Ed. Corrêa, 1939; Preface to Michel de Montaigne, *Essais*, Paris, Gallimard, folio, 1994–95, 3 vols., vol. 1, pp. 7–27.

10. On Montaigne's supposed conservatism, cf. Frieda S. Brown, *Religious and Political Conservatism in the "Essais" of Montaigne*, Geneva, Droz, 1963; Nannerl O. Keohane, *Philosophy and the State in France: The Renaissance to the Enlightenment*, Princeton, Princeton University Press, 1980, pp. 98–116; Judith Shklar, *Ordinary Vices*, Cambridge, MA and London, Belknap Press of Harvard University, 1984; Richard Tuck, *Philosophy and Government, 1572–1651*, Cambridge, Cambridge University Press, 1993, pp. 45 ff; for a contrasting interpretation, cf. David Lewis Schaefer, *The Political Philosophy of Montaigne*, Ithaca and London, Cornell University Press, 1990, pp. 153–76. On the ambiguities of the distinction between public and private sphere, cf. Raymond Geuss, *Public Goods, Private Goods*, Princeton, Princeton University Press, 2001. See also the interesting discussion of this

issue in Ann Hartle, *Michel de Montaigne*, pp. 220 ff. On the structure of conservative arguments, see Albert O. Hirschman, *The Rhetoric of Reaction: Perversity, Futility, Jeopardy*, Cambridge, MA, Harvard University Press, 1991.

11. Cf. for example Diderot's judgment on Montaigne's opportunistic endorsement of "false" opinions in a letter to Etienne Maurice Falconet (5 Aug. 1766): Diderot, *Correspondence*, in *Œuvres*, ed. Laurent Versini, Paris, Robert Laffont, 1997, vol. 5, pp. 663–64. On Montaigne and Diderot, see Jérôme Schwartz, *Diderot and Montaigne: The "Essais" and the Shaping of Diderot's Humanism*, Geneva, Droz, 1966.

12. The text of these inscriptions can be found in the Pléiade edition of Montaigne's works: *Œuvres complètes*, ed. Maurice Rat, Paris, Gallimard, 1962, pp. 1419–27.

13. On Montaigne's and other French Catholic writers' response to the Saint Bartholomew's Day Massacre, see Géralde Nakam, *Montaigne et son temps*, Paris, Gallimard, 1993, pp. 251 ff; Michel Dassonville, ed., *Ronsard et Montaigne: écrivains engagés?* Lexington, KY, French Forum, 1989. See also David El Kenz, "La civilisation des moeurs et les guerres de Religion: un seuil de tolérance aux massacres," in David El Kenz, ed., *Le massacre, objet d'histoire*, Paris, Gallimard, 2005, pp. 183–97. On Montaigne's general attitude to violence, see David Quint, *Montaigne and the Quality of Mercy: Ethical and Political Themes in the "Essais,"* Princeton, Princeton University Press, 1998.

14. Montaigne was a member of the *Académie du palais* sponsored by Henry III of Valois. On French renaissance academies, see Edouard Frémy, *L'Académie des derniers Valois (1570–1585): d'après des documents nouveaux et inédits*, Paris, E. Leroux, 1887; Frances A. Yates, *The French Academies of the Sixteenth Century*, Nendeln, Kraus Reprint, 1973; Robert J. Sealy, *The Palace Academy of Henry III*, Geneva, Droz, 1981.

15. See, for example, the lamentable conditions of Richelieu's diocese of Luçon, in the Poitou, as the newly appointed bishop found it in 1608: Joseph Bergin, *The Rise of Richelieu*, Manchester and New York, Manchester University Press, 1997, ch. 3, "Richelieu and Luçon."

16. The few current biographies of Montaigne are all based upon the same body of historical documents, first collected by Paul Bonnefon in *Montaigne: l'homme et l'œuvre*, Paris, J. Rouam, 1893, then re-elaborated by Donald M. Frame in his *Montaigne: A Biography*, New York, Harcourt Brace & World, 1965 (the French translation of this work—*Montaigne: une vie, une œuvre, 1533–1592*, Paris, Champion, and Geneva, Slatkine, 1994—contains an updated bibliography by François Rigolot). There are in fact more known documents, for example regarding Montaigne's legal activity in Bordeaux, but thus far a new synthesis is missing. Sadly, the late Michel Simonin, who was working on this difficult and ambitious project, died before completing his work: see Michel Simonin, *L'encre et la lumière: quarante-sept articles (1976–2000)*, Geneva, Droz, 2004; John O'Brian and Philippe Desan, eds., *La "familia" de Montaigne (en hommage à Michel Simonin)*, Chicago, University of Chicago, 2001. Some aspects of Montaigne's life, such as his legal studies (it is not known which university he attended) and his confidential diplomatic missions, are probably bound to remain an object of speculation.

17. It is worth pointing out that biographers of Montesquieu do not suggest

that the latter's decision to give up his post at the Bordeaux *parlement* in 1726 was an indication of a lack of political commitment on his part; on the contrary it is generally accepted that Montesquieu's position of *président* in the criminal court of Tournelle (a more prestigious post than Montaigne's) was tedious and unrewarding, and that he was justified in moving on to better things. See Jean Dalat, *Montesquieu magistrat*, Paris, Lettres Modernes, 1971; Rebecca Kingston, *Montesquieu and the Parlement of Bordeaux, 1714–26*, Geneva, Droz, 1996.

18. Montaigne dedicated to Diane de Foix his essay on the education of children (I, 25); to Diane d'Andoins a collection of love sonnets by La Boétie; to Paul de Foix other poems by La Boétie; the "Apology of Raymond Sebond" (II, 12) was apparently inspired by the queen Marguerite de Navarre.

19. See Alphonse Gruen, *La vie publique de Michel de Montaigne* (1855), Geneva, Slatkine, 1970; Donald M. Frame, *Montaigne: A Biography*, ch. 4; see also Pierre Botineau, ed., *Montaigne: maire de Bordeaux, gentilhomme d'Aquitaine, écrivain de France: une évocation à l'aide de quelques documents*, Bordeaux, Bibliothéque Municipale, 1994.

20. On Henry IV's religious attitudes and policies, see the essential study by Michael Wolfe, *The Conversion of Henri IV: Politics, Power and Religious Belief in Early Modern France*, Cambridge, MA, Harvard University Press, 1993; Ronald S. Love, *Blood and Religion: The Conscience of Henri IV, 1553–1593*, Montreal and Kingston, McGill-Queen's University Press, 2001; Mark Greengrass, "The Calvinist Experiment in Béarn," in A. Pettegree, A. Duke, and G. Lewis, eds., *Calvinism in Europe, 1540–1620*, Cambridge, Cambridge University Press, 1994, pp. 119–42.

21. Cf., for example, the judgment formulated by Florimond de Raemond cited in Olivier Millet, *La première réception des "Essais de Montaigne,"* pp. 77–78.

22. On the chronology and evolution of the text of the *Essais*, the essential reference remains Pierre Villey, *Les sources et l'évolution des "Essais" de Montaigne*, Paris, Hachette, 1933; both English translations of the *Essais*, by Frame and Screech, offer helpful corrections or additions to the dating of the essays.

23. Cf. Michel de L'Hospital, *Discours pour la majorité de Charles IX et trois autres discours*, ed. Robert Descimon, Paris, Imprimerie Nationale, 1993; on de l'Hospital's projects of reform, see Denis Crouzet, *La sagesse et le malheur: Michel de l'Hospital, chancelier de France*, Seyssel, Champ Vallon, 1998, pp. 429 ff; the implications of these reforms are discussed in ch. 1 below.

24. The newly established Collège de Guyenne at Bordeaux, where Montaigne was educated, was open to ideas of the Reformation; one of his teachers was George Buchanan: cf. Madeleine Lazard, *Michel de Montaigne*, Paris, Fayard, 1992, pp. 60–61; Louis-Frédéric-Ernest Gaullieur, *Histoire du collège de Guyenne d'àpres un grand nombre de documents inédits*, Paris, Sandoz et Fischbacher, 1874.

25. On the identity and position of the *"politiques,"* see Francis de Crue de Stouz, *Le parti des politiques au lendemain de la Sainte-Barthélemy*, Paris, Plon, 1890; Mack P. Holt, *The French Wars of Religion, 1562–1629*, Cambridge, Cambridge University Press, 1995, in particular the definition given on p. 38 n. 10; and by the same author, *The Duke of Anjou and the Politique Struggle during the Wars of Religion*, Cambridge, Cambridge University Press, 1986; J. Boucher, "Autour de François, duc d'Alençon et d'Anjou, un parti d'opposition à Charles IX et

Henri III," in Robert Sauzet, ed., *Henri III et son temps: Actes du Colloque de Tours, 1989*, Paris, Vrin, 1992; see also R. J. Knecht, *The Rise and Fall of Renaissance France, 1483–1610*, London, Fontana Press, pp. 467–68, for further bibliographical references.

26. For a definition of democratic rule (*domination populaire*) as most natural and equitable, see *Essais* (I, 3), vol. 1, p. 20; Frame, pp. 14–15. Montaigne's mistrust of monarchy is a point on which he parted company with Erasmus; cf. Desiderius Erasmus, *The Education of a Christian Prince*, ed. Lisa Jardine, Cambridge, Cambridge University Press, 1997; on Montaigne's republicanism, see David Lewis Schaefer, *The Political Philosophy of Montaigne,* and the collection of texts edited by the same author: *Freedom over Servitude: Montaigne, La Boétie, and "On Voluntary Servitude,"* Westport, CT and London, Greenwood Press, 1998.

27. On Montaigne's suggestions to Henry of Navarre on legal reform, see Donald M. Frame, *Montaigne: A Biography*, ch. 4. On the reform of the French legal system undertaken by the king in 1604, see Roland Mousnier, *La vénalité des offices sous Henri IV et Louis XIII*, Paris, PUF, 1971.

28. *Essais* (III, 12), vol. 3, p. 1044; Frame, p. 972.

29. For an overview of the diffusion of heresy, see Philip Benedict, "Confessionalisation in France? Critical Reflections and New Evidence," in Raymond A. Mentzer and Andrew Spicer, eds., *Society and Culture in the Huguenot World, 1559–1685*, Cambridge, Cambridge University Press, 2002, pp. 44–61, esp. pp. 51–52. See also Jean Delumeau and Thierry Wanegffelen, *Naissance et affirmation de la Réforme* (1965), Paris, PUF, 1997; Anthony Levi, *Renaissance and Reformation: The Intellectual Genesis*, New Haven and London, Yale University Press, 2002.

30. Estienne de La Boétie, *Mémoire sur la pacification des troubles*, ed. Malcolm Smith, Geneva, Droz, 1983; the original manuscript of this text – legated by La Boétie to Montaigne – has disappeared; a manuscript corresponding to Montaigne's description of this memoir resurfaced in the Bordeaux archives at the beginning of the 20th century, but since it is a copy, the attribution cannot be proved beyond doubt, and has been questioned, though in my view not convincingly: see Anne-Marie Cocula, *Etienne de La Boétie*, Editions Sud Ouest, 1995, pp. 122–27. Compare La Boétie's views on the religious crisis with the positions expressed by Etienne Pasquier, "Exhortation aux princes et seigneurs du conseil privé du roi "(1561), in *Ecrits politiques*, ed. D. Thickett, Geneva, Droz, 1966, pp. 24–95.

31. A similar polarization is apparent in modern interpretations of the French religious wars. Some works stress the spiritual and symbolic dimension of religious violence: see, for example, Natalie Zemon Davies, *Society and Culture in Early Modern France*, Stanford, CA, Stanford University Press, 1965; Denis Crouzet, *Les guerriers de Dieu: la violence au temps des troubles de religion*, Seyssel, Champ Vallon, 1990, 2 vols. Other historians prefer to focus upon the socioeconomic, administrative, or regional factors in the conflict: Barbara Diefendorf, *Beneath the Cross: Catholics and Huguenots in Sixteenth Century Paris*, New York and Oxford, Oxford University Press, 1991; J.H.M. Salmon, *The French Wars of Religion: How Important Were Religious Factors?* Boston, Heath, 1967, and *Society in Crisis: France in the Sixteenth Century*, London, Methuen, 1979. Obviously the two types of approach do not necessarily exclude one another.

32. Pierre Villey, *Les livres d'histoire moderne utilisés par Montaigne: contribution à l'étude des sources des "Essais": suivi d'un appendice sur les traductions françaises d'histoires anciennes utilisées par Montaigne*, Paris, Hachette, 1908, repr. Geneva, Slatkine, 1972; see also Isabelle Konstantinovic, *Montaigne et Plutarque*, Geneva, Droz, 1989. Also: Julian H. Franklin, *Jean Bodin and the Sixteenth Century Revolution in the Methodology of Law and History*, New York, Columbia University Press, 1963.

33. Niccolò Machiavelli, *Discorsi sopra la prima Deca di Tito Livio*, ed. Francesco Bausi, Roma and Salerno, Edizione Nazionale delle Opere di Niccolò Machiavelli, 2001, 2 vols.; on Montaigne and Machiavelli, see Géralde Nakam, *Les "Essais," miroir et procès de leurs temps*, Paris, Nizet, 1984, pp. 245–50; D. L. Schaefer, *The Political Philosophy of Montaigne*, pp. 347–65; Pierre Statius, *Le réel et la joie: essai sur l'oeuvre de Montaigne*, Paris, Kimé, 1997; Thomas Berns, *Violence de la loi à la renaissance: l'originaire du politique chez Machiavel et Montaigne*, Paris, Kimé, 2000.

34. Jean Bodin, *Methodus ad facilem historiarum cognitionem* (1566), French trans.: *La méthode de l'histoire* edited by Pierre Mesnard, Paris, Les Belles Lettres, 1941; see also Philippe Desan, *Naissance de la méthode (Machiavel La Ramée, Bodin, Montaigne, Descartes)*, Paris, Nizet, 1987; Marie-Dominique Couzinet, *Histoire et méthode à la renaissance: une lecture de la "Methodus" de Jean Bodin*, Paris, Vrin, 1996, pp. 114–20.

35. On the different aspects of Montaigne's skepticism, see Richard H. Popkin, *The History of Scepticism: From Erasmus to Spinoza*, Berkeley, University of California Press, 1979; Craig B. Brush, *Montaigne and Bayle: Variations on the Theme of Skepticism*, The Hague, M. Nijhoff, 1966; John Christian Laursen, *The Politics of Scepticism in the Ancients: Montaigne, Hume and Kant*, Leiden, New York, and Cologne, E.J. Brull, 1992; Frédéric Brahami, *Le scepticisme de Montaigne*, and *Le travail du scepticisme*; Sylvia Giocanti, *Penser l'irrésolution: Montaigne, Pascal, La Mothe Le Vayer*, Paris, Honoré Champion, 2001; Hubert Vincent, "Scepticisme et conservatisme chez Montaigne, ou qu'est-ce qu'une philosophie sceptique?" in *Le scepticisme au XVIème et XVIIème siècle: le retour des philosophies antiques à l'age classique*, ed. Pierre-François Moreau, Paris, Albin Michel, 1991–2001, vol. 2, 132–63; Paul Mathias, *Montaigne*, Paris, Vrin, 2006.

36. *Essais*, (II, 1), vol. 2, p. 331; Frame, p. 290.

37. See in particular the essay "Of Physiognomy" ("De la phisionomie," III, 12); the question of the transformation and corruption of language is discussed in ch. 5 below.

38. Erasmus, *Eloge de la folie, adages, colloques, réflexions sur l'art, l'éducation, la religion, la guerre, la philosophie*, ed. Claude Blum, André Godin, Jean-Claude Margolin, and Daniel Ménager, Paris, Robert Laffont, 1992; Léon-Ernest Halkin, *Erasme et l'humanisme chrétien*, Paris, PUF, 1969; Johan Huizinga, *Erasme*, trans. V. Bruncel, preface by Lucien Febvre, Paris, Gallimard, 1955; C. Augustijn, *Erasmus: His Life, Works and Influence*, Toronto, Toronto University Press, 1992.

39. On Montaigne's conception of human nature, see Marie-Luce Demonet, *Montaigne et la question de l'homme*, Paris, PUF, 1999; Emmanuel Faye, *Philosophie et perfection de l'homme, de la Renaissance à Descartes*, Paris, Vrin, 1998, pp. 163–237; Jesse Virgil Mauzey, *Montaigne's Philosophy of Human Nature*, Annandale on Hudson, NY, St. Stephen College, 1933.

40. On the influence of Augustine's thought on Montaigne, see Andrée Comparot, *Augustinisme et Aristotélisme de Sebon à Montaigne*, Paris, Editions du Cerf, 1984, and *Amour et vérité: Sebon, Vives et Michel de Montaigne*, Paris, Klincksieck, 1983. On the Erasmian school, see also Charles Béné, *Erasme et Saint Augustin, ou l'influence de Saint Augustin sur l'humanisme d'Erasme*, Geneva, Droz, 1969; Carlos G. Norena, *Juan Luis Vives*, The Hague, Martinus Nijhoff, 1970, in particular about Vives's commentary of St. Augustine; Robert P. Adams, *The Better Part of Valour: More, Erasmus, Colet and Vives on Humanism, War and Peace, 1496–1535*, University of Washington Press, Seattle, 1962.

41. Montaigne took the view that it was impossible to establish a clear discontinuity between human and animal nature: cf. Thierry Gontier, *De l'homme à l'animal: paradoxes sur la nature des animaux, Montaigne et Descartes*, Paris, Vrin, 1998.

42. Cf., for example, the essays 4, 6, and 11 in Book III: "Of Diversion" ("De la diversion"), "Of Coaches" ("Des coches"), and "Of Cripples" ("Des boyteux"). On Erasmus's views on violence, see J. D. Tracy, *The Politics of Erasmus: A Pacifist Intellectual in His Political Milieu*, Toronto, Toronto University Press, 1992.

43. Cf. essay 26 in Book I, "Of the Education of Children" ("De l'institution des enfans"). Montaigne's interest in a reform of education was one of the concerns he shared with the newly established Society of Jesus; in particular the writer entertained friendly relations with one the pioneers of the Jesuit pedagogical project, Juan Maldonado; see Jacques de Feytaud, "L'Eglise catholique face aux Essais"; William V. Bangert, *A History of the Society of Jesus*, St. Louis, MO, Institute of Jesuit Sources, 1986; Martin A. Lynn, *Henri III and the Jesuit Politicians*, Geneva, Droz, 1973, and *The Jesuit Mind: The Mentality of an Elite in Early Modern France*, Ithaca and London, Cornell University Press, 1988; Paul Schmitt, *La réforme catholique: le combat de Maldonat (1534–1583)*, Paris, Beauchesne, 1985; John C. Olin, *Erasmus, Utopia and the Jesuits: Essays on the Outreach of Humanism*, New York, Fordham University Press, 1994. On the Jesuit pedagogic approach, as it appears in Corneille's work, see Marc Fumaroli, *Héros et orateurs: rhétorique et dramaturgie cornéliennes*, Geneva, Droz, 1990, pp. 63–208. After Montaigne's death the Society remained loyal to his memory notwithstanding the condemnation of the *Essais* by the Vatican in 1676.

44. The main source of this theory is Arthur Armaingaud, *Montaigne pamphlétaire: l'enigme du contr'un*, Paris, Hachette, 1910; see also David Lewis Schaefer, *Freedom over Servitude*.

45. On Montaigne and the Tacitean tradition, see Marc Fumaroli, *L'age de l'éloquence* (1980), Paris, Albin Michel, 1993; on Montaigne and Lipsius, see Richard Tuck, *Philosophy and Governement, 1572–1615*, pp. 45 ff; see also Jason Lewis Sanders, *Justus Lipsius: The Philosophy of Renaissance Stoicism*, New York, Liberal Arts Press, 1955.

46. *Essais* (III, 6), vol. 3, p. 910; Frame, p. 844.

47. See, for example, Tzvetan Todorov, *Le jardin imparfait: la pensée humaniste en France*, Paris, Grasset, 1998.

48. Bernard Mouralis, *Montaigne et le mythe du bon sauvage, de l'antiquité à Rousseau*, Paris, Bordas, 1989; Edwin M. Duval, "Lessons for the New World: Design and Meaning in Montaigne's 'Des cannibales' (I,31) and 'Des coches' (III,6)," in Gerard Défaux, *Montaigne: Essays in Reading, Yale French Studies* 64

(1984), pp. 180–87; Frank Lestringant, *L'Huguenot et le sauvage: l'Amérique et la controverse coloniale en France au temps des guerres de religion (1555–1589)*, Geneva, Droz, 2004, and *Le Cannibale, grandeur et decadence*, Paris, Perrin, 1994; see also Anthony Pagden, *The Fall of Natural Man: The American Indian and the Origins of Comparative Ethnology*, Cambridge, Cambridge University Press, 1982.

49. Montaigne's views on nonviolence as an essential Christian value show in particular the influence of Juan Luis Vives: cf. Andrée Comparot, *Augustinisme et Aristotelisme*, pp. 189–99 and the references given in n. 40 above. See also the differences between Montaigne and the censors who examined the *Essais* on the question of torture and cruel punishments in Malcolm Smith, *Montaigne and the Roman Censors*, pp. 75–86.

50. Cf. Allan M. Boase, *The Fortunes of Montaigne*, p. 2. Montaigne used the word *essais* to describe the general character of his work: see Ullrich Langer, "Introduction" to *The Cambridge Companion to Montaigne*, p. 3.

51. "C'est icy un livre de bonne foy, lecteur. Il t'avertit dès l'entrée, que je ne m'y suis proposé aucune fin, que domestique et privée . . . Je l'ay voué à la commodité particuliere de mes parens et amis: à ce que m'ayant perdu (ce qu'ils ont à faire bien tost) ils y puissent retrouver aucuns traits de mes conditions et humeurs, et que par ce moyen ils nourrissent plus entiere et plus vifve, la connoissance qu'ils ont eu de moy." "Au lecteur," *Essais*, vol. 1, p. 3; Frame, p. 2.

52. "Sied-il pas bien à deux consuls Romains, souverains magistrats de la chose publique emperiere du monde, d'employer leur loisir à ordonner et fagoter gentiment une belle missive, pour en tirer la reputation de bien entendre le langage de leur nourrisse?" *Essais* (I, 40), vol. 1, p. 249; Frame, p. 222. For an essential reference on the Ciceronian tradition in the Renaissance, see Quentin Skinner, *The Foundations of Modern Political Thought*, Cambridge, Cambridge University Press, 1978, vol. 1, part III.

53. Montaigne's use of autobiography is possibly the most widely studied aspect of his work and is the object of an immense critical literature; for an essential reference, see Antoine Compagnon, *Nous, Michel de Montaigne*, Paris, Seuil, 1980; see also Craig B. Brush, *From the Perspective of the Self: Montaigne's Self-Portrait*, New York, Fordham University Press, 1994; Ian J. Winter, *Montaigne's Self-Portrait and Its Influence in France: 1580–1630*, Lexington, KY, French Forum, 1976.

54. The phrase attributed to Montaigne is: "Il faut donc que je plaise à Votre Majesté, puisque mon livre lui est agreeable, car il ne contient autre chose qu'un discours de ma vie et de mes actions." La Croix du Maine, "Michel de Montaigne," *Bibliothèque Française*, 1584, cited in Pierre Villey, *Montaigne devant la posterité*, pp. 18–19.

55. Cf., for example, the judgment expressed by Estienne Pasquier in Olivier Millet, *La première réception des Essais*, p. 144.

56. Jean Starobinski, *Montaigne en mouvement*, Paris, Gallimard, 1982.

57. *Essais* (I, 23), vol. 1, p. 120; Frame, p. 105.

58. "Nostre intelligence se conduisant par la seule voye de la parolle, celuy qui la fauce, trahit la societé publique. C'est le seul util par le moien duquel se communiquent nos volontez et nos pensées, c'est le truchement de nostre ame: s'il

nous faut, nous ne nous tenons plus, nous ne nous entreconnoissons plus. S'il nous trompe, il rompt tout nostre commerce et dissoult toutes les liaisons de nostre police." *Essais* (II, 18), vol. 2, pp. 666–67; Frame, p. 614. On the role of speech and dialogue in Montaigne's work, cf. Marc Fumaroli, *La diplomatie de l'esprit: de Montaigne à La Fontaine*, Paris, Hermann, 2001; David Quint, *Montaigne and the Quality of Mercy*; Yves Delègue, *Montaigne et la mauvaise foi: l'écriture de la vérité*, Paris, Honoré Champion, 1998; also, on the word as social link, Carlo Cappa, *Michel de Montaigne, l'appartenenza della scrittura: il dialogo tra vita e opera negli Essais*, Milano, Franco Angeli, 2003, pp. 123–40; Philip Knee, *La parole incertaine: Montaigne en dialogue*, Saint Nicolas (Quebec), Presses de l'Université de Laval, 2003.

59. "Les autheurs se communiquent au peuple par quelque marque particuliere et estrangere; moy le premier par mon estre universel, comme Michel de Montaigne, non comme grammarien ou poete ou jurisconsulte. Si le monde se plaint de quoy je parle trop de moy, je me plains de quoy il ne pense seulement pas à soy." *Essais* (III, 2), vol. 3, p. 805; Frame, p. 741.

60. "Je suis absorbé dans un compte que je me rends à moi-même par ordre alphabétique, de tout ce que je dois penser sur ce monde-ci et sur l'autre, le tout, pour mon usage, et peut-être, après ma mort, pour l'usage des honnêtes gens. Je vas *[sic]* dans ma besogne aussi franchement que Montaigne va dans la sienne." François-Marie Arouet de Voltaire, *Correspondance choisie*, ed. Jacqueline Helleguarc'h, Paris, Librairie Générale Française, 1990–97, p. 535.

61. *Essais* (III, 8), vol. 3, p. 921; Frame, p. 854.

62. "Je fais la même enterprise que Montagne *[sic]*, mais avec un but tout contraire au sien; car il n'écrivait ses essais que pour les autres, et je n'écris mes rêveries que pour moi." Jean-Jacques Rousseau, *Les rêveries du promeneur solitaire*, in *Oeuvres complètes*, ed. B. Gagnebin, and M. Raymond, Paris, Gallimard, 1959–69, 1959, vol. 1, p. 1001.

63. Marie de Gournay, *Oeuvres complètes*, ed. Jean Claude Arnould, Paris, Honoré Champion, 2002; Mario Schiff, *La fille d'alliance de Montaigne: Marie de Gournay*, Geneva, Slatkine, 1978.

64. "En mon climat de Gascongne, on tient pour drolerie de me veoir imprimé. D'autant que la connoissance qu'on prend de moy s'esloigne de mon giste, j'en vaux d'autant mieux. J'achette les imprimeurs en Guiene, ailleurs ils m'achettent." *Essais* (III, 2), vol. 3, p. 809; Frame, p. 744. The first edition of the *Essais* was probably printed privately at the author's expense.

65. After Montaigne's death the *Essais* went through several editions between 1595 and 1635, but there is no comprehensive information about the actual circulation.

66. "Ainsi, lecteur, je suis moy-mesmes la matiere de mon livre: ce n'est pas raison que tu employes ton loisir en un subject si frivole et si vain." *Essais*, "Au lecteur," vol. 1, p. 3; Frame, p. 2.

67. "Ce livre n'est point fait pour circuler dans le monde, et convient à très peu de lecteurs. Le style rebutera le gens de gout; la matière alarmera les gens sévères; . . . Il doit déplaire aux dévots, aux libertins, aux philosophes." Jean-Jacques Rousseau, Preface to *Julie, ou La Nouvelle Héloïse*, ed. Michel Launey, Paris, Garnier Flammarion, 1953, p. 3. Rousseau's views on authorship and responsibility

are discussed in Christopher Kelly, *Rousseau as Author: Consecrating One's Life to the Truth*, Chicago and London, University of Chicago Press, 2003.

CHAPTER 1

1. On the forms of legal training current in Montaigne's time, see Roland Mousnier, *Les institutions de la France sous la monarchie absolue*, Paris, PUF, 1980, vol. 2, pp. 331–33. On Montaigne's legal activities, see Fortunat Strowski, *Montaigne: sa vie publique et privée*, Paris, Editions Nouvelle Revue Critique, 1938; Roger Trinquet, *La jeunesse de Montaigne: ses origines familiales, son enfance et ses études*, Paris, Nizet, 1972; Donald M. Frame, *Montaigne: A Biography*, ch. 4; Madeleine Lazard, *Michel de Montaigne*, pp. 83–104; François Roussel, *Montaigne: magistrat sans juridiction*, Paris, Michalon (Le Bien Commun), 2006.

2. The exact date is unknown: Montaigne was only twenty-one in 1554, while the minimal legal age for a *conseiller* was twenty-five, but exceptions were often made.

3. Charles-Bon-François Boscheron des Portes, *Histoire du parlement de Bordeaux depuis sa création jusqu'à sa suppression (1451–1790)*, Geneva, Megariotis, 1978 (repr. of the Bordeaux edition of 1877–78), vol. 1, pp. 1–239; Bernard Barbiche, *Les institutions de la monarchie française à l'époque moderne*, Paris, PUF, 1999, pp. 342–43; D. Bège-Seurin, "La cour des Aides de Périgueux, 1553–1561," in *Sarlat et le Périgord, actes du XXXIXème congrès d'études régionales* (Sarlat, 26–27 Apr. 1987), Société Historique et Archéologique du Périgord, 1987, pp. 321–30.

4. For a documentation of Montaigne's legal activity, cf. his "Les arrêts des Enquêtes rédigés (10), dictés (40) ou contresignés (341) par Montaigne, récemment découverts par Katherine Almquist," ed. Katherine Almquist, *Bulletin de la Société des Amis de Montaigne*, Jan. 1998, pp. 13–38.

5. *Essais* (III, 13), vol. 3, pp. 1066–67, Frame pp. 993–94. The questions of the "excess" of legislation and of the intelligibility of laws has not disappeared from contemporary debates: cf. the articles by Pierre Avril and others, collected in "La Loi," special issue of *Pouvoirs*, 114 (2005), Seuil.

6. On the defects of French legislation, see also *Essais* I, 23, *passim*; on the debate on Roman and customary law and its implications, see Julian H. Franklin, *Jean Bodin and the Sixteenth Century Revolution in the Methodology of Law and History*; see also Jean Bodin, *La méthode de l'histoire*, trans. and ed. by Pierre Mesnard; cf. François Hotman, *Anti-tribonien ou discours pour l'estude des loix*, Cologne, Bruxelles, 1681; cf. Philippe Desan, *Naissance de la méthode (Machiavel, La Ramée, Bodin, Montaigne, Descartes)*; Marie-Dominique Couzinet, *Histoire et méthode à la renaissance: une lecture de la "Méthodus" de Jean Bodin*, pp. 114–20.

7. *Essais* (III, 13), vol. 3, p. 1072; Frame, p. 1000.

8. A post could be recalled, for example, if the holder died suddenly, before making arrangements for its sale or transfer to a successor; in some cases posts were not actually sold, but "leased" for a limited number of years. Cf. Roland Mousnier, *La vénalité des offices sous Henri IV et Louis XIII*, pp. 35 ff.

9. "Cette vénalité est bonne dans les Etats monarchiques, parce qu'elle fait faire, comme un métier de famille, ce qu'on ne voudroit pas entreprendre pour la vertu;

qu'elle destine chacun à son devoir, et rend les ordres de l'Etat plus permanents." Montesquieu went on to argue that in a monarchy, where corruption was inevitable, judicial offices, like all other posts and distinctions, would necessarily become the object of an illegal market, if they were not sold openly by the crown. Montesquieu, *L'Esprit des lois*, Book V, ch. 19, in *Oeuvres complètes*, ed. Roger Caillois, Paris, Gallimard, 1951, vol. 2, pp. 305–6. For a wider perspective on venality in the 18th century, see William Doyle, *Venality: The Sale of Offices in Eighteenth-Century France*, Oxford, Clarendon Press, 1996.

10. *Essais* (I, 23), vol. 1, pp. 117–18, and (III, 13), vol. 3, pp. 1070–71; Frame, pp. 998–99.

11. Robert Jean Knecht, *The Rise and Fall of Renaissance France: 1483–1610*, London, Fontana Press, 1996, pp. 248–50; on the repression of heresy, see also Ole Peter Grell and Bob Scribner, eds., *Tolerance and Intolerance in the European Reformation*, Cambridge, Cambridge University Press, 1996; Diarmaid MacCulloch, *Reformation: Europe's House Divided, 1490–1700*, London, Allen Lane, 2003; Patrick Collinson, *The Reformation*, London, Weidenfeld and Nicolson, 2003.

12. See the essays II, 11, "Of Cruelty" ("De la cruauté"), and II, 27, "Cowardice Mother of Cruelty" ("Couardise mere de la cruauté"); on Montaigne's critique of violence as a feature of contemporary society, see David Quint, *Montaigne and the Quality of Mercy*.

13. On Michel de l'Hospital's career, see Ernest Dupré Lasale, *Michel de l'Hospital avant son élévation au poste de chancelier de France*, Paris, E. Thorin, A. Fontemoing, 1875–99; Seong-Hak Kim, *Michel de l'Hôpital: The political vision of a reformist chancellor, 1560–1568*, Minneapolis, University of Minnesota Press, 1991; Denis Crouzet, *La sagesse et le malheur*, pp. 429 ff. On the background of the Paris parliament, cf. J. H. Shennan, *The Parlement of Paris* (1968), Phoenix Mill, Sutton Publishing, 1998; Nancy Lyman Roelker, *One King, One Faith: The Parlement of Paris and the Religious Reformations of the Sixteenth Century*, Berkeley, University of California Press, 1996.

14. On Montaigne and the *édit de janvier*, see Malcolm Smith, *Montaigne and Religious Freedom; The Dawn of Pluralism*, Geneva, Droz, 1991. On the Reformation in Bordeaux, see L.F.E. Gaullieur, *Histoire de la Réformation à Bordeaux, et dans le ressort du parlement de Guyenne*, Paris, H. Champion, 1884, vol. 1, "Les origines et la première guerre de Religion jusqu'à la paix d'Amboise (1523–1563)"; see also Joel Cornette, *Le livre et le Glaive: chronique de la France moderne, le XVI siècle*, Paris, Armand Colin, 1995, pp. 363–75 for further bibliographical references.

15. *Essais* (II, 17), vol. 2, p. 661; Frame, p. 609.

16. L'Hospital visited Bordeaux and addressed the local *parlement* in 1562: cf. Géralde Nakam, *Montaigne et son temps*, pp. 211 ff.

17. "L'on dit bien qu'il est besoin de réformer l'Eglise, mais la justice a aussi grand besoin de réformation que l'Eglise." Michel de l'Hospital, "Harangue au Parlement de Rouen" (17 Aug. 1563), in *Discours pour la majorité de Charles IX*, ed. Robert Descimon, p. 107.

18. *Essais* (II, 17), vol. 2, p. 656; Frame, p. 604.

19. *Essais* (I, 23), vol. 1, p. 120; Frame, p. 105.

20. "To King Henry III: Letter of Remonstrance from the Mayor and Jurats of Bordeaux" (31 Aug. 1583), Frame, pp. 1304–7; "Au Roy," in *Oeuvres complètes,* ed. Maurice Rat, pp. 1373–78; for a version in modern French, cf. Montaigne, *Lettres,* ed. Claude Pinganaud, Paris, Arléa, 2004, pp. 63–70. The letter was jointly signed by Montaigne and the other members of the Town Council.

21. "La justice bien et dévouement administrée fait régner hereusement les rois et contenir leur sujets en l'obéissance qu'ils lui doivent, les faisant vivre en bonne union, concorde et amitié: aussi est-ce la principale colonne sur laquelle nous voulons appuyer les fondements de notre Etat, que nous penserions ne pouvoir subsister autrement, n'ayant rien en si grande recommandation, après l'honneur de Dieu, que la faire distribuer également et en toutes saisons à nos sujets, comme nous y sommes tenus de le faire." Quoted in: Michel de Waele, *Les relations entre le parlement de Paris et Henri IV,* Paris, Editions Publisud, 2000, p. 176, my translation.

22. On the resolution passed by the King's Council cf. R. Mousnier, *La vénalité des offices,* p. 234; originally secretary of the *chambre du roi,* Paulet became the new "*fermier*" in charge of offices.

23. On the practice of venality, see also Michel Antoine, *Le coeur de l'Etat: surintendence, contrôle général et intendence des finances, 1552–1791,* Paris, Fayard, 2003, pp. 149 ff.

24. *Essais* (III, 12), vol. 3, p 1043; Frame, p. 971.

25. *Essais* (III, 9), vol. 3, p. 966; Frame, p. 897.

26. On the question of the attribution of the text, see Paul Bonnefon, *Estienne de la Boétie, sa vie, ses ouvrages et ses relations avec Montaigne* (1888), Geneva, Slatkine, 1970; Arthur Armaingaud, *Montaigne pamphlétaire;* Anne-Marie Cocula, *Etienne de la Boétie;* Simone Goyard Fabre, introduction to Etienne de La Boétie, *Discours de la servitude volontaire,* Paris, Flammarion, 1983, pp. 17–122; David Lewis Schaefer, ed., *Freedom over Servitude,* ch. 1, "Montaigne and La Boétie."

27. Estienne de la Boétie, *Discours de la servitude volontaire ou contr'un,* ed. Malcolm Smith and Michel Magnien, Geneva, Droz, 2001, pp. 67–68; "On Voluntary Servitude," trans. David Lewis Schaefer, in D. L. Schaefer, ed., *Freedom over Servitude,* pp. 189–222.

28. Cf. Théodore de Bèze, *Du droit des magistrats,* ed. Robert M. Kingdon, Geneva, Droz, 1971; François Hotman, *Francogallia,* ed. R. E. Giesey and J.H.M. Salmon, Cambridge, Cambridge University Press, 1972; *Vindiciae, contra tyrannos,* trans. and ed. George Garnett, Cambridge, Cambridge University Press, 1994. For an overview of this debate, see Quentin Skinner, *The Foundations of Modern Political Thought,* vol. 2, ch. 9, "The Right to Resist"; Simone Goyard Fabre, "Au tournant de l'idée de démocratie: l'influence des Monarchomaques," *Cahiers de philosophie politique et juridique de l'université de Caen,* no. 1, 1982, pp. 27–48; J.H.M. Salmon, *Renaissance and Revolt: Essays in the Intellectual and Social History of Early Modern France,* Cambridge, Cambridge University Press, 1987, ch. 5, pp. 119–35.

29. *Essais* (I, 23), vol. 1, p. 115; Frame, p. 100.

30. On Bodin's methodology, see the references given in n. 5 above; cf. also Pierre Villey, *Les livres d'histoire moderne utilisés par Montaigne,* p. 58.

31. Jean Bodin, *La méthode de l'histoire,* ed. Pierre Mesnard, p. xxxvi.

32. *Essais* (II, 32), vol. 2, pp. 722–24; Frame, pp. 662–64.

33. Henricii Cornelii Agrippae, *De incertitude et vanitate scientiarum et artium atque excellentia verbi Dei declamatio*, Antwerp, Loan Grapheus, 1530; Heinrich Cornelius Agrippa von Nettlesheim, *Opera*, ed. Richard H. Popkin, Hildesheim and New York, G. Holms, 1970; see also Charles G. Nauert Jr., *Agrippa and the Crisis of Renaissance Thought*, Urbana, University of Illinois Press, 1965.

34, *Essais* (I, 23), vol. 1, p. 111; Frame, p. 95.

35. "Les loix de la conscience, que nous disons naistre de la nature, naissent de la coustume: chacun ayant en veneration interne les opinions et moeurs approuvées et receües autour de luy, ne s'en peut desprendre sans remors, ny s'y appliquer sans applaudissement . . . Mais le principal effect de sa puissance, c'est de nous saisir et empieter de telle sorte, qu'a peine soit-il en nous de nous r'avoir de sa prinse et de r'entrer en nous, pour discourir et raisonner de ses ordonnances." *Essais*, vol. 1, p. 115; Frame, p. 100.

36. "Puisqu'il pleu à Dieu de nous doüer de quelque capacité de discours, affin que, comme les bestes, nous ne fussions pas servilement assujectis aux loix communes, ainsi que nous nous y appliquassions par jugement et liberté volontaire, nous devons bien prester un peu à la simple authorité de la nature, mais non pas nous laisser tyranniquement emporter à elle; la seule raison doit avoir la conduite de nos inclinations." *Essais* (II, 8), vol. 2, p. 387, Frame, p. 339.

37. *Essais* (III, 12), vol. 3, p. 1049, Frame, p. 978.

38. *Essais* (III, 13), vol. 3, p. 1072, Frame, p. 1000. On the background to Montaigne's understanding of natural justice, see Antonina Alberti, "The Epicurian Theory of Law and Justice," in A. Laks and M. Schofield, eds., *Justice and Generosity: Studies in Hellenistic Social and Political Philosophy*, Cambridge, Cambridge University Press, 1995, pp. 161–90.

39. *Essais* (I, 23), vol. 1, p. 117, Frame, pp. 101–2.

40. On the law as a form of tyranny of the past over the present cf. Marcel Conche, *Montaigne et la philosophie*, Paris, PUF, 1996, p. 59.

41. "Les peuples nourris à la liberté et à se commander eux mesmes, estiment toute autre forme de police monstrueuse et contre nature. Ceux qui sont duits à la monarchie en font de mesme. Et quelque facilité que leur preste fortune au changement, lors mesme qu'ils se sont, avec grandes difficultez, deffaitz de l'importunité d'un maistre, ils courent à en replanter un nouveau avec pareilles difficultez, pour ne se pouvoir resoudre de prendre en haine la maistrise." *Essais*, vol. 1, p. 116, Frame, p. 101.

42. *Essais* (I, 23), vol. 1, pp. 118–19, Frame, pp. 104–5; on the same theme of the danger and futility of change, see also essay III, 9, "Of Vanity," *passim*.

43. *Essais*, vol. 1, p. 119, Frame, p. 105.

44. The question of royal derogation to the law is discussed in particular in the essay III, 1, "Of the Useful and the Honorable" ("De l'utile et de l'honneste"); see in particular the passage in vol. 3, p. 799, Frame, p. 736.

45. On the uneasy position of rulers and the frequent absence of merit and abilities in the people of rank see the essays I, 42, "Of the Inequality That Is between Us" ("De l'inequalité qui est entre nous"), and III, 7, "Of the Disadvantages of Greatness" ("De l'incommodité de la grandeur"). The question of the limitations and unsatisfactory training of monarchs is discussed in ch. 5 below.

46. *Essais* (II, 19), vol. 2, p. 672, Frame, p. 619.

47. The tensions and conflicts between the private interests and opinions of individuals and the imperatives of the law is discussed more particularly in the essays III, 1, "Of the Useful and the Honorable," and III, 10, "Of Husbanding Your Will" ("De mesnager sa volonté").

48. "La justice en soy, naturelle et universelle, est autrement reiglée, et plus noblement, que cet autre justice speciale, nationale, contrainte au besoing de nos polices. *'Veri juris germanaeque justitiae solidam et expressam effigiem nullam tenemus; umbra et imaginibus utimur.'*" *Essais* (III, 1), vol. 3, p. 796, Frame, p. 732.

49. For an influential illustration of this view, see the work by Claude de Seyssel, *La grande monarchie de France*, written around 1519 for the king François I: Claude de Seyssel, *La monarchie de France et deux autres fragments politiques*, ed. Jacques Poujol, Paris, d'Argences, 1961.

50. The instinctive capacity of human conscience to recognize right from wrong is illustrated in essay II, 5, "Of Conscience" ("De la conscience"). There Montaigne clearly implies that such capacity is present in all human beings, regardless of their religious beliefs, as some of the examples in the essay refer to pagans, infidels, or heretics. In his edition Screech suggests that the inspiration for this essay comes from Juan Luis Vives's commentary of the *City of God*: cf. Michel de Montaigne, *The Complete Essays*, ed. M. A. Screech, p. 411. On a different level, the question of the relation between the individual conscience and God is discussed in essay II, 12, "Apology for Raymond Sebond" ("Apologie de Raimond Sebond"), in which Montaigne famously defends the view that God's truth is accessible to man through faith, not reason. However the writer makes a rather idiosyncratic use of the notion of "faith," since in the examples he provides, infidels and pagans are often shown to be more aware of God's justice than Christians. "Faith" seems in fact to indicate in broad terms the aspiration to "rise . . . above humanity." *Essais*, vol. 2, p. 604, Frame, p. 556. Cf. also Vincent Carraud, "Imaginer l'inimaginable: le Dieu de Montaigne," in Vincent Carraud and Jean-Luc Marion, eds., *Montaigne: scepticisme, métaphysique, théologie*, Paris, PUF, 2004, pp. 49–87.

51. On Montaigne's different approaches to the notion of law, see also my articles "The Rule of Law and the Problem of Legal Reform in Montaigne's *Essais,*" in José Maria Maraval and Adam Przeworski, eds., *Democracy and the Rule of Law*, Cambridge, Cambridge University Press, 2003, pp. 302–15, and "Loi, in *Dictionnaire de Michel de Montaigne*, ed. Philippe Desan, Paris, Honoré Champion, 2004, pp. 601– 3.

CHAPTER 2

1. "Ce siècle auquel nous vivons, au moins dans notre climat, est si plombé, que, je ne dis pas l'execution, mais l'imagination mesme de la vertu en est à dire; et semble que ce ne soit autre chose qu'un jargon de colliege . . . Il ne se recognoit plus d'action vertueuse: celles qui en portent le visage, elles n'en ont pas pourtant l'essence, car le profit, la gloire, la crainte, l'accoutumance et autres telles causes estrangeres nous acheminent à les produire." *Essais*, I, 37 ("Du jeune Caton"), vol. 1, p. 230, Frame, pp. 205–6.

2. Juan Luis Vives, *D. Aurelii Augustini Hipponensis episcopi De civitate Dei libri XXII*, Geneva, Jacobus Stoer, 1610; *The Selected Works of J. L. Vives*, ed. C.

Matheeussen, Leiden and New York, E. J. Brill, 1987– ; see also Alan Guy, ed., *Vivès ou l'humanisme engagé*, Paris, Seghers, 1972; Carlos G. Norena, *Juan Luis Vives*, The Hague, Martinus Nijhoff, 1970.

3. Augustine, *The City of God against the Pagans*, ed. R. W. Dyson, Cambridge, Cambridge University Press, 1998, Book XIX, ch. 4, pp. 853–54.

4. *Essais* (I, 37), vol. 1, pp. 230–31, Frame, pp. 205–6.

5. "Comparez nos meurs à un Mahometan, à un Payen; vous demeurez tousjours au dessoubs: là ou', au regard de l'avantage de nostre religion, nous devrions luire en excellence, d'une extreme et incomparable distance; et devroit on dire: Sont ils si justes, si charitables, si bons? Ils sont donq Chrestiens." *Essais* (II, 12), vol. 2, p. 442, Frame, p. 391.

6. *Essais* (II, 11), vol. 2, p. 432, Frame, p. 385.

7. Steven Ozment, *The Age of Reform 1250–1550: An Intellectual and Religious History of Late Medieval and Reformation Europe*, New Haven, Yale University Press, 1980; Anthony Levi, *Renaissance and Reformation;* Andrée Comparot, *Amour et vérité,* and *Augustinisme et Aristotelisme de Sebon à Montaigne.*

8. The only classical author Montaigne seems to have reread systematically after 1580 is Caesar; cf. Pierre Villey, *Les livres d'histoire moderne utilisés par Montaigne.*

9. Cf. Pierre Villey, *Les sources et l'évolution des "Essais" de Montaigne.*

10. See, for example, essay I, 1, "By Diverse Means We Arrive at the Same End" ("Par divers moyens on arrive à pareille fin"); I, 14, "That the Taste of Good and Evil Depends in Large Part on the Opinion We Have of Them" ("Que le goust des biens et des maux depend en bonne partie de l'opinion que nous en avons"); I, 24, "Various Outcomes of the Same Plan" ("Divers evenemens de mesme conseil"); I, 27, " It Is Folly to Measure the True and False by Our Own Capacity" ("C'est folie de rapporter le vray et le faux à nostre suffisance"); I, 47, "Of the Uncertainty of our Judgement" ("De l'incertitude de nostre jugement").

11. *Essais*, (I, 26), vol. 1, p. 157, Frame, p. 141.

12. *Essais*, (II, 17), vol. 2, p. 655, Frame, pp. 603–4.

13. Francesco Guicciardini, *Storia d'Italia*, ed. Seidel Menchi, Torino, Einaudi, 1971, and *Ricordi*, ed. Emilio Pasquini, Milano, Garzanti, 1984; Felix Gilbert, *Machiavelli and Guicciardini, Politics and History in Sixteenth-Century Florence*, Princeton, Princeton University Press, 1965; Emanuela Scarano Lagnani, *Guicciardini e la crisi del Rinascimento*, Bari, Laterza, 1973; Donald J. Wilcox, "Guicciardini and the Humanist Historians," in *Annali di Italianistica*, Department of Modern and Classical Languages, University of Notre Dame, 1984, vol. II, pp. 110–22; Mario Perniola, *Del sentire cattolico: la forma culturale di una religione universale*, Bologna, Il Mulino, 2001, ch. 7, "Il pensiero della differenza," pp. 77–95. See also Timothy Hampton, *Writing from History: The Rhetoric of Exemplarity in Renaissance Literature*, Ithaca, Cornell University Press, 1990.

14. *Essais* (III, 9), vol. 3, pp. 959–61, Frame, pp. 890–92.

15. "Dieu, qui est en soy toute plenitude et le comble de toute perfection, il ne peut s'augmenter et accroistre au dedans; mais son nom se peut augmenter et accroistre par la benediction et louange que nous donnons à ses ouvrages exterieurs. Laquelle louange, puis que nous ne la pouvons incorporer en luy, d'autant qu'il n'y peut avoir accession de bien, nous l'attribuons à son nom, qui est la piece hors de luy la plus voisine. Voilà comment c'est à Dieu seul à qui gloire et honneur appar-

tient; et il n'est rien si esloigné de raison que de nous metre en queste pour nous."
Essais (II, 16), vol. 2, p. 618, Frame, p. 569.

16. Cicero, *On Duties*, ed. M. T. Griffin and E. M. Atkins, Cambridge, Cambridge University Press, 1991, Book I, §74 ff; see also A.A. Long, "Cicero's politics in *De Officiis*," in A. Laks and M. Schofield, eds., *Justice and Generosity: Studies in Hellenistic Social and Political Philosophy*, Cambridge, Cambridge University Press, 1995, pp. 213–40; J.H.M. Salmon, "Cicero and Tacitus in Sixteenth-Century France," *Renaissance and Revolt*, pp. 27–53. For an overview of the humanist reinterpretation of the notion of virtue, see Quentin Skinner, *The Foundations of Modern Political Thought*, vol. 1, pp. 88 ff.

17. *Essais* (II, 33), vol. 2, p. 733, Frame, p. 673.

18. *Essais* (II, 16), vol. 2, pp. 626–27, Frame, pp. 578–79; cf. Erasmus, *Ecstasy and "The Praise of Folly,"* ed. M. A. Screech, London, Duckworth, 1980, ch. XXIII.

19. *Essais* (II, 23), vol. 2, pp. 684–85, Frame, pp. 629–30.

20. Essais (I, 20), vol. 1, p. 85, Frame, p. 80.

21. *Essais* (II, 23), vol. 2, p. 685, Frame, p. 630. See also James J. Supple, *Arms versus Letters: The Military and Literary Ideals in the "Essais" of Montaigne*, Oxford, Oxford University Press, 1984.

22. "Combien voit-on de personnes populaires, conduictes à la mort, et non à une mort simple, mais meslée de honte et quelque fois de griefs tourmens, y apporter une telle assurance, qui par opiniatreté, qui par simplesse naturelle, qu'on n'y apperçoit rien de change de leur estat ordinaire: establissans leurs affaires domestiques, se recommandans à leurs amis, chantans, preschans et entretenans le peuple: voire y meslans quelque-fois des mots pour rire, et beuvans à leurs cognoissans, aussi bien que Socrates . . . Toute opinion est assez forte pour se faire espouser au pris de la vie." *Essais* (I, 14), vol. 1, pp. 51–53, Frame, p. 40–41. On violence at the time of the religious wars, cf. the fundamental study by Denis Crouzet, *Les guerriers de Dieu*, vol. II.

23. *Essais* (I, 23), vol. 1, p. 110, Frame, p. 94.

24. *Essais* (II, 27), vol. 2, p. 695, Frame, p. 638. On the attitudes to dueling in French culture, see François Billacois, *Le duel dans la société française des XVIe-XVIIe siècles: essai de psychosociologie historique*, Paris, Edition de l'Ecole d'Hautes Etudes, 1986; Nicolas Le Roux, *La faveur du roi: mignons et courtisans au temps des derniers Valois (vers 1547–vers 1589)*, Seyssel, Champ Vallon, 2001; see also, on the logic of duelling, Russell Hardin, *One for All: The Logic of Group Conflict*, Princeton, Princeton University Press, 1995, pp. 91–106.

25. On the changing identity of the French nobility, see Arlette Jouanna, *Le devoir de révolte: la noblesse française et la gestation de l'Etat moderne, 1559–1661*, Paris, Fayard, 1989; Laurent Bourquin, *La noblesse dans la France moderne (XVI–XVIII siècles)*, Paris, Belin, 2002; see also Kristen B. Neuschel, *Word of Honor: Interpreting Noble Culture in Sixteenth-Century France*, Ithaca, Cornell University Press, 1986; Jonathan Dewald, *The European Nobility, 1400–1800*, Cambridge, Cambridge University Press, 1996.

26. *Essais* (II, 17), vol. 2, p. 647, Frame, p. 596. On Erasmus's pacifism, see Robert P. Adams, *The Better Part of Valour;* Philip C. Dust, *Three Renaissance Pacifists: Essays in the Theories of Erasmus, More and Vives*, New York and Bern,

Peter Lang, 1987; Jean-Claude Margolin, ed., *Guerre et paix dans la pensée d'Erasme*, Paris, Aubier, 1973; James D. Tracy, *The Politics of Erasmus*.

27. "La corruption du siecle se faict par la contribution particuliere de chacun de nous: les uns y conferment la trahison, les autres l'injustice, l'irreligion, la tyrannie, l'avarice, la cruauté, selon qu'ils sont plus puissans; les plus foibles y apportent la sottise, la vanité, l'oisiveté, desquels je suis." *Essais* (III, 9), vol. 3, p. 946, Frame, p. 877.

28. "Nous ne pouvons pas tout. Ainsi comme ainsi nous faut il souvent, comme à la derniere anchre, remettre la protection de nostre vaisseau à la pure conduitte du ciel. A quelle plus juste necessité se reserve il? Que luy est il moins possible à faire que ce qu'il ne peut faire qu'aux despens de sa foy et de son honneur, choses qui à l'aventure luy doivent estre plus cheres que son propre salut, ouy, et que le salut de son peuple? Quand, les bras croizes, il appellera Dieu simplement à son aide, n'aura il pas à esperer que la divine bonté n'est pour refuser faveur de sa main extraordinaire à une main pure et juste?" *Essais* (III, 1), vol. 3, pp. 799–800, Frame, p. 736.

29. Montaigne would have been familiar with Innocent Gentillet's *Anti-Machiavel*: Innocent Gentillet, *Anti-Machiavel* (1576), ed. C. Edward Rathé, Geneva, Droz, 1968. On the anti-Machavellian debate, see Robert Bireley, *The Counter-Reformation Prince: Anti-Machiavellianism or Catholic Statecraft in Early Modern Europe*, Chapel Hill and London, University of North Carolina Press, 1990. On Montaigne and Machiavelli, see Hugo Frederich, *Montaigne*, Paris, Gallimard, 1968, pp. 161–63; Géralde Nakam, *Les "Essais" de Montaigne*, pp. 198 ff; S. G. Sanders, "Montaigne et les idées politiques de Machiavel," *Bulletin de la Société des Amis de Montaigne*, 18–19 (1976), pp. 97–98; J. H. Whitfield, "Machiavelli, Guicciardini, Montaigne," *Italian Studies* 28 (1973), pp. 31–47; Thomas Berns, *Violence de la loi à la renaissance*, pp. 232–55.

30. *Essais* (II, 36), vol. 2, p. 756, Frame, p. 695. On Montaigne and moral judgment, cf. Raymond La Charité, *The Concept of Judgment in Montaigne*, The Hague, Martinus Nijhoff, 1968, pp. 134–35; Clément Sclafert, *L'âme religieuse de Montaigne*, part II.

31. See the essay III, 2, "Of Repenting" ("Du repentir"), *passim*.

32. On the concept of "honneteté," the classical reference is Maurice Magendie, *La politesse mondaine et les théories de l'honnêteté en France au XVIIème siècle* (1925), Geneva, Slatkine Reprints, 1993; see also Marc Fumaroli, *L'age de l'éloquence* (1980), Paris, Albin Michel, 1993; Emmanuel Bury, *Littérature et politesse: l'invention de l'honnête homme, 1580–1750*, Paris, PUF, 1996; Robert Muchembled, *La société policée: politesse et politique en France du XVIème au XX siècle*, Paris, Seuil, 1998; Benedetta Craveri, *L'arte della conversazione*, Milano, Adelphi, 2001. The study by Bérengère Parmentier, *Le siècle des moralistes, de Montaigne à La Bruyère* (Paris, Seuil, 2000), contains a useful bibliography and a glossary of terms.

33. "My virtue is a virtue, or I should say an innocence, that is accidental and fortuitous. If I had been born with a more unruly disposition, I fear it would have gone pitifully with me. For I have not experienced much firmness in my soul to withstand passions, if they are even the least bit vehement. I do not know how to foster quarrels and conflict within me. Thus I cannot give myself any great thanks

because I find myself free from many vices." ("Ma vertu, c'est une vertu, ou inno-cence, pour mieux dire, accidentale et fortuite. Si je fusse nay d'une complexion plus déreglée, je crains qu'il fut allé piteusement de mon faict. Car je n'ay essayé guiere de fermeté en mon ame pour soustenir des passions, si elles eussent esté tant soit peu vehementes. Je ne sçay point nourrir des querelles et du debat chez moy. Ainsi, je ne puis dire nul granmercy dequoy je me trouve exempt de plusieurs vices.") *Essais* (II, 11), vol. 2, p. 427, Frame, p. 377.

34. Ibid., vol. 2, p. 426, Frame p. 376.

35. On the influence of ancient philosophy on Montaigne, the classical refer-ence remains Hugo Friedrich, *Montaigne*, trans. Robert Rovini, Paris, Gallimard, 1968, ch. 2, "Tradition et culture"; on the modern revival of ancient philosophy, see Richard H. Popkin, *The History of Scepticism: From Erasmus to Spinoza*, Berke-ley, University of California Press, 1979, and *The History of Scepticism: From Savonarola to Bayle*, Oxford, Oxford University Press, 2003; Tom Sorell, ed., *The Rise of Modern Philosophy*, Oxford, Clarendon Press, 1993; Pierre-François Moreau, ed., *Le retour des philosophies antiques à l'age classique*, 2 vols., Paris, Albin Michel, 1999–2001; see also Marcel Conche, *Montaigne et la philosophie*; Philippe Desan, ed., *La philosophie et Montaigne*, special issue of *Montaigne Studies*, 12 (2000); Patrick Henry, ed., *Montaigne and Ethics*, special issue of *Montaigne Stud-ies*, 14 (2002); Ann Hartle, *Michel de Montaigne: Accidental Philosopher*, pp. 11–38.

36. *Essais* (II, 11), vol. 2, pp. 422 and 425, Frame, pp. 372 and 375.

37. *Essais* (I, 30), vol. 1, p. 197, Frame, p. 177.

38. "Gaigner une bresche, conduire une ambassade, regir un peuple, ce sont des actions esclatantes. Tancer, rire, vendre, payer, aymer, hayr et converser avec les siens et avec soymesme doucement et justement, ne rélacher point, ne se desmen-tir poinct c'est une chose plus rare, plus difficile et moins remerquable." *Essais* (III, 2), vol. 3, p. 809, Frame, p. 744.

39. *Essais* (I, 42), vol. 1, p. 260, Frame, p. 231.

40. *Essais* (III, 7), *passim*.

41. ". . . ils avoyent aperçeu qu'il y avoit parmy nous des hommes pleins et gorgez de toutes sortes de commoditez, et que leurs moitiez estoient mendians à leurs portes, décharnez de faim et de pauvreté; et trouvoient estrange comme ces moitiez icy necessiteuses pourvoient souffrir une telle injustice, qu'ils ne prinsent les autres à la gorge, ou missent le feu à leurs maisons." *Essais* (I, 31), vol. 1, pp. 214, Frame, p. 193.

42. *Essais* (III, 2), vol. 2, p. 811, Frame, p. 747.

43. "Sire Vostre Majeste me fera sil luy plaist ceste grace de croyre que je ne plaindray jamais ma bource aux occasions ausquelles je ne voudrois espargner ma vie Je n'ai jamais receu bien quelconque de la liberalite des Rois non plus que de-mandé ny merité et nay receu nul payment des pas que j'ay employes à leur service desquels Vostre Majeste a heu en partie cognoissance ce que jay faict pour ses pre-dessesseurs je le feray encores beaucoup plus volontiers pour elle. Je suis Sire aussi riche que je me souhaite." Montaigne to Henry of Navarre, 2 Sept. 1590, in *Oeu-vres complètes*, ed. Maurice Rat, p. 1400, Frame, p. 1334.

44. "Je suis desgousté de maistrise et active et passive. Otanez, l'un des sept qui avoient droit de pretendre au royaume de Perse, print un party que j'eusse prins

volontiers; c'est qu'il quitta à ses compagnons son droit d'y pouvoir arriver par election ou par sort, pourveu que luy et les siens vescussent en cet empire hors de toute subjection et maistrise, sauf celle des loix antiques, et y eussent toute liberté qui ne porteroit prejudice à icelles, impatient de commander comme d'estre commandé." *Essais* III, 7, vol. 3, p. 917, Frame, p. 850; see also III, 9, vol. 3, p. 966, Frame, p. 897.

45. David Quint, *Montaigne and the Quality of Mercy.*

46. "Il n'a jamais en la bouche que cochers, menuisiers, savetiers et maçons. Ce sont inductions et similitudes tirées des plus vulgaires et cogneues actions des hommes; chacun l'entend." *Essais* III, 12, vol. 3, p. 1037, Frame, p. 965.

47. *Essais* (III, 7), vol. 3, p. 919, Frame, p. 853.

48. Cf. Timothy Reiss, "Montaigne et le sujet politique," in *Oeuvres et Critiques*, 8/1–2 (1983), pp. 127–52; see also Raymond Geuss, *Public Goods, Private Goods*, Princeton, Princeton University Press, 2001.

CHAPTER 3

1. For a recent discussion of the symbolic (numerical as well as cosmological) significance of the order and sequence of the different essays in Montaigne's work see D. L. Schaefer, ed., *Freedom over Servitude.*

2. On the Edict of Nantes, see in particular Janine Garrison, *L'édit de Nantes: chronique d'une paix attendue*, Paris, Fayard, 1998, and her edition of the text of the edict published by the Société Henri IV, *L'édit de Nantes*, Biarritz, Editions Atlantica, 1997; Thierry Wanegffelen, *L'édit de Nantes: une histoire européenne de la tolérance*, Paris, Librairie Générale Française, 1998; on the Edict of 17 Nov. 1787 and the debates of 1789 on the rights of Protestants, cf. John McManners, *Church and Society in Eighteenth century France*, Oxford, Clarendon Press, 1998, vol. 2, pp. 644–57.

3. For the text of the various edicts, see André Stegmann, ed., *Edits des guerres de religion*, Paris, Vrin, 1979 (in particular on the edict of Beaulieu, pp. 125–30); see also the texts collected in David Potter, ed., *The French Wars of Religion: Selected Documents*, London, Macmillan, 1997, pp. 160 ff. On the approval of the edict, cf. Sarah Hanley, *The "Lit de Justice" of the Kings of France: Constitutional Ideology in Legend, Ritual and Discourse*, Princeton, Princeton University Press, 1983, ch. 9, and Mack Holt, *The French Wars of Religion, 1562–1629*, p. 68, n. 122. The edict was registered by the *parlement* of Paris on 14 Feb. 1576. On the practice of repression of heresy, see also Elena Brambilla, *Alle origini del Sant'Uffizio: penitenza, confessione e giustizia spirituale dal medioevo al XVI secolo*, Bologna, Il Mulino, 2000, ch. 15, "La laicizzazione dell'eresia in Francia."

4. Quoted in David Potter, ed., *The French Wars of Religion*, p. 33; on the disputes that followed the proclamation of the edict, cf. Denis Crouzet, *La sagesse et le malheur: Michel de L'Hospital, Chancelier de France*, pp. 450 ff. See also Mario Turchetti, "Une question mal posée: la tolérance dans les edits de janvier (1562) et d'Amboise (1563): les premiers commentaries et interprétations," in Henry Méchoulan et al., eds., *La formazione storica dell'alterità*, Florence, L. S. Olski, 2001, vol. 1, pp. 245–94.

5. The personality, intellectual background, and political views of Catherine de

Médicis have recently become the object of a series of new studies; see in particular R. J. Knecht, *Catherine de' Medici*, London, Longman, 1998; Jean-François Solnon, *Catherine de Médicis*, Paris, Perrin, 2003; Jean-Hippolyte de Mariéjol, *Catherine de Médicis*, Paris, Tallandier, 2005; Denis Crouzet, *Le haut de coeur de Catherine de Médicis*, Paris, Albin Michel, 2005; Thierry Wanegffelen, *Catherine de Médicis: le pouvoir au féminin*, Paris, Payot, 2005; Leonie Frieda, *Catherine de Medici: A Biography*, London, Weidenfeld and Nicolson, 2003. See also the older study by Ivan Cloulas, *Catherine de Médicis*, Paris, Fayard, 1979.

6. On the colloque de Poissy, see Alain Dufour, "Le colloque de Poissy," in *Mélanges d'histoire du 16ème siècle offerts à Henri Meylan*, Geneva, Droz, 1970, pp. 127–37; Mario Turchetti, "Concorde ou tolérance? Les Moyenneurs à la veille des guerres de religion en France," *Revue de Théologie et Philosophie* 118 (1986), pp. 255–67; Donald Nugent, *Ecumenism in the Age of the Reformation: The Colloquy of Poissy*, Cambridge, MA, Harvard University Press, 1974; Corrado Vivanti, *Guerre civile et paix religieuse dans la France d'Henri IV*, Paris, Desjonquères, 2006. See also W. H. Huseman, "A Lexicological Study of the Expression of Toleration in French at the time of the Colloque of Poissy," in *Cahiers de Lexicologie*, 1986, pp. 89–109; Laurent Bourquin, "Les défis des guerres de religion, 1559–1610," in Joël Cornette, ed., *La monarchie entre Renaissance et Révolution, 1515–1792*, Paris, Seuil, 2000, pp. 63–150; Olivier Christin, *La paix de religion: l'autonomisation de la raison politique au XVIème siècle*, Paris, Seuil, 1997.

7. On the different aspects of this debate, cf. Joseph Lecler, *Histoire de la tolérance au siècle de la Réforme* (1955), Paris, Albin Michel, 1994, pp. 453–66. On the position of l'Hospital, see his *Discours politiques pendant les guerres de religion: 1560–1568*, Clermont-Ferrand, Paleo, 2001; on his religious policy, see Thierry Wanegffelen, ed., *De Michel de l'Hospital à l'édit de Nantes: politique et religion face aux églises*, Clermont-Ferrand, Presses Universitaires Blaise Pascal, 2002; Seong-Hak Kim, *Michel de l'Hôpital*.

8. Michel de l'Hospital, *Discours (1560–1562)*, in Loris Petris, *La Plume et la Tribune: Michel de l'Hospital et ses discours (1559–1562)*, Geneva, Droz, 2002, p. 439. On the circumstances in which the speech was given, see Malcolm C. Smith, *Montaigne and Religious Freedom*, note to p. 38, p. 197.

9. The requirement, for the *conseillers*, of making a profession of fidelity to the Catholic religion had been introduced in 1543; the *parlement* of Bordeaux enforced it only on 25 July 1562: cf. Donald M. Frame, *Montaigne: A Biography*, ch. 4. The episode of the councillor disguising his true beliefs is in *Essais* (I, 56), vol. 1, p. 320, Frame, pp. 280–81.

10. Estienne Pasquier, "Exhortation aux princes et seigneurs du conseil privé du roi" (1561), in *Ecrits politiques*, ed. D. Thickett, pp. 24–95. On Pasquier, see Dorothy Thickett, *Estienne Pasquier (1529–1615): The Versatile Barrister of 16th Century France*, London and New York, Regency Press, 1979; cf. the influential pamphlet by Sébastien Castellion, *Conseil à la France désolée* (1562), ed. Marius F. Valkhoff, Geneva, Droz, 1967.

11. Estienne Pasquier, *Ecrits politiques*, p. 69.

12. Estienne de La Boétie, *Mémoire sur la pacification des troubles*, ed. Malcolm C. Smith, in particular, the introduction by Malcolm Smith on the question of the authorship of the text; see also the edition by Annie Prassloff, *Mémoire touchant à*

l'édit de janvier, published in an appendix to Etienne de La Boétie, *De la servitude volontaire ou Contr'un*, ed. Nadia Gontarbert, Paris, Gallimard, 1993. La Boétie's authorship of the *Mémoire* is contested by some scholars, though, it seems to me, unconvincingly: cf. Anne-Marie Cocula, *Etienne de La Boétie*, pp. 122 ff, and Arlette Jouanna, "La Boétie," in *Histoire et dictionnaire des guerres de religion*, ed. A. Jouanna, J. Boucher, D. Biloghi, and G. de Thiec, Paris, Robert Laffont, 1998, p. 1005. On La Boétie's relations to the parliament, see also André Toulemon, *Etienne de La Boétie: un enfant de Sarlat: président du Parlement de Bordeaux*, Paris, Librairies Techniques, 1980. For the letter of dedication of La Boétie's poems addressed to de l'Hospital (30 Apr. 1570), see Michel de Montaigne, *Oeuvres complètes*, ed. Maurice Rat, pp. 1363–65, and *Lettres*, ed. Claude Pinganaud, pp. 39–43.

13. Estienne de La Boétie, *Mémoire*, ed. Malcolm Smith, p. 54.

14. Ibid., pp. 50–56.

15. See Denis Crouzet, "Identity and Violence: French Protestants and the Early Wars of Religion," in Ruth Wheland and Carol Baxter, eds., *Toleration and Religious Identity: The Edict of Nantes and Its Implications in France, Britain and Ireland*, Dublin, Four Courts Press, 2003, pp. 73–91; Raymond A. Mentzer and Andrew Spicer, eds., *Society and Culture in the Huguenot World, 1559–1685*. On the breakdown of social order at the beginning of the wars, see Pierre Miquel, *Les guerres de religion*, Paris, Fayard, 1980, pp. 201 ff.

16. Maturin Dréano, *La religion de Montaigne*, pp. 137–40; Joseph Lecler, *Histoire de la tolérance au siècle de la Réforme*, pp. 539–47.

17. Cf. Alain Legros, introduction to Michel de Montaigne, *Des prierès*, Geneva, Droz, 2003.

18. On Montaigne's attitude to Anglicanism, see Malcolm C. Smith, *Montaigne and Religious Freedom*, pp. 87–89.

19. See the speech made by Rabaut de Saint-Etienne to the Constituent Assembly on 23 Aug. 1789 on the articles 16 and 18 of the project of the 6th bureau (articles 10 and 11 in the Declaration of Rights), where he rejects the notion of "toleration" as applicable to the position of French Protestants; see Stéphane Rials, ed., *La déclaration des droits de l'homme et du citoyen*, Paris, Hachette, 1988, pp. 236–47; Jean-Albert Dartigue, *Rabaut de Saint Etienne à l'Assemblée constituante de 1789*, Nantes, Salières, 1903; André Dupont, *Rabaut Saint Etienne, 1743–1793: un protestant défenseur de la liberté religieuse*, Geneva, Labor et Fides, 1989; Dale K. Van Kley, *The Religious Origins of the French Revolution: From Calvin to the Civil Constitution, 1560–1791*, New Haven, Yale University Press, 1996; Patrick Cabanel, *Les Protestants et la République*, Paris, Editions Complexe, 2000.

20. Quoted in Pierre Chevallier, *Henri III*, Paris, Fayard, 1985, p. 287.

21. Mack P. Holt, *The Duke of Anjou and the Politique Struggle during the Wars of Religion*; J. Boucher, "Autour de François, duc d'Alençon et d'Anjou"; Stuart Carroll, *Noble Power during the French Wars of Religion: The Guise Affinity and the Catholic Cause in Normandy*, Cambridge, Cambridge University Press, 1998. See also R. J. Knecht, *The Rise and Fall of Renaissance France, 1483–1610*, pp. 467–88, for further bibliographical references. On the international perspectives, see David El Kenz and Claire Gantet, *Guerres et paix de religion en Europe, 16ème*

et 17ème siècles, Paris, Armand Colin, 2003; Henry Kamen, *Philip of Spain*, New Haven, Yale University Press, 1997.

22. Cf. Pierre Chevallier, *Henri III*, p. 323.

23. On the wording and dispositions of the edict, see A. Stegmann, ed., *Edits des guerres de religion*, pp. 95–120.

24. On the enforcement of Nantes, cf. M. Grandjean and Bernard Roussel, eds., *Coexister dans l'intolérance: l'Edit de Nantes (1598)*, Geneva, Labor et Fides, 1998; Raymond A. Mentzer and Andrew Spicer, eds., *Society and Culture in the Huguenot World, 1559–1685*, in particular, Raymond A. Mentzer, "The Edict of Nantes and Its Institutions," pp. 98–116; Paul Mironneau and Isabelle Pébay-Clottes, eds., *Paix des armes, paix des âmes: Colloque de Pau*, Société Henri IV, Edition Imprimérie Nationale, 2000; Ruth Whelan and Carol Baxter eds., *Toleration and Religious Identity;* Olivier Chistin, "La réception de l'Edit de Nantes: illusions et désillusions de la 'tolérance,'" in A. Pettegree, P. Nelles, and P. Conner, eds., *The Sixteenth Century French Religious Book*, Aldershot (UK) and Burlington, VT, Ashgate, 2001, pp. 197–209; Pierre Bolle, ed., *L'Edit de Nantes: un compromis reussi?* Grenoble, Presses Universitaires de Grenoble, 1999.

25. See Claude Tienant, *Le gouverneur de Languedoc pendant les premières guerres de religion, Henri de Montmorency-Damville*, Paris, Publisud, 1993. On the Ligues, see Jean-Marie Constant, *La Ligue*, Paris, Fayard, 1996; and Jacqueline Boucher, "Ligues," in A. Jouanna, J. Boucher, D. Biloghi, and G. de Thiec, eds., *Histoire et dictionnaire des guerres de religion*, pp. 1042–44, for further bibliographical references.

26. Henry IV, letter to Henry of Bourbon, prince of Condé (? October 1576), in Jean-Pierre Babelon, *Henri IV: lettres d'amour et écrits politiques*, Paris, Fayard, 1988, p. 56.

27. Mack P. Holt, "Attitudes of the French Nobility at the Estates General of 1576," *Sixteenth Century Journal*, 18 (1987), pp. 489–504; on the Estates of Blois and the nobility, see also Manfred Orléa, *La noblesse aux états généraux de 1576 et de 1588*, Paris, PUF, 1980. On the third estate, see O. Ulph, "Jean Bodin and the Estates General in 1576," *Journal of Modern History*, 19 (1947), pp. 289–96; M. Greengrass, "A Day in the Life of the Third Estate, Blois, 26 Dec. 1576," in Adrianna E. Bakos, ed., *Politics, Ideology and the Law in Early Modern Europe: Essays in Honour of J.H.M. Salmon*, Rochester, NY, University of Rochester Press, 1994, pp. 73–90. See also J. Russell Major, *From Renaissance Monarchy to Absolute Monarchy: French Kings, Nobles and Estates*, Baltimore and London, Johns Hopkins University Press, 1994.

28. Quoted in Mack P. Holt, *The Duke of Anjou and the Politique Struggle*, p. 78.

29. "Remontrance aux Etats de Blois pour la paix, sous la personne d'un catholique romain, l'an 1576," in André Stegmann, ed., *Edits des guerres de religion*, pp. 125–30. Among the negative consequences of the war, Mornay indicated in particular the corruption of justice, since the prolongation of the conflict would inevitably lead to the perpetuation of the venality of offices—an argument to which Montaigne would have been especially sympathetic.

30. On the instability of French legislation, see in particular the essays II, 7, "Of Presumption"("De la praesumption"), and III, 13, "Of experience" ("De l'-expérience").

31. On Anjou's involvement in the Netherlands, in addition to Mack P. Holt, *The Duke of Anjou and the Politique Struggle*, see Pieter Geyl, *The Revolt of the Netherlands, 1555–1609*, London, Barnes and Noble Books, 1980, and Geoffrey Parker, *The Dutch Revolt*, Harmondsworth, Penguin Books, 1981.

32. Quoted in Arlette Jouanna's article "Politiques," in *Histoire et dictionnaire des guerres de religion*, p. 1211.

33. Pierre Viret, *L'Interim fait par dialogues (1565)*, ed. Guy R. Mermier, New York and Bern, Peter Lang, 1985, p. 19. Cf. the interpretation set forth by the Sorbonne doctor Claude d'Espence, for whom the *moyenneur* (mediator) was in fact Christ himself: see Thierry Wanegffelen, *Catherine de Médicis*, p. 276. On the respective positions of *politiques* and *ligueurs*, see also Peter Ascoli's introduction to François Cromé, *Dialogue d'entre le maheustre et le manant*, ed. Peter M. Ascoli, Geneva, Droz, 1977.

34. Francis de Crue de Stouz, *Le parti des politiques au lendemain de la Saint-Barthélemy*; Joseph Lecler, *Histoire de la tolérance au siècle de la Réforme*, pp. 482 ff; Mario Turchetti, "Une question mal posée: l'origine et l'identité des 'Politiques' au temps des guerres de religion," in Thierry Wanegffelen, ed., *De Michel de l'Hospital à l'édit de Nantes: politique et religion face aux églises*, pp. 357–90; Mack P. Holt, *The French Wars of Religion, 1562–1629*, and *The Duke of Anjou and the Politique Struggle*.

35. Myriam Yardeni, *La conscience nationale en France pendant les guerres de religion (1559–1598)*, Louvain and Paris, Nauwelaerts, 1971.

36. ". . . n'ayans peu ce qu'ils vouloient, ils ont fait semblant de vouloir ce qu'ils pouvoient." *Essais* (II, 19), vol. 2, p. 672, Frame, p. 619.

37. See, for example, Joseph Lecler, *Histoire de la tolérance au siècle de la Réforme*, and Malcolm C. Smith, *Montaigne and Religious Freedom*.

38. Cf. the following passage, which denounces the dangers of the "novelty" (*nouvelleté*) represented by the Reformation: "The one that has been oppressing us for so many years is not the sole author of our troubles, but one may say with good reason that it has accidentally produced and endangered everything, even the troubles and ruins that have been happening since without it, and against it; it has itself to blame." ("Celle qui nous presse depuis tant d'ans, elle n'a pas tous exploicté, mais on peut dire avec apparence, que par accident elle a tout produict et engendré: voir et les maux et ruines, qui se font depuis sans elle, et contre elle; c'est à elle à s'en prendre au nez.") *Essais* (I, 23), vol. 1, p. 119, Frame, p. 104.

39. See, for example, the following comment on the cruel executions of criminals: "All that is beyond plain death seems to me pure cruelty. Our justice cannot hope that the man who will not be deterred from doing wrong by the fear of dying on the block or the gallows will be prevented by the idea of a slow fire, or pincers, or the wheel. And I do not know but that meanwhile we drive them to despair." ("Tout ce qui est au delà de la mort simple, me semble pure cruauté; nostre justice ne peut esperer que celuy que la crainte de mourir et d'estre decapité ou pendu ne gardera de faillir, en soit empesché par l'imagination d'un feu languissant, ou des tenailles, ou de la roue. Et je ne sçay cependant si nous les jettons au desespoir.") *Essais* (II, 27), vol. 2, pp. 700–701, Frame, p. 643.

40. "A tuer les gens, il faut une clarté lumineuse et nette; et est nostre vie trop réele et essentielle pour garantir ces accidens supernaturels et fantastiques . . . En

ces autres accusations extravagantes, je dirois volontiers que c'est bien assez qu'un homme, quelque recommendation qu'il aye, soit creu de ce qui est humain." *Essais* (III, 11, "Des boyteux"), vol. 3, p. 1031, Frame, p. 960.

41. For some modern discussions of the concept of toleration, see John Dunn, The Claim to Freedom of Conscience, Freedom of Speech, Freedom of Thought, Freedom of Worship?" in Ole Peter Grell, Jonathan I. Israel, and Nicholas Tyacke, eds., *From Persecution to Toleration: The Glorious Revolution and Religion in England*, Oxford, Clarendon Press, 1991, pp. 171–93; Michael Walzer, *On Toleration*, New Haven and London, Yale University Press, 1997; Raymond Geuss, *History and Illusion in Politics*, Cambridge, Cambridge University Press, 2001, pp. 73 ff.

CHAPTER 4

1. Julianus, *Misopogon*, ed. C. Lacombrade and Aude de Saint-Loup, Paris, Les Belles Lettres, 2003. On Julian in French culture, see René Braun and Jean Richer, eds., *L'Empereur Julien*, Paris, Les Belles Lettres, 1978–81, vol. 1, De l'histoire à la légende Julien dans les textes du XVIème siècle, pp. 303–19; Géralde Nakam, "Figures du risque. Deux héros des *Essais*: Julien l'Apostat, Alcibiade," in: *Montaigne: la manière et la matière*, Paris, Klincksieck, 1992, pp. 95–108; Michel Butor, *Essais sur les Essais*, Paris, Gallimard, 1968, pp. 131–39. On Julian and Paris, see Ignazio Tantillo, *L'Imperatore Giuliano*, Bari, Laterza, 2001, pp. 53–55.

2. See the essay "Defense of Seneca and Plutarch" (II, 32); cf. Jean Bodin, *La méthode de l'histoire*, ed. Pierre Mesnard, ch. 4, "Du choix des historiens," pp. 65–66.

3. Joseph Lecler, *Histoire de la tolérance au siècle de la Réforme*, pp. 464–65.

4. On the figure of Julian in the works of Protestant writers, see in particular Innocent Gentillet, *Anti-Machiavel*, part II, 1ère maxime: "Un prince sur toutes choses doit appeter d'estre estimé devot, bien qu'il ne le soit pas," pp. 190–202; *Vindiciae, contra tyrannos*, trans. and ed. George Garnett, p. 36; Pierre Viret, "Le cinquième dialogue," in *L'Interim fait par dialogues (1565)*, ed. Guy R. Mermier, pp. 221–39.

5. See, for example, François de La Mothe le Vayer, *De la vertu de païens*: "De Julien l'Apostat," in *Libertins du XVIIème siècle*, ed. Jacques Prévot, Paris, Gallimard, vol. 2, pp. 151–73; Gabriel Naudé, *Advis pour dresser une bibliothèque* (repr. of the 1644 ed.), Paris, Klincksieck, 1994; Denis Diderot, *Pensées philosophiques*, in *Oeuvres*, ed. Laurent Versini, vol. 1, pp. 30–31; François-Marie Arouet de Voltaire, "Baptême" and "Julien le philosophe," in *Dictionnaire philosophique*, ed. René Pomeau, Paris, Garnier Flammarion, 1986; see also René Pomeau, *La religion de Voltaire*, Paris, Nizet, 1995, pp. 280–81; cf. E. M. Haag, "Diderot et Voltaire, lecteurs de Montaigne: du jugement suspendu à la raison libre," in *Revue de Métaphysique et de Morale*, 3, 1997, pp. 365–83, and Jérôme Schwartz, *Diderot and Montaigne: The "Essais" and the Shaping of Diderot's Humanism*, Geneva, Droz, 1966.

6. *Essais* (II, 17), vol. 2, p. 659, Frame, p. 608.

7. "Il est ordinaire de voir les bonnes intentions, si elles sont conduites sans moderation, pousser les hommes à des effects tres-vitieux. En ce debat par lequel la France est à present agitée de guerres civiles, le meilleur et plus sain party est sans

doubte celuy qui maintient et la religion et la police ancienne du pays. Entre les gens de bien toutes-fois qui le suyvent . . . il s'en voit plusieurs que la passion pousse hors les bornes de la raison. Et leur faict par fois prendre les conseils injustes, violents et encore temeraires." *Essais* (II, 19), vol. 2, p. 668, Frame, p. 615.

8. *Essais* (II, 5), vol. 2, p. 366, Frame, p. 320.

9. *Essais* (II, 19), vol. 2, p. 671, Frame, p. 619.

10. On the general issue of conversion and apostasy, see Arthur Darby Nock, *Conversion: The Old and New in Religion from Alexander the Great to Augustine of Hippo* (1933), London and Baltimore, Johns Hopkins University Press, 1998; Arnaldo Momigliano, ed., *The Conflict of Paganism and Christianity*, Oxford, Oxford University Press, 1963. On conversions in the French Reformation, see Thierry Wanegffelen, *Ni Rome ni Genève: des fidèles entre deux chaires en France au XVIème siècle*, Paris, Champion, and Geneva, Slatkine, 1997; Philip Benedict, "Confessionalisation in France? Critical Reflections and New Evidence," pp. 44–61; see also Joseph Bergin, *The Making of the French Episcopate, 1589–1661*, New Haven and London, Yale University Press, 1996, pp. 335–64.

11. For an exhaustive and illuminating study of Navarre's conversion, see Michael Wolfe, *The Conversion of Henri IV*.

12. For a recent assessment of the circumstances of the designation of Navarre as Henry III's heir, see Nicolas Le Roux, *Un regicide au nom de Dieu: l'assassinat d'Henri III, 1er août 1589*, Paris, Gallimard, 2006, pp. 25–31; see also Pierre Chevallier, *Henri III, roi shakespearien*, pp. 701–4; Jean-François Solnon, *Henri III: un désir de majesté*, Paris, Perrin, 2001, pp. 364–81.

13. On the accusations of atheism directed toward Henry IV, cf. Michael Wolfe, *The Conversion of Henri IV*, pp. 32 ff.; more generally, on the political use of such accusations, see François Hotman, *Brutum fulmen papae Sixti V: adversus Henricum regem Navarrae et Henricum Borbonium: principem Condaeum*, Geneva, 1585; *Vindiciae, contra tyrannos*, trans. and ed. George Garnett, pp. 140 ff, "Who Tyrants Are." See also Roland Mousnier, *L'assassinat de Henri IV: le problème du tyrannicide et l'affermissement de la monarchie absolue*, Paris, Gallimard, 1964. On the general question of political assassination, see Thierry Sol, *Fallait-il tuer César? L'argumentation politique de Dante à Machiavel*, Paris, Dalloz, 2005.

14. Quoted in Jean-Pierre Babelon, *Henri IV*, Paris, Fayard, 1982, p. 333.

15. On the Protestant response to the conversion, see in particular Hugues Daussy, *Les Huguenots et le Roi: le combat politique de Philippe Duplessis-Mornay (1572–1600)*, Geneva, Droz, 2002, pp. 477–512.

16. On the notion of "catholique," see Michael Wolfe, *The Conversion of Henri IV*, pp. 85–87, on Henry's use of "Christianisme," cf. Jean-Pierre Babelon, *Henri IV*, pp. 336–37.

17. Jean-Pierre Babelon, *Henri IV*, p. 532.

18. ". . . it is dangerous to do evil to make good out of it," Elizabeth Regina to Henry IV, July 1593, in Elizabeth I, *Collected Works*, ed. Leah S. Marcus, Janel Mueller, and Mary Beth Rose, Chicago and London, University of Chicago Press, 2000, pp. 370–71.

19. Cited in Henri Carré, *Sully, sa vie, son oeuvre (1559–1641)*, Paris, Payot, 1932, pp. 314–16; on Sully, see also Bernard Barbiche and Ségolène de Dainville-Barbiche, *Sully, l'homme et ses fidèles*, Paris, Fayard, 1997.

20. Yves Cazaux, ed., *Mémoires et autres écrits de Marguerite de Valois*, Paris, Mercure de France, 1986, pp. 155–56. On the court of Nérac, see Eliane Viennot, *Marguerite de Valois: histoire d'une femme, histoire d'un mythe*, Paris, Payot, 1993, pp. 119–38. Marguerite's chief literary inspiration would have been *L'Honneste amour*, the French translation and adaptation, by Guy Le Fèvre de la Boderie, of Marsilio Ficino's "Christian" version of Plato's *Symposium*: cf. Philippe Erlanger, *La Reine Margot, ou la rébellion*, Paris, Perrin, 1972, p. 211.

21. *Essais* (II, 12), vol. 2, pp. 557–58, Frame, p. 508.

22. Shakespeare's original source for the play is generally identified as Pierre de la Primaudaye, *L'académie française* (1577), a work dedicated to Henry III that was translated into English in 1586; see G. R. Hibbard, introduction to William Shakespeare, *Love's Labour's Lost*, Oxford, Oxford University Press, 1990, p. 47. On the connection between Montaigne's and Shakespeare's work, see Pierre Villey, "Montaigne et Shakespeare," in Sir Israel Gollancz, ed., *A Book of Homage to Shakespeare*, London, Shakespeare Association, 1916, pp. 417–20; Hugh Grady, *Shakespeare, Machiavelli and Montaigne: Power and Subjectivity from Richard II to Hamlet*, Oxford, Oxford University Press, 2002; see also Gilberto Sacerdoti, *Sacrificio e sovranità. Teologia e politica nell'Europa di Shakespeare e Bruno*, Torino, Einaudi, 2002, pp. 3–11.

23. See Montaigne's letters to the marshal of Matignon in *Oeuvres complètes*, ed. Maurice Rat, pp. 1373–96, Frame, pp. 1309–31.

24. Quoted in Malcolm Smith, *Montaigne and Religious Freedom*, p. 174; cf. Jacques Auguste de Thou, *Mémoires*, in Joseph-François Michaud and Jean-Joseph-François Poujoulat, eds., *Nouvelle collection des mémoires pour servir à l'histoire de France*, Paris, 1838, vol. XI, p. 331; see also DavidMaskell, "Montaigne médiateur entre Navarre et Guise," in *Bibliothèque d'Humanisme et Renaissance*, 41, 1979, pp. 541–53.

25. "J'ay de tout temps regardé en vous cette mesme fortune ou vous estes et vous peut souvenir que lors mesme quil m'en faloit confesser à mon cure je ne laissois de voir aucunemant de bon euil vos succez a presant aveq plus de raison et de liberté je les embrasse de pleine affection." Montaigne to Henry IV, in *Oeuvres complètes*, ed. Maurice Rat, p. 1397; also in Montaigne, *Lettres*, ed. Claude Pinganaud, p. 123; Frame, pp. 1332–33. The date of the letter is given as either 1589 or 1590.

26. See for example Don Cameron Allen, *Doubt's Boundless Sea*, ch. 3, "Three French Atheists: Montaigne, Charron, Bodin," pp. 75–110; Mathurin Dreano, "La crise sceptique de Montaigne?" *Bibliothèque d'Humanisme et Renaissance*, XXIII, 1961, pp. 252–64; J. Casals, "La théologie de Montaigne? Ou que Dieu n'existe pas dans les *Essais*," in *Bulletin de la Société des Amis de Montaigne*, ser. VII, no. 33–34 (July–Dec. 1993).

27. *Essais* (II, 19), vol. 2, p. 670, Frame, p. 618; Montaigne's sources on Julian were essentially Ammianus Marcellinus and Eutropius.

28. Ibid., vol. 2, p. 671, Frame, p. 619.

29. Ibid., vol. 2, p. 668, Frame, p. 615.

30. "On peut dire, d'un costé, que de lâcher la bride aux pars d'entretenir leur opinion, c'est espandre et semer la division; c'est prêter quasi la main à l'augmenter, n'y ayant aucune barriere ny coerction des loix qui bride et empesche sa

course. Mais, d'austre costé, on diroit aussi que de lascher la bride aux pars d'entretenir leur opinion, c'est les amolir et relàcher par la facilité et par l'aisance, et que c'est émousser l'éguillon qui s'affine par la rareté, la nouvelleté et la difficulté." Ibid., pp. 671–72, Frame, p. 619.

31. *Essais* (II, 12), vol. 2, pp. 441–42, Frame, pp. 389–90. On the background of the distinction between "creed" and "spirituality" in contemporary debates, see Anthony Levi, *Renaissance and Reformation,* and Henri Busson, *La pensée religieuse française de Charron à Pascal,* Paris, Vrin, 1933.

32. On the figure of Socrates, see *Essais* (III, 12), vol. 3, pp. 1052–53, Frame, pp. 965–66; cf. Joshua Scodel, "The Affirmation of Paradox: a Reading of Montaigne's 'De la phisionomie,'" in Gérard Defaux, ed., *Montaigne: Essays in Reading,* special issue of *Yale French Studies,* 64, 1983, pp. 209–37.

33. "If those (laws) that I serve, threatened even the tip of my finger, I should instantly go and find others, wherever it might be." ("Si celles que je sers me menassoissent seulement le bout du doigt, je m'en irois incontinent en trouver d'autres, où que ce fut.") *Essais* (III, 13), vol. 3, p. 1072, Frame, p. 1000.

34. From a somewhat different perspective, references to sanctity in the text present the saint as someone who is completely impervious to the attitudes and motives of his environment; see for example the description of Carlo Borromeo in essay I, 14, vol. 1, p. 61, Frame, p. 50.

35. *Essais* (I, 23), vol. 1, p. 122, Frame, p. 107.

36. "Et nous trouvons estrange si, aux guerres qui pressent à cette heure nostre estat, nous voyons flotter les evenements et diversifier d'une maniere commune et ordinaire. C'est que nous n'y apportions rien que le nostre . . . Dieu doibt son secours extraordinaire à la foy et à la religion, non pas à nos passions. Les hommes y sont conducteurs et s'y servent de la religion: ce devroit ester tout le contraire." *Essais* (II, 12), vol. 2, pp. 442–43, Frame, p. 391.

37. Ibid., vol. 2, p. 445, Frame, p. 394.

38. "Any opinion is strong enough to make people espouse it at the price of life." ("Toute opinion est assez forte pour se faire espouser au pris de la vie.") *Essais* (I, 14), vol. 1, p. 53, Frame, p. 41.

39. See the examples provided in the essay I, 14, *passim.*

40. Cf. *Essais* (I, 21), vol. 1, p. 99, Frame, p. 84, and the examples of credulity provided in it.

41. "L'erreur particuliere faict premierement l'erreur publique, et à son tour après, l'erreur publique faict l'erreur particuliere. Ainsi va tout ce bastiment, s'estoffant et formant de main en main: de maniere que le plus esloigné tesmoin en est mieux instruict que le plus voisin, et le dernier informé mieux persuade que le premier. C'est un progrez naturel." *Essais* (III, 11), vol. 3, pp. 1027–28, Frame, p. 956.

42. Ibid., vol. 3, p. 1031, Frame, p. 960.

43. *Essais,* (I, 51), vol. 1, p. 305, Frame, p. 269. On the role of classical rhetoric see Nicole Loraux, *L'invention d'Athènes,* Paris, Payot, 1993; Robert Morstein-Marx, *Mass Oratory and Political Power in the Late Roman Republic,* Cambridge, Cambridge University Press, 2004.

44. On these themes, in addition to the essays already cited I, 21 ("Of the Power of the Imagination") and I, 23 ("Of Custom"), see essay III, 4 ("Of Diversion").

45. On Montaigne's attitude to witchcraft and supernatural phenomena, see Alan M. Boase, "Montaigne et la sorcellerie," in *Humanisme et Renaissance*, 4, 1935, pp. 386–402; Fausta Garavini, *Monstres et chimères: Montaigne, le texte et le fantasme*, Geneva, Slatkine, 1993. On the background of the renaissance debate on witchcraft, see Robin Briggs, *Witches and Neighbours: The Social and Cultural Context of European Witchcraft*, London, Fontana, 1996; Stuart Clark, *Thinking with Demons: the Idea of Witchcraft in Early Modern Europe*, Oxford, Oxford University Press, 1997.

46. See the important study by Frank Lestringant, *Lumière des martyrs: Essai sur le martyre au siècle des Réformes*, Paris, Honoré Champion, 2004.

47. "Toutes autres apparences sont communes à toutes religions: esperance, confiance, evenemens, ceremonies, penitence, martyres." *Essais* (II, 12), vol. 2, p. 442, Frame, p. 391.

48. *Essais* (I, 14), vol. 1, p. 60, Frame p. 49; see also the essay "Of Moderation" (I, 30), *passim*.

49. *Essais* (III, 10), vol. 3, p. 1013, Frame, p. 943.

50. For an overview of the "material" aspects of the religious conflict in France, see Emmanuel Le Roy Ladurie, *L'état royal, 1460–1610*, Paris, Hachette, 1987.

51. On the theme of moral education in the *Essais*, see David Quint, *Montaigne and the Quality of Mercy*; Max Gauna, *Montaigne and the Ethics of Compassion*, Lewiston, NY, Mellen Press, 2000. On Montaigne's views on educational practices, see Hubert Vincent, *Education et scepticisme chez Montaigne, ou pédantisme et l'exercice du jugement*, Paris, L'Harmattan, 1997; Gabriel Compayré, *Montaigne et l'éducation du jugement*, Paris, P. Delaplane, 1904; see also Pierre Villey, *L'influence de Montaigne sur les idées pédagogiques de Locke et de Rousseau*, Paris, Hachette, 1911.

52. On the issue of violence against children, see also the essay II, 31, "Of Anger" ("De la colere"); in March 1582, when he was mayor of Bordeaux, the writer intervened in a case of malpractice at the priory of Saint Jacques, an orphanage, where inadequate funding had resulted in the ill-treatment of the children; it was unusual for the municipal authorities to interfere with the affairs of a religious institution, but in this case they did so with considerable energy, imposing a higher payment towards the children's diet and ruling that any suspect death must in the future be reported to the town council. See Donald Frame, *Montaigne: A Biography*, ch. 13.

53. *Essais* (I, 2), vol. 1, p. 176, Frame, p. 159. On theatrical experience as part of education, see Marc Fumaroli, *Héros et orateurs*, ch. 2, "Corneille et la Société de Jesus," pp. 63–208.

54. See C. Sclafert, "Montaigne et Maldonat," in *Bulletin de littérature ecclésiastique*, 1951, pp. 65–93 and 129–46. On Jesuit schooling and education, see Luce Giard, ed., *Les jésuites à la Renaissance: système éducatif et production du savoir*, Paris, PUF, 1995; Jean Lacouture, *Jésuites: une multibiographie*, Paris, Seuil, vol. I, "Les conquérants," pp. 259–96; Vincent J. Duminuco, ed., *The Jesuit "Ratio Studiorum": 400th Anniversary Perspectives*, New York, Fordham University Press, 2000. On Jesuit ideology and politics, see also John C. Olin, *Erasmus, Utopia and the Jesuits*; William V. Bangert, *A History of the Society of Jesus*; Harro

Hopfl, *Jesuit Political Thought: The Society of Jesus and the State, c. 1540–1630*, Cambridge, Cambridge University Press, 2004.

CHAPTER 5

1. Stéphane-Claude Gigon, *La révolte de la gabelle en Guyenne, 1548–1549: contribution à l' histoire de l'impôt sous l'ancien régime*, Paris, Champion, 1906; see also J. Pasquier, *L'impôt des gabelles en France aux XVIIe et XVIIIe siècles* (1905), Geneva, Slatkine, 1978; Robert Boutruche, ed., *Histoire de Bordeaux de 1453 à 1715*, Bordeaux, Fédération Historique du Sud-Ouest, 1966.

2. The Collège de Guyenne, which Montaigne attended at the time, was closed following the beginning of the riots, and it seems unlikely that the fifteen-year-old boy might have actually witnessed the killings. On the other hand, Montaigne's future father in law, Geoffroy de La Chassaigne, was president of the town council at the time of Moneins's murder (it was rumored that the disastrous initiative of going to the town hall had been his idea) and had barely escaped with his life. Montaigne must have heard his account of the events, and probably talked to other eyewitnesses. Donald Frame points out that the term "childhood" is often used rather vaguely; also the expression "je vis" (I saw) is sometimes employed in the *Essais* to mean "j'ai appris que" (I learned that): Donald M. Frame, *Montaigne: A Biography*, ch. 3, note 51.

3. Louppes de Villeneuve (a cousin of Montaigne's on his mother's side) had replaced the moderate Lagebaston at the head of the *parlement*; he had been one of the notables who opposed Montaigne's reelection to the post of mayor. On the difficult situation in Bordeaux in 1585 see Montaigne's letter of 27 May 1585 to the absent marshal of Matignon, governor of the Guyenne, where he urged him to return as soon as possible to the town: "I have spent every night either around the town in arms, or outside of town at the port, and before your warning I had already kept watch there one night on the news of a boat loaded with armed men which was due to pass." Michel de Montaigne, *Oeuvres complètes*, ed. Maurice Rat, pp. 1392–93; Frame, p. 1327; *Lettres*, ed. Claude Pinganaud, pp. 109–10. See also Madeleine Lazard, *Michel de Montaigne*, pp. 70–71 and 289–91; Jean Lacouture, *Montaigne à cheval*, Paris, Seuil, 1996, pp. 275–310; Géralde Nakam, *Montaigne et son temps*, pp. 79–85.

4. *Essais* (I, 24), vol. 1, pp. 130–31; Frame, pp. 115–16.

5. On the notion of "Fortune" in Machiavelli's work, see Thomas Flanagan, "The Concept of *Fortuna* in Machiavelli," in Anthony Parel, ed., *The Political Calculus*, Toronto, Toronto University Press, 1972, pp. 127–56; Rudolf Wittkower, "Chance, Time and Virtue," *Journal of the Warburg Institute* 1 (1937–38), pp. 313–21; Quentin Skinner, "Machiavelli on Virtù and the Maintenance of Liberty," in *Visions of Politics*, Cambridge, Cambridge University Press, 2002, vol. 2, *Renaissance Virtues*, pp. 160–85; and *Machiavelli*, Oxford, Oxford University Press, 1981, pp. 96–97, for further bibliographical references.

6. On the general issue of trust, see John Dunn, "Trust and Political Agency," in *Interpreting Political Responsibility: Essays, 1981–1989*, Cambridge, Polity Press,

1990, pp. 26–44; Diego Gambetta, ed., *Trust: Making and Breaking Cooperative Relations*, Oxford, Basil Blackwell, 1990.

7. On these questions see, for example, *Essais* (I, 21), vol. 1, p. 106, Frame, pp. 91–92; (II, 10), vol. 2, p. 418, Frame, pp. 369–70; (III, 12), vol. 3, p. 1037, Frame, pp. 964–65.

8. *Essais* (II, 32), vol. 2, pp. 722–23, Frame, pp. 662–63.

9. *Essais* (I, 27), vol. 1, p. 181, Frame, p. 163.

10. *Essais* (III, 12), vol. 3, p. 1037, Frame, p. 964.

11. *Essais* (I, 14), vol. 1, p. 52, Frame, p. 41.

12. *Essais* (I, 42), vol. 1, pp. 266–67, Frame, pp. 236–37.

13. *Essais* (I, 23), *passim;* (I, 42), vol. 1, p. 266, Frame, p. 237. On the notion of authority in relation to legitimacy, cf. Raymond Geuss, *History and Illusion in Politics*, pp. 37–42.

14. "Or je tiens qu'il faut vivre par droict et par auctorité, non par recompence ny par grace. Combien de galans hommes ont mieux aimé perdre la vie que la devoir! Je fuis à me submettre à toute sorte d'obligation, mais sur tout à celle qui m'attache par devoir d'honneur. Je ne trouve rien si cher que ce qui m'est donné et ce pourquoy ma volonté demeure hypothequée par tiltre de gratitude, et reçois plus volontiers les offices qui sont à vendre. Je croy bien: pour ceux-cy je ne donne que de l'argent; pour les autres je me donne moy-mesme. Le neud qui me tient par la loy d'honnesteté me semble bien plus pressant et plus poisant que n'est celuy de la contrainte civile." *Essais* (III, 9), vol. 3, p. 966, Frame, p. 897. On Montaigne and the practice of donation, see Natalie Zemon Davies, *The Gift in Sixteenth Century France*, Oxford, Oxford University Press, 2000, pp. 123–25.

15. *Essais* (III, 12), vol. 3, p. 1044, Frame, p. 972.

16. *Essais* (III, 9), vol. 3, pp. 956 ff, Frame pp. 887 ff.

17. See, for example, Estienne Pasquier, "Exhortation aux princes et seigneurs du conseil privé du roi," in *Ecrits politiques*, ed. D. Thickett, pp. 80–81, and the texts collected in David Potter, ed., *The French Wars of Religion*, pp. 34–64. On the climate of fear before and after the Saint Bartholomew's Day Massacre, cf. Nicolas Le Roux, *Un regicide au nom de Dieu*, pp. 11–57; cf. Penny Roberts, "Huguenot Petitioning during the Wars of Religion," in Raymond A. Mentzer and Andrew Spicer, eds., *Society and Culture in the Huguenot World, 1559–1685*, pp. 62–77.

18. "On n'y oyoit que cris et voix effrayées. On voyoit les habitans sortir de leurs maisons, comme à l'alarme, et se charger, blesser et entretuer les uns les autres, comme si ce fussent ennemis qui vinssent à occuper leur ville." *Essais* (I, 18), vol. 1, p. 77, Frame, p. 64. On the psychological aspects of religious violence, see Denis Crouzet's seminal works: *Les guerriers de Dieux,* and *La nuit de la Saint-Barthélemy: un rêve perdu de la Renaissance*, Paris, Fayard, 1994; see also Philip Erlanger, *Le massacre de la Saint-Barthélemy*, Paris, Gallimard, 1960.

19. *Essais* (III, 9), vol. 3, p. 946, Frame, p. 877.

20. *Essais* (II, 18), vol. 2, pp. 666–67, Frame, pp. 613–15. The most developed discussion of the topic of conversation is essay 8 of Book III, "Of the Art of Discussion"; on the linguistic aspects of trust in Montaigne's work, see Antoine Compagnon, "Montaigne ou la parole donnée," in Frank Lestringant, ed., *Rhétorique de Montaigne*, Paris, Honoré Champion, 1985; see also Philip Knee, *La parole in-*

certaine, ch. 1, pp. 7–63; Carlo Cappa, *Michel de Montaigne: l'appartenenza della scrittura,* pp. 123 ff.

21. See the essay "Of the Useful and the Honest" (III, 1), *passim;* cf. Bernard Williams, *Truth and Truthfulness: An Essay in Genealogy,* Princeton, Princeton University Press, 2002; Paolo Di Lucia, "La fiducia nelle parola," in Giuseppe Galli, ed., *Interpretazione e fiducia: atti del XIX colloquio sull'interpretazione,* Pisa and Rome, Istituti Editoriali e Poligrafici Internationali, 1999, pp. 109–32.

22. *Essais* (III, 1), vol. 3, p. 791, Frame, p. 727.

23. *Essais* (I, 23), vol. 1, p. 120, Frame, p. 105; (III, 12) vol. 3, p. 1043, Frame, pp. 971–72.

24. "Nostre monde n'est formé qu'à l'ostentation; les hommes ne s'enflent que de vent, et se manient à bonds, comme les balons. Cettuy-cy ne se propose point des vaines fantaisies; sa fin fut nous fournir de choses et de preceptes qui reelement et plus jointement servent à la vie . . . il n'y a rien d'emprunté de l'art et des sciences; les plus simples y recognoissent leurs moyens et leur force." *Essais* (III, 12), vol. 3, pp. 1037–38, Frame, pp. 965–66.

25. *Essais* (III, 1), vol. 3, p. 803, Frame, p. 739.

26. *Essais* (I, 24), vol. 1, pp. 124–25, Frame, p. 109. François of Lorraine, duke of Guise, was finally murdered in 1563, by the Protestant Poltrot de Méré; Montaigne was acquainted with his son, Henry of Lorraine (1550–88). A. Jouanna, J. Boucher, D. Biloghi, and G. de Thiec, eds., *Histoire et Dictionnaire des guerres de religion,* pp. 956–58.

27. *Essais* (III, 12), vol. 3, pp. 1060–62, Frame, pp. 988–91.

28. Edouard Frémy, *L'Académie des derniers Valois (1570–1585);* Frances A. Yates, *The French Academies of the Sixteenth Century,* Nendeln, Kraus Reprint, 1973; Robert J. Sealy, *The Palace Academy of Henri III;* in particular, on the role of the king in restoring peace, see Nuccio Ordine, *Giordano Bruno, Ronsard et la religion,* Paris, Albin Michel, 2004, pp. 69 ff; M. Dossonville, ed., *Ronsard et Montaigne. Ecrivains engagés?* Lexington, KY, French Forum, 1989.

29. On the general question of obedience and fidelity in relation to royal and religious authority, see the articles collected in the special issue of the *Nouvelle Revue du XVIème Siècle,* "Métaphysique et politique de l'obéissance dans la France du XVIème siècle," 22/1 (2004).

30. On the acceptance of Henry IV as legitimate sovereign, see S. Annette Finley-Croswhite, *Henry IV and the Towns: The Pursuit of Legitimacy in French Urban Society, 1589–1610,* Cambridge, Cambridge University Press, 1999; Michel de Waele, *Les relations entre le parlement de Paris et Henri IV.* See also Janine Garrison, *Henri IV,* Paris, Seuil, 1984, pp. 55–80.

31. *Essais* (III, 7), vol. 3, pp. 917–18, Frame, p. 851.

32. *Essais* (III, 8), vol. 3, pp. 932–33, Frame, pp. 864–65.

33. *Essais* (I, 42), vol. 1, pp. 265–66, Frame, pp. 235–36.

34. *Essais,* III, 7, Villey, vol. 3, p. 918, Frame, p. 851. Both Buchanan's and Blackwood's works were translated into French: see Michel de Montaigne, *The Complete Essays,* ed. M. A. Screech, p. 1040, n. 6; Roger A. Mason and Martin S. Smith, eds., *A Dialogue on the Law of Kingship among the Scots. A Critical Edition and Translation of George Buchanan's "De Iure Regni apud Scotos Dialogus,"* Aldershot, St Andrews Studies in Reformation History, Ashgate, 2004; cf. Hugh

R. Trevor-Roper, *George Buchanan and the Ancient Scottish Constitution*, London, Longmans, 1966.

35. "J'eusse bien desire que le guein particulier des soldats de vostre armee et le besouin de les contanter ne vous eut desrobe nomecmant en cette ville principale la belle recomandation d'avoir treté vos subjects mutins en pleine victoire aveq plus de solagemant que ne font leurs protecteurs & qu'a la difference d'un credit passagier et usurpé vous eussiez montré qu'ils estoint vostres par une protection paternelle et vraïment royalle." Montaigne to Henry of Navarre, in *Oeuvres complètes*, ed. Maurice Rat, p. 1398, Frame, pp. 1332–33, *Lettres,* ed. Claude Pinganaud, p. 124. The dating of the letter is given by the different editors as 1589 or 1590.

36. On Epaminondas, see *Essais* (II, 36), vol. 2, pp. 756–57, Frame, pp. 694–96.

37. On France's ancient monarchy, see (III, 9), vol. 3, p. 994, Frame, p. 925.

38. "Je ne vous ai point appelés, comme faisaient mes prédécesseurs, pour vous faire approuver leur volontés; je vous ai assemblés pour recevoir vos conseils, pour les croire, pour les suivre, bref, pour me mettre en tutelle entre vos mains." Henry IV, *Lettres d'amour et écrits politiques*, ed. Jean-Pierre Babelon, p. 223. Navarre's correspondence is collected in Henry IV, *Recueil des letters missives de Henri IV*, ed. Jules Berger de Xivrey and Joseph Guadet, Paris, 1843–76, 9 vols. As was often the case in troubled times, the assembly of notables was summoned as a short-term solution, instead of the more cumbersome Estates-General.

39. Germaine de Staël, *Considérations sur la Révolution française*, ed. Jacques Godechot, Paris, Tallandier, 2000, p. 74. In the same text de Staël gave a nationalist twist to her celebration of Henry IV by claiming that his superior qualities as king were connected to the fact that, unlike his Bourbon descendants, he had wholly French origins (i.e., a French mother) and had received a truly French education. On Henry IV as a mythic figure in French history, see Christian Biet, *Henri IV: la vie, la légende*, Saint-Germain de Puy, Larousse, 2000.

40. "Je viens parler à vous non point en habit royal, ou avec l'épée et la cape, comme mes prédécesseurs, ni comme un prince qui vient parler aux ambassadeurs étrangers, mais vetu comme un père de famille, en pourpoint, pour parler familièrement à ses enfants." in Henry IV, *Lettres d'amour et écrits politiques*, ed. Jean-Pierre Babelon, p. 238.

41. Michel de Waele, "Henri IV, politicien monarchomaque? Les contrats de fidélité entre le roi et les Français," in Jean-François Labourdette, Jean-Pierre Poussons, and Marie-Catherine Vignal, eds., *Le traité de Vervins*, Presses de l'Université de Paris-Sorbonne, 2000, pp. 117–31; Michel Cassan, "La réduction des villes ligueuses à l'obéissance," *Nouvelle Revue du XVIè Siècle*, 22/1 (2004), pp. 159–74.

42. Laurent Bourquin, "Les défis des guerres de religion, 1559–1610," pp. 63–134.

43. Léonce Anquez, *Histoire des assemblées politiques des Réformés en France: 1573–1622*, Geneva, Slatkine, 1970; *Vindiciae, contra Tyrannos, concerning the legitimate power of a prince over the people, and of the people over a prince*, ed. and trans. George Garnett. For a recent assessment of the authorship of this work, see Hugues Daussy's major study of Duplessis-Morney's political career: *Les*

Huguenots et le Roi: le combat politique de Philippe Duplessis-Mornay (1572–1600), pp. 241–56.

44. "Popular inclinations go in waves; if the leaning in your favour is once established, it will gather its own momentum and go all the way." ("Les inclinations des peuples se manient a ondees si la pente est une fois prinse en votre faveur elle s'emportera de son propre branle jusques au bout.") Montaigne to Henry of Navarre, in *Oeuvres complètes*, ed. Maurice Rat, p. 1398; Frame, p. 1333; *Lettres*, ed. Claude Pinganaud, pp. 124.

CHAPTER 6

1. Michel de Montaigne, *Notes sur les "Ephémerides,"* in *Oeuvres complètes*, ed. Maurice Rat, pp. 1408–9; see also *Journal de voyage en Italie*, ed. Fausta Garavini, Paris, Gallimard, 1983; for the English translation of the *Journal*, see Frame, pp. 1049–1270.

2. *Essais* (III, 9), vol. 3, p. 956, Frame p. 886.

3. Donald M. Frame, *Montaigne: A Biography*, ch. 13.

4. On the same occasion it was decided that the marshal of Matignon—a moderate, like Montaigne—should replace Biron as lieutenant of the Guyenne, while the king of Navarre retained his hereditary entitlement to the *"gouvernement"* of the region. The treatise of Fleix was signed on 26 Nov. 1580 in a castle in Périgord (possibly the residence of the Marquis de Trans, one of Montaigne's patrons): cf. Jean-Pierre Babelon, *Henri IV*, p. 277; Madeleine Lazard, *Michel de Montaigne*, p. 284.

5. George Hoffmann, *Montaigne's Career*, pp. 8–38; Ullrich Langer, "Montaigne's Political and Religious Context," in U. Langer, ed., *The Cambridge Companion to Montaigne*, pp. 9–26.

6. Pierre Eyquem de Montaigne had been elected mayor in 1554, at the age of 59 (he was born in 1495), when his son was already in his 20s; before that, however, he had occupied various municipal posts (especially during the difficult period of the *gabelle* riots around 1548), a fact that justifies his son's childhood memories of him as a man crushed by his public responsibilities. Madeleine Lazard, *Michel de Montaigne*, pp. 30 ff.

7. *Essais* (III, 10), vol. 3, p. 1006, Frame, p. 935.

8. "En somme, les occasions, en cette charge, ont suivy ma complexion; dequoy je leur sçay tres bon gré. Est-il quelqu'un qui desire ester malade pour voir son medecin en besoigne, et faudroit-il pas foyter le medecin qui nous desireroit la peste, pour mettre son art en practique? Je n'ay point eu cett'humeur inique et assez commune, de desirer que le trouble et maladie des affaires de cette cite rehaussast et honnorat mon gouvernement: . . . Qui ne me voudra sçavoir gré de l'ordre, de la douce et muette tranquillité qui a accompaigné ma conduitte, aumoins ne peut-il me priver de la part qui m'en appartient par le titre de ma bonne fortune. Et je suis ainsi faict, qui j'ayme autant ester heureux que sage, et devoir mes succez purement à la grace de Dieu, qu'à l'entremise de mon operation." *Essais* (III, 10), vol. 3, pp. 1023–24, Frame, p. 953.

9. Nannerl O. Keohane writes, for example: "Machiavelli made an influential distinction between the public and the private realms of morality and action, and

gave exclusive attention to the former. Montaigne made the same distinction, and the opposite choice; he recommended a course of self-absorption, with only a limited and measured involvement in public life. This was the primary legacy he left for his successors." *Philosophy and the State in France*, p. 99.

10. *Essais* (III, 8), vol. 3, p. 933, Frame p. 865.

11. See the initial paragraph of the essay I, 56, "Of Prayers," in which Montaigne explained his position in relation to the dogmas of the Catholic Church; cf. Malcolm Smith, *Montaigne and the Roman Censors*, for a detailed and illuminating discussion of the potentially controversial issues in the *Essais*.

12. *Essais* (I, 31), vol. 1, pp. 213–14, Frame, p. 193; and (III, 6) *passim*.

13. Silvia Giocanti, *Penser l'irrésolution: Montaigne, Pascal, La Mothe Le Vayer*, pp. 93–116.

14. See the essay I, 34, "Fortune Is Often Met in the Path of Reason"; see also Silvia Giocanti, *Penser l'irrésolution*, pp. 157–59; cf. Daniel Martin, *Montaigne et la fortune: essai sur le hazard et le langage*, Paris, H. Champion, 1977.

15. Montaigne's use of the notion of "fortune" was one of the points that the Roman censors found objectionable in the *Essais:* see Malcolm Smith, *Montaigne and the Roman Censors*, pp. 23–35.

16. See in particular the essay II, 1, "Of the Inconsistency of Our Actions."

17. "Just observe who are the most powerful in the cities and who do their jobs best: you will ordinarily find that they are the least able. It has happened to women, children and madmen to rule great states just as well as the ablest princes." ("Qu'on regarde qui sont les plus puissans aus villes, et qui font mieux leurs besongnes: on trouvera ordinairement que ce sont les moins habiles. Il est advenu aux femmes, aux enfans et aux insensez, de commander des grands estats, à l'esgal des plus suffisans Princes.") *Essais* (III, 8), vol. 3, p. 934, Frame p. 867.

18. *Essais* (III, 10), vol. 3, p. 1008, Frame, pp. 937–38.

19. For a contemporary discussion of these issues, see John Dunn, *The Cunning of Unreason: Making Sense of Politics*, Harper Collins Publishers, London, 2001, pp. 242–44.

20. "Puisque les loix ethiques, qui regardent le devoir particulier de chacun en soy, sont si difficiles à dresser, comme nous voyons qu'elles sont, ce n'est pas merveille si celles qui gouvernent tant de particuliers le sont d'avantage." *Essais* (III, 13), vol. 3, p. 1070, Frame, p. 998.

21. The conquest of Mexico and its comparison to the experience of ancient conquests is discussed in particular in *Essais*, III, 6 ("Of Coaches"). On Montaigne and America, see Claude Blum, Marie-Luce Demonet, and André Tournon, eds., *Montaigne et le Nouveau Monde: actes du colloque de Paris*, Mont-de-Marsan, Editions InterUniversitaires, 1994; Philippe Desan, *Montaigne, les cannibales et les conquistadores*, Paris, Nizet, 1994; Tzvetan Todorov, "Les morales de la conquête," *Diogène*, 125 (1984), pp. 93–107; François Rigolot, "Montaigne lecteur européen de l'Amérique," *Diogène*, 164 (1993), pp. 3–15; Tom Conley, "The Essays and the New World," in Ullrich Langer, ed., *The Cambridge Companion to Montaigne*, pp. 74–95; Franck Lestringant, *Le Huguenot et le sauvage*, and Lestringant, ed., *Le Bresil de Montaigne: le Nouveau Monde des "Essais,"* Paris, Chandeigne, 2005.

22. On the concept of "diversion," see the essays II, 23, "Of Evil Means Employed to a Good End," and III, 4, "Of Diversion."

23. "And quite in contrast with that other [Julius Caesar] I would perhaps prefer to be second or third in Périgueux rather than first in Paris; at least, without prevarication, rather the third in Paris than the first in responsibility." ("Et, tout à l'opposite de l'autre, m'aimerois à l'avanture mieux deuxiesme ou troisiesme à Perigeus que premier à Paris; au moins, sans mentir, mieux troisiesme à Paris, que premier en charge.") *Essais* (III, 7), vol. 3, pp. 916–17, Frame, p. 850.

24. *Essais* (I, 42), vol. 1, p. 267, Frame, p. 237; (III, 7), *passim*.

25. In the essay "Of Experience" (III, 13) Montaigne describes "*opiniastreté*" as a mark of stupidity: vol. 3, p. 1075, Frame, p. 1003; in contemporary debates the same word describes the attitude of heretics, who are such not because they hold or express unorthodox beliefs, but because they are obstinately attached to them.

26. See the essay I, 30, "Of Moderation."

27. See Paul Mathias, *Montaigne*, chs. 3 and 4; on the philosophical background, see Sextus Empiricus, *Outlines of Scepticism*, ed. Julia E. Annas and Julian Barnes, Cambridge, Cambridge University Press, 2000; Julia E. Annas, *Hellenistic Philosophy of Mind*, Berkeley, University of California Press, 1992, and *The Morality of Happiness*, Oxford, Oxford University Press, 1993; Barry Stroud, *The Significance of Philosophical Scepticism*, Oxford, Clarendon Press, 1996; Gisela Striker, *Essays on Hellenistic Epistemology and Ethics*, Cambridge, Cambridge University Press, 1996; Jean-Paul Dumont, *Le scepticisme et le phenomène*, Paris, Vrin 1985.

28. On the uncertainty of human calculation, see in particular the essays I, 47, "Of the Uncertainty of Our Judgment," I, 54, "Of Vain Subtleties," and II, 20, "We Taste Nothing Pure."

29. *Essais* (III, 1), vol. 3, pp. 802–3, Frame, p. 739; (III, 10), vol. 3, pp. 1012 ff, Frame, pp. 942 ff.

30. On Montaigne's skepticism, see in particular Frédéric Brahami, *Le scepticisme de Montaigne*, and *Le travail du scepticisme*; Silvia Giocanti, *Penser l'irrésolution: Montaigne, Pascal, La Mothe Le Vayer*; Vincent Carraud and Jean-Luc Marion, eds., *Montaigne: scepticisme, métaphysique, théologie*; Ann Hartle, "Montaigne and Scepticism," in Ullrich Langer, ed., *The Cambridge Companion to Montaigne*, Cambridge, Cambridge University Press, 2005, pp. 183–206; see also Christopher Hookway, *Scepticism*, London, Routledge, 1990; Tullio Gregory, *Genèse de la raison classique: de Charron à Descartes*, Paris, PUF, 2000; Bernard Williams, *Moral Luck*, pp. 20–39.

31. "J'ay veu de mon temps merveilles en l'indiscrete et prodigieuse facilité des peuples à se laisser mener et manier la creance et l'esperance où il a pleu et servy à leurs chefs, par desssus cent mescontes les uns sur les autres, par dessus les fantosmes et les songes. Je ne m'estonne plus de ceux que les singeries d'Apollonius et de Mehumet enbufflarent. Leur sens et entandement est entierement estouffé en leur passion." *Essais* (III, 10), vol. 3, p. 1013, Frame, p. 943.

32. *Essais* (III, 1), vol. 3, pp. 791–92, Frame, pp. 728–29.

33. ". . . que la mémoire de toutes choses passés d'une part et d'autre . . . demeurera éteinte et assoupie, comme de chose non advenue." Janine Garrisson, ed., *L'édit de Nantes*, p. 29, article I. In the text of the edict this obliviousness began at a specific date (March 1595), that of Henry IV's accession to the throne.

34. Emmanuel Naya and Anne-Pascale Pouey-Monou, eds., *Eloge de la médiocrité: le juste milieu à la Renaissance*, Paris, Editions Rue d'Ulm, 2005.

35. *Essais* (III, 13), vol. 3, p. 1065, Frame, p. 992.

36. Ibid., p. 1073, Frame, p. 1001.

37. Ibid., p. 1071, Frame, p. 999. Montaigne's source on China was Juan Gonzales, *Historia de las cosas mas notables de la China* (Rome, 1585), French trans. by L. de la Porte, Paris, 1588.

38. *Essais* (III, 13), vol. 3, p. 1082, Frame, p. 1011.

39. Ibid., p. 1069, Frame, p. 996.

40. Ibid., p. 1070, Frame, p. 998.

41. Ibid., p. 1079, Frame, p. 1007.

42. For some contemporary views on the education of princes, cf. Ran Halévi, ed., *Le savoir du prince: du moyen age aux lumières*, Paris, Fayard, 2002; Robert Damien, *Le conseiller du Prince: de Machiavel à nos jours*, Paris, PUF, 2003, pp. 29–126; see also Erasmus, *The Education of a Christian Prince*, ed. Lisa Jardine, Cambridge, Cambridge University Press, 1997.

43. "J'eusse eu assez de fidelité, de jugement et de liberté pour cela. Ce seroit un office sans nom; autrement il perdroit son effect et sa grace. Et est un rolle qui ne peut indifferemment appartenir à tous." *Essais* (III, 13), vol. 3, p. 1078, Frame, p. 1006.

44. Warren Boutcher, "Montaigne's Legacy," in Ullrich Langer ed., *The Cambridge Companion to Montaigne*, pp. 27–52.

45. Gilles Achache, ed., *La Prudence: une morale du possible*, Paris, Editions Autrement, 1996; Francis Goyet, "Montaigne and the Notion of Prudence," in Ullrich Langer, ed., *The Cambridge Companion to Montaigne*, Cambridge, Cambridge University Press, 2005, pp. 118–41.

46. On the notion of human nature in Montaigne's thought, see Marcel Conche, *Montaigne ou la conscience heureuse* (1967), Paris, PUF, 2002; Emmanuel Faye, *Philosophie et perfection de l'homme*; Thierry Gontier, *De l'homme à l'animal*.

47. "Il n'y a piece indigne de nostre soin en ce present que Dieu nous a faict; nous en devons conte jusques à un poil. Et n'est pas une commission par acquit à l'homme de conduire l'homme selon sa condition: elle est expresse, naïfve et tres principale, et nous l'a le createur donnée serieusement et severement." *Essais* (III, 13), vol. 3, p. 1114, Frame, p. 1043.

48. Blaise Pascal, "Entretien de Pascal avec M. de Sacy sur Epictète et Montaigne," in *Œuvres complètes*, ed. Michel Le Guern, vol. 1, pp. 82–98; Léon Brunschvicg, *Descartes et Pascal lecteurs de Montaigne*; see also Philippe Sellier, *Pascal et Saint Augustin* (1970), Paris, Albin Michel, 1995.

BIBLIOGRAPHY

BIBLIOGRAPHIC NOTE

The existing literature on Montaigne is immense, and only a limited selection of titles features in this list; on the other hand, the number of works dedicated to the writer's political experience and views is surprisingly small. Regrettably, the recent *Cambridge Companion to Montaigne* (edited by Ullrich Langer, 2005), while offering a helpful general introduction to the *Essais*, does not attempt to place the work in the context of the history of political thought. For the reader interested in this particular perspective, the best introduction to the circumstances of Montaigne's life remains the old biography by Donald Frame (1965); Géralde Nakam's works (1984 and 1993), though distant from the style of Anglo-Saxon academic literature, provide invaluable information on the historical background. The studies by Malcolm Smith (1991), David Schaefer (1990 and 1998), and David Quint (1998) have greatly contributed to renewing our understanding of Montaigne's political morality, while those by Frédéric Brahami (1997 and 2001), Sylvia Giocanti (2001), and John Christian Laursen (1992) have helpfully brought to light the practical and political implications of Montaigne's skepticism. Andrée Comparot's works (1983 and 1984) provide an essential connection between the *Essais* and the Christian tradition. Among the many excellent historical works on France at the time of the religious wars, I found those by Denis Crouzet (1990, 1994, and 1998), Mack Holt (1986), Michael Wolfe (1993), Michael de Waele (2000) and Thierry Wanegffelen (1997 and 1998) especially instructive about the predicament of those who, like Montaigne himself, worked hard to bring the conflict to an end. The long-awaited new edition of the *Essais* in the "Bibliothèque de la Pléiade" has finally been published in May 2007, when this book was already in proofs: Michel de Montaigne, *Les Essais (texte de 1595)*, ed. Jean Balsamo, Michel Magnien, and Catherine Magnien-Simonin, Paris, Gallimard, 2007.

WORKS CITED

Achache, Gilles, ed. *La Prudence: une morale du possible*, Paris, Editions Autrement, 1996.

Adams, Robert P. *The Better Part of Valour: More, Erasmus, Colet and Vives on Humanism, War and Peace, 1496–1535*, Seattle, University of Washington Press, 1962.

Agrippa, von Nettlesheim, Heinrich Cornelius. *Opera*, ed. Richard H. Popkin, Hildesheim and New York, G. Holms, 1970.

Alberti, Antonina. "The Epicurean Theory of Law and Justice," in A. Laks and M. Schofield, eds., *Justice and Generosity: Studies in Hellenistic Social and Political Philosophy*, Cambridge, Cambridge University Press, 1995, pp.161–90.

Allen, Don Cameron. *Doubt's Boundless Sea: Skepticism and Faith in the Renaissance*, Baltimore, Johns Hopkins Press, 1964.

Annas, Julia E. *Hellenistic Philosophy of Mind*, Berkeley, University of California Press, 1992;

————. *The Morality of Happiness*, Oxford, Oxford University Press, 1993.

Antoine, Michel. *Le coeur de l'état: surintendance, contrôle général et intendence des finances, 1552–1791*, Paris, Fayard, 2003.

Anquez, Léonce. *Histoire des assemblées politiques des Réformés en France: 1573–1622*, Geneva, Slatkine, 1970.

Armaingaud, Arthur. *Montaigne pamphlétaire: l'enigme du contr'un*, Paris, Hachette, 1910.

Augustijn, Cornelis. *Erasmus: His Life, Works and Influence*, Toronto, Toronto University Press, 1992.

Augustine. *The City of God against the Pagans*, ed. R.W. Dyson, Cambridge, Cambridge University Press, 1998.

Avril, Pierre, et al.. "La Loi," special issue of *Pouvoirs*, 114 (2005).

Babelon, Jean-Pierre. *Henri IV*, Paris, Fayard, 1982.

Bady, René. *L'homme et son "institution" de Montaigne à Berulle: 1580–1625*, Paris, Les Belles Lettres, 1964.

Bangert, William V. *A History of the Society of Jesus*, St. Louis, MO, Institute of Jesuit Sources, 1986.

Barbiche, Bernard. *Les institutions de la monarchie française à l'époque moderne*, Paris, PUF, 1999.

Barbiche, Bernard, and Segolène de Dainville-Barbiche. *Sully, l'homme et ses fidèles*, Paris, Fayard, 1997.

Bége-Seurin, D. "La cour des Aides de Périgueux, 1553–1561," in *Sarlat et le Périgord, actes du XXXIXème congrès d'études régionales* (Sarlat, 26–27 April 1987), Société Historique et Archéologique du Périgord, 1987, pp. 321–30.

Béné, Charles. *Erasme et Saint Augustin, ou l'influence de Saint Augustin sur l'humanisme d'Erasme*, Geneva, Droz, 1969.

Benedict, Philip. "Confessionalisation in France? Critical Reflections and New Evidence," in Raymond A. Mentzer and Andrew Spicer, eds., *Society and Culture in the Huguenot World, 1559–1685*, Cambridge, Cambridge University Press, 2002, pp. 44–61.

Bergin, Joseph. *The Making of the French Episcopate, 1589–1661*, New Haven and London, Yale University Press, 1996.

————. *The Rise of Richelieu*, Manchester and New York, Manchester University Press, 1997.

Berns, Thomas. *Violence de la loi à la renaissance: l'originaire du politique chez Machiavel et Montaigne*, Paris, Kimé, 2000.

Bèze, Théodore de. *Du droit des magistrats*, ed. Robert M. Kingdon, Geneva, Droz, 1971.

Biet, Christian. *Henri IV: la vie, la légende*, Saint-Germain de Puy, Larousse, 2000.

Billacois, François. *Le duel dans la société française des XVIe-XVIIe siècles: essai de psychosociologie historique*, Paris, Editions de l'Ecole d'Hautes Etudes, 1986.

Bireley, Robert. *The Counter-Reformation Prince: Anti-Machiavellianism or Catholic Statecraft in Early Modern Europe*, Chapel Hill and London, University of North Carolina Press, 1990.

Blum, Claude, Marie-Luce Demonet, and André Tournon, eds. *Montaigne et le Nouveau Monde: actes du colloque de Paris*, Mont-de-Marsan, Editions InterUniversitaires, 1994.

Boase, Alan M. *The Fortunes of Montaigne: A History of the Essays in France, 1580–1669,* London, Methuen, 1935.

———. "Montaigne et la sorcellerie," *Bibliothèque d'Humanisme et Renaissance,* 4 (1935), pp. 386–402.

Bodin, Jean. *Methodus ad facilem historiarum cognitionem* (1566); French trans.: *La méthode de l'histoire,* ed. Pierre Mesnard, Paris, Les Belles Lettres, 1941.

Bolle, Pierre, ed. *L'Edit de Nantes: un compromis reussi?* Grenoble, Presses Universitaires de Grenoble, 1999.

Bonnefon, Paul. *Estienne de la Boétie, sa vie, ses ouvrages et ses relations avec Montaigne* (1888), Geneva, Slatkine, 1970.

———. *Montaigne: l'homme et l'œuvre,* Paris, J. Rouam, 1893;

———. *Montaigne et ses amis: La Boétie, Charron, Mlle de Gournay,* Paris, Armand Colin, 1898.

Boscheron des Portes, Charles-Bon-François. *Histoire du parlement de Bordeaux depuis sa création jusqu'à sa suppression (1451–1790),* 2 vols., Geneva, Megariotis, 1978 (reprint of the 1877–78 Bordeaux edition).

Botineau, Pierre, ed. *Montaigne: maire de Bordeaux, gentilhomme d'Aquitaine, écrivain de France: une évocation à l'aide de quelques documents,* Bordeaux, Bibliothèque Municipale, 1994.

Boucher, J. "Autour de François, duc d'Alençon et d'Anjou, un parti d'opposition à Charles IX et Henri III," in Robert Sauzet, ed., *Henri III et son temps: Actes du Colloque de Tours, 1989,* Paris, Vrin, 1992.

Bourquin, Laurent. "Les défis des guerres de religion, 1559–1610," in Joël Cornette, ed., *La monarchie entre Renaissance et Révolution, 1515–1792,* Paris, Seuil, 2000, pp. 63–150.

———. *La noblesse dans la France moderne (XVI–XVIII siècles),* Paris, Belin, 2002.

Boutcher, Warren. "Montaigne's Legacy," in Ullrich Langer, ed., *The Cambridge Companion to Montaigne,* Cambridge, Cambridge University Press, 2005, pp. 27–52.

Boutruche, Robert ed. *Histoire de Bordeaux de 1453 à 1715,* Bordeaux, Fédération Historique du Sud-Ouest, 1966.

Brahami, Frédéric. *Le scepticisme de Montaigne,* Paris, PUF, 1997.

———. *Le travail du scepticisme, Montaigne, Bayle, Hume,* Paris, PUF, 2001.

Brambilla, Elena. *Alle origini del Sant'Uffizio: penitenza, confessione e giustizia spirituale dal medioevo al XVI secolo,* Bologna, Il Mulino, 2000.

Braun, René, and Jean Richter, eds. *L'Empereur Julien,* 2 vols., Paris, Les Belles Lettres, 1978–81.

Briggs, Robin. *Witches and Neighbours: The Social and Cultural Context of European Witchcraft,* London, Fontana Books, 1996.

Brown, Frieda S. *Religious and Political Conservatism in the "Essais" of Montaigne,* Geneva, Droz, 1963.

Brunschvicg, Léon. *Descartes et Pascal lecteurs de Montaigne* (1942–45), Paris, Presses Pocket, 1995.

Brush, Craig B. *From the Perspective of the Self: Montaigne's Self-Portrait,* New York, Fordham University Press, 1994.

————. *Montaigne and Bayle: Variations on the Theme of Skepticism*, The Hague, M. Nijhoff, 1966.

Bury, Emmanuel. *Littérature et politesse: l'invention de l'honnête homme, 1580–1750*, Paris, PUF, 1996.

Busson, Henri. *Littérature et théologie: Montaigne, Bossuet, La Fontaine, Prévost*, Paris, PUF, 1962.

————. *La pensée religieuse française de Charron à Pascal*, Paris, Vrin, 1933.

————. *Le Rationalisme dans la Littérature Française de la Renaissance, 1533–1601*, Paris, Vrin, 1971.

Butor, Michel. *Essais sur les Essais*, Paris, Gallimard, 1968.

Cabanel, Patrick. *Les Protestants et la République*, Paris, Editions Complexe, 2000.

Cappa, Carlo. *Michel de Montaigne, l'appartenenza della scrittura: il dialogo tra vita e opera negli Essais*, Milano, Franco Angeli, 2003.

Carraud, Vincent, and Jean-Luc Marion, eds. *Montaigne: scepticisme, métaphysique, théologie*, Paris, PUF, 2004.

Carré, Henri. *Sully, sa vie, son œuvre (1559–1641)*, Paris, Payot, 1932.

Carroll, Stuart. *Noble Power during the French Wars of Religion: The Guise Affinity and the Catholic Cause in Normandy*, Cambridge, Cambridge University Press, 1998.

Casals, Jaume. "La théologie de Montaigne? Ou que Dieu n'existe pas dans les *Essais*," *Bulletin de la Société des Amis de Montaigne*, ser. VII, no. 33–34 (July–Dec. 1993).

Cassan, Michel. La Réduction des villes ligueuses à l'obéissance," *Nouvelle Revue du XVIè siècle*, 22/1 (2004), pp. 159–74.

Castellion, Sébastien. *Conseil à la France désolée* (1562), ed. Marius F. Valkhoff, Geneva, Droz, 1967.

Cazaux, Yves, ed. *Mémoires et autres écrits de Marguerite de Valois*, Paris, Mercure de France, 1986.

Chevallier, Pierre. *Henri III, roi shakespearien*, Paris, Fayard, 1985.

Christin, Olivier. *La paix de religion: l'autonomisation de la raison politique au XVIème siècle*, Paris, Seuil, 1997.

————. "La réception de l'Edit de Nantes: illusions et désillusions de la 'tolérance,'" in A. Pettegree, P. Nelles, and P. Conner, eds., *The Sixteenth Century French Religious Book*, Aldershot (UK) and Burlington, VT, Ashgate, 2001, pp. 197–209.

Cicero, Marcus Tullius. *On Duties*, ed. M. T. Griffin and E. M. Atkins, Cambridge, Cambridge University Press, 1991.

Clark, Stuart. *Thinking with Demons: The Idea of Witchcraft in Early Modern Europe*, Oxford, Oxford University Press, 1997.

Cloulas, Ivan. *Catherine de Médicis*, Paris, Fayard, 1979.

Cocula, Anne-Marie. *Etienne de La Boétie*, Luçon, Editions Sud Ouest, 1995.

Collinson, Patrick. *The Reformation*, London, Weidenfeld and Nicolson, 2003.

Compagnon, Antoine. "Montaigne ou la parole donnée," in Frank Lestringant, ed., *Rhétorique de Montaigne*, Paris, Honoré Champion, 1985.

————. *Nous, Michel de Montaigne*, Paris, Seuil, 1980.

Comparot, Andrée. *Amour et vérité: Sebon, Vives et Michel de Montaigne*, Paris, Klincksieck, 1983.

——. *Augustinisme et Aristotélisme de Sebon à Montaigne*, Paris, Editions du Cerf, 1984.

Compayré, Gabriel. *Montaigne et l'éducation du jugement*, Paris, P. Delaplane, 1904.

Conche, Marcel. *Montaigne et la philosophie*, Paris, PUF, 1996.

——. *Montaigne ou la conscience heureuse* (1967), Paris, PUF, 2002.

Tom Conley, "The Essays and the New World," in Ullrich Langer, ed., *The Cambridge Companion to Montaigne*, Cambridge, Cambridge University Press, 2005, pp. 74–95.

Constant, Jean-Marie. *La Ligue*, Paris, Fayard, 1996.

Cornette, Joël. *Le livre et le Glaive: chronique de la France moderne, le XVI siècle*, Paris, Armand Colin, 1995.

——,ed. *La monarchie entre Renaissance et Révolution, 1515–1792*, Paris, Seuil, 2000.

Couzinet, Marie-Dominique. *Histoire et méthode à la renaissance: une lecture de la 'Methodus' de Jean Bodin*, Paris, Vrin, 1996.

Craveri, Benedetta. *L'arte della conversazione*, Milano, Adelphi, 2001.

Cromé, François. *Dialogue d'entre le maheustre et le manant*, ed. Peter M. Ascoli, Geneva, Droz, 1977.

Croquette, Bernard. *Pascal et Montaigne: étude des réminescences des "Essais" dans l'oeuvre de Pascal*, Geneva, Droz, 1974.

Crouzet, Denis. *Les guerriers de Dieu: la violence au temps des troubles de religion*, 2 vols., Seyssel, Champ Vallon, 1990.

——. *Le haut de cœur de Catherine de Médicis*, Paris, Albin Michel, 2005.

——. *La nuit de la Saint-Barthélemy: un rêve perdu de la Renaissance*, Paris, Fayard, 1994.

——. *La sagesse et le malheur: Michel de l'Hospital, Chancelier de France*, Seyssel, Champ Vallon, 1998.

Dalat, Jean. *Montesquieu magistrat*, Paris, Lettres Modernes, 1971.

Damien, Robert. *Le conseiller du prince: de Machiavel à nos jours*, Paris, PUF, 2003.

Dartigue, Jean-Albert. *Rabaut de Saint Etienne à l'Assemblée constituante de 1789*, Nantes, Salières, 1903.

Dassonville, Michel, ed. *Ronsard et Montaigne: écrivains engagés?* Lexington, KY, French Forum, 1989.

Daussy, Hugues. *Les Huguenots et le Roi: le combat politique de Philippe Duplessis-Mornay (1572– 1600)*, Geneva, Droz, 2002.

Defaux, Gérard, ed. *Montaigne: Essays in Reading*, special issue of *Yale French Studies*, no. 64, 1983.

Delègue, Yves. *Montaigne et la mauvaise foi: l'écriture de la vérité*, Paris, Honoré Champion, 1998.

Delumeau, Jean and Wanegffelen, Thierry, eds. *Naissance et affirmation de la Réforme* (1965), Paris, PUF, 1997.

Demonet, Marie-Luce. *Montaigne et la question de l'homme*, Paris, PUF, 1999.

Desan, Philippe. *Montaigne, les cannibales et les conquistadores*, Paris, Nizet, 1994.

——. *Naissance de la méthode (Machiavel, La Ramée, Bodin, Montaigne, Descartes)*, Paris, Nizet, 1987.

————, ed. *La philosophie et Montaigne*, special issue of *Montaigne Studies*, 12 (2000).

Dewald, Jonathan. *The European Nobility, 1400–1800*, Cambridge, Cambridge University Press, 1996.

Diderot, Denis. *Œuvres*, ed. Laurent Versini, 5 vols., Paris, Robert Laffont, 1997.

Diefendorf, Barbara B. *Beneath the Cross: Catholics and Huguenots in Sixteenth Century Paris*, New York and Oxford, Oxford University Press, 1991.

Di Lucia, Paolo. "La fiducia nelle parola," in Giuseppe Galli, ed., *Interpretazione e fiducia: atti del XIX colloquio sull'interpretazione*, Pisa and Rome, Istituti Editoriali e Poligrafici Internationali, 1999, pp. 109–32.

Doyle, William. *Venality: The Sale of Offices in Eighteenth-Century France*, Oxford, Clarendon Press, 1996.

Dréano, Maturin. "La crise sceptique de Montaigne?" *Bibliothèque d'Humanisme et Renaissance*, 23 (1961), pp. 252–64.

————. *La pensée religieuse de Montaigne*, Paris, G. Beauchesne, 1936;

————. *La Renommée de Montaigne en France au XVIIIème siècle (1677–1802)*, Angers, Editions de l'Ouest, 1952.

Dufour, Alain. "Le colloque de Poissy," in *Mélanges d'histoire du 16ème siècle offerts à Henri Meylan*, Geneva, Droz, 1970, pp. 127–37.

Duminuco, Vincent J., ed. *The Jesuit "Ratio studiorum": 400th Anniversary Perspectives*, New York, Fordham University Press, 2000.

Dumont, Jean-Paul. *Le scepticisme et le phenomène*, Paris, Vrin, 1985.

Dunn, John M. "The Claim to Freedom of Conscience, Freedom of Speech, Freedom of Thought, Freedom of Worship?" in Ole Peter Grell, Jonathan I. Israel, and Nicholas Tyacke, eds., *From Persecution to Toleration: The Glorious Revolution and Religion in England*, Oxford, Clarendon Press, 1991, pp. 171–93.

————. *The Cunning of Unreason: Making Sense of Politics*, London, Harper Collins Publishers, 2001.

————. *Interpreting Political Responsibility: Essays, 1981–1989*, Cambridge, Polity Press, 1990.

Dupont, André. *Rabaut Saint Etienne, 1743–1793: un protestant défenseur de la liberté religieuse*, Geneva, Labor et Fides, 1989.

Dust, Philip C. *Three Renaissance Pacifists: Essays in the Theories of Erasmus, More and Vives*, New York and Bern, Peter Lang, 1987.

Duval, Edwin M. "Lessons for the New World: Design and Meaning in Montaigne's 'Des cannibales' (I,31) and 'Des coches' (III,6)," in Gérard Defaux, ed., *Montaigne: Essays in Reading*, special issue of *Yale French Studies* 64 (1983), pp.180–87.

Elizabeth I, *Collected Works*, ed. Leah S. Marcus, Janel Mueller, and Mary Beth Rose, Chicago and London, University of Chicago Press, 2000.

El Kenz, David, ed. *Le massacre, objet d'histoire*, Paris, Gallimard, 2005.

El Kenz, David, and Claire Gantet, eds. *Guerres et paix de religion en Europe, 16ème et 17ème siècles*, Paris, Armand Colin, 2003.

Erasmus, Desiderius. *Ecstasy and "The Praise of Folly"* (1511), ed. M. A. Screech, London, Duckworth, 1980.

————. *The Education of a Christian Prince* (1516), ed. Lisa Jardine, Cambridge, Cambridge University Press, 1997.

————. *Eloge de la folie, adages, colloques, réflexions sur l'art, l'éducation, la religion, la guerre, la philosophie,* ed. Claude Blum, André Godin, Jean-Claude Margolin, and Daniel Ménager, Paris, Robert Laffont, 1992.

Erlanger, Philippe, *Le massacre de la Saint-Barthélemy,* Paris, Gallimard, 1960.

————. *La Reine Margot ou la rébellion,* Paris, Perrin, 1972.

Faye, Emmanuel. *Philosophie et perfection de l'homme: de la Renaissance à Descartes,* Paris, Vrin, 1998.

Feytaud, Jacques de. "L'Eglise catholique face aux *Essais,*" in Jacques Lemaire, ed., *Montaigne et la révolution philosophique du XVIème siècle,* Brussels, Editions de l'Université de Bruxelles, 1992, pp. 105–22.

Finley-Croswhite, S. Annette. *Henri IV and the Towns: The pursuit of Legitimacy in French Urban Society, 1589–1610,* Cambridge, Cambridge University Press, 1999.

Flanagan, Thomas. "The Concept of *Fortuna* in Machiavelli," in Anthony Parel, ed., *The Political Calculus,* Toronto, Toronto University Press, 1972, pp. 127–56.

Fleuret, Colette. *Rousseau et Montaigne,* Paris, Nizet, 1980.

Fontana, Biancamaria. "Loi," in *Dictionnaire de Michel de Montaigne,* ed. Philippe Desan, Paris, Honoré Champion, 2004, pp. 601–3.

————. "The Rule of Law and the Problem of Legal Reform in Montaigne's *Essais,*" in José Maria Maraval and Adam Przeworski, eds., *Democracy and the Rule of Law,* Cambridge, Cambridge University Press, 2003, pp. 302–15.

Frame, Donald M. *Montaigne: A Biography,* New York, Harcourt Brace & World, 1965; French trans.: *Montaigne, une vie, une œuvre, 1533–1592,* Paris, Champion, and Geneva, Slatkine, 1994, with an updated bibliography by François Rigolot.

————. *Montaigne in France: 1812–1852,* New York, Columbia University Press, 1940.

Franklin, Julian H. *Jean Bodin and the Sixteenth Century Revolution in the Methodology of Law and History,* New York, Columbia University Press, 1963.

Frémy, Edouard. *L'Académie des derniers Valois (1570–1585): d'après des documents nouveaux et inédits,* Paris, E. Leroux, 1887.

Frieda, Leonie. *Catherine de Medici: A Biography,* London, Weidenfeld and Nicolson, 2003.

Friedrich, Hugo. *Montaigne* (1949), trans. Robert Rovini, Paris, Gallimard, 1968.

Fumaroli, Marc. *L'âge de l'éloquence: rhétorique et "res literaria" de la Renaissance au seuil de l'époque classique* (1980), Paris, Albin Michel, 1993.

————. *La diplomatie de l'esprit: de Montaigne à La Fontaine,* Paris, Hermann, 2001.

————. *Héros et orateurs: rhétorique et dramaturgie cornéliennes* (1990), Geneva, Droz, rev. ed., 1996.

————. "Preface," in Blaise Pascal, *"L'art de persuader," précédé de "L'art de conférer" de Montaigne,* Paris, Rivages, 2001.

Galli, Giuseppe, ed. *Interpretazione e fiducia: atti del XIX colloquio sull'interpretazione,* Pisa and Rome, Istituti Editoriali e Poligrafici Internazionali, 1999.

Gambetta, Diego, ed. *Trust: Making and Breaking Cooperative Relations*, Oxford, Basil Blackwell, 1990.

Garavini, Fausta. *Monstres et chimères: Montaigne, le texte et le fantasme*, Geneva, Slatkine, 1993.

Garrison, Janine. *L'édit de Nantes: chronique d'une paix attendue*, Paris, Fayard, 1998.

———. *Henri IV*, Paris, Seuil, 1984.

———, ed. *L'édit de Nantes*, Biarritz, Editions Atlantica, 1997.

Gaullieur, Louis-Frédéric-Ernest. - *Histoire de la Réformation à Bordeaux, et dans le ressort du parlement de Guyenne*, 2 vols., Paris, H. Champion, 1884.

———. *Histoire du collège de Guyenne d'àpres un grand nombre de documents inédits*, Paris, Sandoz et Fischbacher, 1874.

Gauna, Max. *The Dissident Montaigne*, New York and Bern, Peter Lang, 1989.

———. *Montaigne and the Ethics of Compassion*, Lewiston, NY, Mellen Press, 2000.

Gentillet, Innocent. *Anti-Machiavel* (1576), ed. C. Edward Rathé, Geneva, Droz, 1968.

Geuss, Raymond. *History and Illusion in Politics*, Cambridge, Cambridge University Press, 2001.

———. *Public Goods, Private Goods*, Princeton, Princeton University Press, 2001.

Geyl, Pieter. *The Revolt of the Netherlands, 1555–1609*, London, Barnes and Noble Books, 1980.

Giard, Luce, ed. *Les jésuites à la Renaissance: système éducatif et production du savoir*, Paris, PUF, 1995.

Gide, André. *Les pages immortelles de Montaigne, choisies et expliquées par André Gide*, Paris, Ed. Corrêa, 1939.

Gigon, Stéphane-Claude. *La révolte de la gabelle en Guyenne, 1548–1549: contribution à l'histoire de l'impôt sous l'ancien régime*, Paris, H. Champion, 1906.

Gilbert, Felix. *Machiavelli and Guicciardini: Politics and History in Sixteenth Century Florence*, Princeton, Princeton University Press, 1965.

Giocanti, Sylvia. *Penser l'irrésolution: Montaigne, Pascal, La Mothe Le Vayer*, Paris, Honoré Champion, 2001.

Gontier, Thierry. *De l'homme à l'animal: paradoxes sur la nature des animaux, Montaigne et Descartes*, Paris, Vrin, 1998.

Goyard Fabre, Simone. "Au tournant de l'idée de démocratie: l'influence des Monarchomaques," *Cahiers de philosophie politique et juridique de l'université de Caen*, 1 (1982), pp. 27–48.

Gournay, Marie de. *Oeuvres complètes*, ed. Jean Claude Arnould, 2 vols., Paris, Honoré Champion, 2002.

Goyet, Francis. "Montaigne and the Notion of Prudence," in Ullrich Langer, ed., *The Cambridge Companion to Montaigne*, Cambridge, Cambridge University Press, 2005, pp. 118–41.

Grady, Hugh. *Shakespeare, Machiavelli and Montaigne: Power and Subjectivity from Richard II to Hamlet*, Oxford, Oxford University Press, 2002.

Grandjean, M., and Bernard Roussel, eds. *Coexister dans l'intolérance: L'Edit de Nantes (1598)*, Geneva, Labor et Fides, 1998.

Greengrass, Mark. "The Calvinist Experiment in Béarn," in A. Pettigree, A. Duke, and G. Lewis, eds., *Calvinism in Europe, 1540–1620*, Cambridge, Cambridge University Press, 1994, pp.119–42.

———. "A Day in the Life of the Third Estate, Blois, 26 Dec. 1576," in Adrianna E. Bakos, ed., *Politics, Ideology and the Law in Early Modern Europe: Essays in Honor of J.H.M. Salmon*, Rochester, NY, Rochester University Press, 1994, pp. 73–90.

Gregory, Tullio. *Genèse de la raison classique: de Charron à Descartes*, Paris, PUF, 2000.

Grell, Ole Peter, and Bob Scribner, eds. *Tolerance and Intolerance in the European Reformation*, Cambridge, Cambridge University Press, 1996.

Gruen, Alphonse. *La vie publique de Michel de Montaigne* (1855), Geneva, Slatkine, 1970.

Guicciardini, Francesco. *Storia d'Italia*, ed. Seidel Menchi, Torino, Einaudi, 1971; ———. *Ricordi*, ed. Emilio Pasquini, Milano, Garzanti, 1984.

Guy, Alan, ed. *Vivès ou l'humanisme engagé*, Paris, Seghers, 1972.

Haag, E. M. "Diderot et Voltaire, lecteurs de Montaigne: du jugement suspendu à la raison libre," *Revue de Métaphysique et de Morale*, 3 (1997), pp. 365–83.

Halévi, Ran, ed. *Le savoir du prince: du moyen age aux lumières*, Paris, Fayard, 2002.

Halkin, Léon-Ernest. *Erasme et l'humanisme chrétien*, Paris, PUF, 1969.

Hampton, Timothy. *Writing from History: The Rhetoric of Exemplarity in Renaissance Literature*, Ithaca, NY, Cornell University Press, 1990.

Hanley, Sarah. *The "Lit de Justice" of the Kings of France: Constitutional Ideology in Legend, Ritual and Discourse*, Princeton, Princeton University Press, 1983.

Hardin, Russell. *One for All: The Logic of Group Conflict*, Princeton, Princeton University Press, 1995.

Hartle, Ann. *Michel de Montaigne: Accidental Philosopher*, Cambridge, Cambridge University Press, 2003.

———. "Montaigne and Scepticism," in Ullrich Langer, ed., *The Cambridge Companion to Montaigne*, Cambridge, Cambridge University Press, 2005, pp. 183–206.

Henry IV. *Lettres d'amour et écrits politiques*, ed. Jean-Pierre Babelon, Paris, Fayard, 1988.

———. *Recueil des lettres missives de Henri IV*, ed. Jules Berger de Xivrey and Joseph Guadet, 9 vols., Paris, 1843–76.

Henry, Patrick, ed. *Montaigne and Ethics*, special issue of *Montaigne Studies*, 14 (2002).

Hibbard, G. R. "Introduction," in William Shakespeare, *Love's Labour's Lost*, Oxford, Oxford University Press, 1990, pp. 1–83.

Hirschman, Albert O. *The Rhetoric of Reaction: Perversity, Futility, Jeopardy*, Cambridge, MA, Harvard University Press, 1991.

Hoffmann, George. *Montaigne's Career*, Oxford, Oxford University Press, 1998.

Holt, Mack P. "Attitudes of the French Nobility at the Estates General of 1576," *Sixteenth Century Journal*, 18 (1987), pp. 489–504.

———. *The Duke of Anjou and the Politique Struggle during the Wars of Religion*, Cambridge, Cambridge University Press, 1986.

———. *The French Wars of Religion, 1562–1629*, Cambridge, Cambridge University Press, 1995.

Hookway, Christopher. *Scepticism*, London, Routledge, 1990.

Hopfl, Harro. *Jesuit Political Thought: The Society of Jesus and the State, c. 1540–1630*, Cambridge, Cambridge University Press, 2004.

Hotman, François. *Anti-tribonien ou discours pour l'estude des loix*, Cologne and Brussels, Bruxelles, 1681.

———. *Brutum fulmen papae Sixti V: adversus Henricum regem Navarrae et Henricum Borbonium: principem Condaeum*, Geneva, 1585.

———. *Francogallia*, ed. R. E. Giesey and J.H.M. Salmon, Cambridge, Cambridge University Press, 1972.

Huizinga, Johan. *Erasme*, trans. V. Bruncel, preface by Lucien Febvre, Paris, Gallimard, 1955.

Huseman, William H. "A Lexicological Study of the Expression of Toleration in French at the time of the Colloque of Poissy," *Cahiers de Lexicologie*, 1986, pp. 89–109.

Jouanna, Arlette. "La Boétie," in A. Jouanna, J. Boucher, D. Biloghi, and G. de Thiec, eds., *Histoire et dictionnaire des guerres de religion*, Paris, Robert Laffont, 1998, pp. 1004–6.

———. *Le devoir de révolte: la noblesse française et la gestation de l'Etat moderne, 1559–1661*, Paris, Fayard, 1989;

———. "Politiques," in A. Jouanna, J. Boucher, D. Biloghi, and G. de Thiec, eds., *Histoire et dictionnaire des guerres de religion*, Paris, Robert Laffont, 1998, pp. 1210–1213.

Jouanna, Arlette, et al. *Métaphysique et politique de l'obéissance dans la France du XVIème siècle*, special issue, *Nouvelle Revue du XVIème siècle*, 22/1 (2004).

Jouanna, A., J. Boucher, D. Biloghi, and G. de Thiec, eds. *Histoire et dictionnaire des guerres de religion*, Paris, Robert Laffont, 1998.

Julianus, *Misopogon*, ed. C. Lacombrade and Aude de Saint-Loup, Paris, Les Belles Lettres, 2003.

Kelly, Christopher. *Rousseau as Author: Consecrating One's Life to the Truth*, Chicago and London, University of Chicago Press, 2003.

Keohane, Nannerl O. *Philosophy and the State in France: The Renaissance to the Enlightenment*, Princeton, Princeton University Press, 1980.

Kim, Seong-Hak. *Michel de l'Hôpital: The political vision of a reformist chancellor, 1560–1568*, Minneapolis, University of Minnesota Press, 1991.

Kingston, Rebecca. *Montesquieu and the Parlement of Bordeaux, 1714–26*, Geneva, Droz, 1996.

Knecht, R. J. *Catherine de' Medici*, London, Longman, 1998.

———. *The Rise and Fall of Renaissance France, 1483–1610*, London, Fontana Press, 1996.

Knee, Philip. *La parole incertaine: Montaigne en dialogue*, Saint Nicolas (Quebec), Presses de l'Université de Laval, 2003.

Konstantinovic, Isabelle. *Montaigne et Plutarque*, Geneva, Droz, 1989.

La Boétie, Estienne de. *De la servitude volontaire ou Contr'un*, ed. Nadia Gonterbert, Paris, Gallimard, 1993.

———. *Discours de la servitude volontaire*, ed. Simone Goyard-Fabre, Paris, Flammarion, 1983.

———. *Discours de la servitude volontaire ou contr'un,* ed. Malcolm Smith and Michel Magnien, Geneva, Droz, 2001.

———. *Mémoire sur la pacification des troubles,* ed. Malcolm Smith, Geneva, Droz, 1983.

———. "On Voluntary Servitude," trans. David Lewis Schaefer, in D. L. Schaefer, ed., *Freedom over Servitude, Montaigne, La Boétie and "On Voluntary Servitude,"* Westport, CT, and London, Greenwood Press, 1998, pp. 189–222.

La Charité, Raymond. *The Concept of Judgement in Montaigne,* The Hague, Martinus Nijhoff, 1968.

Lacouture, Jean. *Les Jésuites: une multibiographie,* 2 vols., Paris, Seuil, 1991–92.

———. *Montaigne à cheval,* Paris, Seuil, 1996.

La Mothe le Vayer, François de. *De la vertu de païens:* "De Julien l'Apostat," in *Libertins du XVIIème siècle,* ed. Jacques Prévot, 2 vols., Paris, Gallimard, vol. 2, pp. 151–73.

Langer, Ullrich, ed. *The Cambridge Companion to Montaigne,* Cambridge, Cambridge University Press, 2005.

Lasale, Ernest Dupré. *Michel de l'Hospital avant son élévation au poste de chancelier de France,* Paris, E. Thorin, A. Fontemoing, 1875–99.

Laursen, John Christian. *The Politics of Scepticism in the Ancients: Montaigne, Hume and Kant,* Leiden, New York, and Cologne, E. J. Brull, 1992.

Lazard, Madeleine. *Michel de Montaigne,* Paris, Fayard, 1992.

Lecler, Joseph. *Histoire de la tolérance au siècle de la Réforme* (1955), Paris, Albin Michel, 1994.

Le Roux, Nicolas. *La Faveur du Roi: mignons et courtisans au temps des derniers Valois (vers 1547–vers 1589),* Seyssel, Champ Vallon, 2001.

———. *Un régicide au nom de Dieu: l'assassinat d'Henri III, 1er août 1589,* Paris, Gallimard, 2006.

Le Roy Ladurie, Emmanuel. *L'état royal, 1460–1610,* Paris, Hachette, 1987.

Lestringant, Frank. *Le Cannibale, grandeur et décadence,* Paris, Perrin, 1994.

———. *L'Huguenot et le sauvage: l'Amérique et la controverse coloniale en France au temps des guerres de religion (1555–1589)* (1990), Geneva, Droz, 2004.

———. *Lumière des martyrs: essai sur le martyre au siècle des Réformes,* Paris, Honoré Champion, 2004.

———, ed. *Le Bresil de Montaigne: le Nouveau Monde des "Essais,"* Paris, Chandeigne, 2005.

———, ed. *Rhétorique de Montaigne: actes du Colloque de la Société des Amis de Montaigne,* Paris, Honoré Champion, 1985.

Levi, Anthony. *Renaissance and Reformation: The Intellectual Genesis,* New Haven and London, Yale University Press, 2002.

L'Hospital, Michel de. *Discours (1560–1562),* in Loris Petris, *La Plume et la Tribune: Michel de l'Hospital et ses discours (1559–1562),* Geneva, Droz, 2002, pp. 359–439.

———. *Discours pour la majorité de Charles IX et trois autres discours,* ed. Robert Descimon, Paris, Imprimerie Nationale, 1993.

———. *Discours politiques pendant les guerres de religion: 1560–1568,* Clermont-Ferrant, Paleo, 2001.

Long, A. A. "Cicero's Politics in *De Officiis*," in A. Laks and M. Schofield, eds., *Justice and Generosity: Studies in Hellenistic Social and Political Philosophy*, Cambridge, Cambridge University Press, 1995, pp. 213–40.

Loraux, Nicole. *L' invention d'Athènes*, Paris, Payot, 1993.

Love, Ronald S. *Blood and Religion: The Conscience of Henri IV, 1553–1593*, Montreal and Kingston, McGill-Queen's University Press, 2001.

Lynn, Martin A. *Henri III and the Jesuit Politicians*, Geneva, Droz, 1973.

———. *The Jesuit Mind: The Mentality of an Elite in Early Modern France*, Ithaca and London, Cornell University Press, 1988.

MacCulloch, Diarmaid. *Reformation: Europe's House Divided, 1490–1700*, London, Allen Lane, 2003.

Machiavelli, Niccolò. *Discorsi sopra la prima Deca di Tito Livio*, ed. Francesco Bausi, 2 vols., Roma and Salerno, Edizione Nazionale delle Opere di Niccolò Machiavelli, 2001.

McManners, John. *Church and Society in Eighteenth Century France*, 2 vols., Oxford, Clarendon Press, 1998.

Magendie, Maurice. *La politesse mondaine et les théories de l'honnêteté en France au XVIIème siècle* (1925), Geneva, Slatkine, 1993.

Major, J. Russell. *From Renaissance Monarchy to Absolute Monarchy: French Kings, Nobles and Estates*, Baltimore and London, Johns Hopkins University Press, 1994.

Marchi, Dudley M. *Montaigne among the Moderns: Reception of the "Essays,"* Providence and Oxford, Berghahn Books, 1994.

Margolin, Jean-Claude, ed. *Guerre et paix dans la pensée d'Erasme*, Paris, Aubier, 1973.

Mariéjol, Jean-Hippolyte de. *Catherine de Médicis*, Paris, Tallandier, 2005.

Martin, Daniel. *Montaigne et la fortune: essai sur le hazard et le langage*, Paris, H. Champion, 1977.

Maskell, David. "Montaigne médiateur entre Navarre et Guise," *Bibliothèque d'Humanisme et Renaissance*, 41 (1979), pp. 541–53.

Mason, Roger A., and Martin S. Smith, eds. *A Dialogue on the Law of Kingship among the Scots: A Critical Edition and Translation of George Buchanan's "De Iure Regni apud Scotos Dialogus,"* St Andrews Studies in Reformation History, Aldershot, Ashgate, 2004.

Mathias, Paul. *Montaigne*, Paris, Vrin, 2006.

Mauzey, Jesse Virgil. *Montaigne's Philosophy of Human Nature*, Annandale-on-Hudson, NY, St. Stephen College, 1933.

Mentzer, Raymond A., and Andrew Spicer, eds. *Society and Culture in the Huguenot World, 1559–1685*, Cambridge, Cambridge University Press, 2002.

Millet, Olivier. *La première réception des "Essais" de Montaigne (1580–1640)*, Paris, Honoré Champion, 1995.

Miquel, Pierre. *Les guerres de religion*, Paris, Fayard, 1980.

Mironneau, Paul, and Isabelle Pébay-Clottes, eds. *Paix des armes, paix des âmes: Colloque de Pau*, Société Henri IV, Edition Imprimerie Nationale, 2000.

Momigliano, Arnaldo, ed. *The Conflict of Paganism and Christianity*, Oxford, Oxford University Press, 1963.

Montaigne, Michel de. "Les arrêts des Enquêtes rédigés (10), dictés (40) ou contresignés (341) par Montaigne, récemment découverts par Katherine Almquist," ed. Katherine Almquist, *Bulletin de la Société des Amis de Montaigne*, Jan. 1998, pp. 13–38.

———.*The Complete Essays*, trans. and ed. M. A. Screech, Harmondsworth, Penguin Books, 1987.

———.*The Complete Works, Essays, Travel Journals, Letters*, trans. and ed. Donald M. Frame, London, Everyman's Library, 2003.

———. *Des prières*, ed. Alain Legros, Geneva, Droz, 2003.

———. *Les essais: édition conforme au texte de l'exemplaire de Bordeaux* (1924), ed. Pierre Villey, 3 vols., rev. ed., Paris, Quadrige, 1988.

———. *Essais: Michel de Montaigne*. 3 vols., Paris, Gallimard, 1994–95.

———. *Journal de voyage en Italie*, ed. Fausta Garavini, Paris, Gallimard, 1983.

———. *Lettres*, ed. Claude Pinganaud, Paris, Arléa, 2004.

———. *Œuvres complètes*, ed. Maurice Rat, Paris, Gallimard, 1962.

Montesquieu, Charles Secondat de. *L'esprit des lois*, in *Oeuvres complètes*, ed. Roger Caillois, 2 vols., Paris, Gallimard, 1951, vol. 2.

Moreau, Pierre-François, ed. *Le retour des philosophies antiques à l'age classique*, 2 vols., Paris, Albin Michel, 1999–2001.

Morstein-Marx, Robert. *Mass Oratory and Political Power in the Late Roman Republic*, Cambridge, Cambridge University Press, 2004.

Mouralis, Bernard. *Montaigne et le mythe du bon sauvage, de l'antiquité à Rousseau*, Paris, Bordas, 1989.

Mousnier, Roland. *L'assassinat de Henri IV: le problème du tyrannicide et l'affermissement de la monarchie absolue*, Paris, Gallimard, 1964.

———. *Les institutions de la France sous la monarchie absolue*, 2 vols., Paris, PUF, 1980.

———. *La vénalité des offices sous Henri IV et Louis XIII*, Paris, PUF, 1971.

Muchembled, Robert. *La société policée: politesse et politique en France du XVIème au XX siècle*, Paris, Seuil, 1998.

Nakam, Géralde. *Les "Essais" de Montaigne miroir et procès de leurs temps: témoignage historique et création littéraire*, Paris, Nizet, Publications de la Sorbonne, 1984.

———. *Montaigne: la manière et la matière*, Paris, Klincksieck, 1992.

———. *Montaigne et son temps: les événements et les "Essais": l'histoire, la vie, le livre*, Paris, Gallimard, 1993.

Naudé, Gabriel. *Advis pour dresser une bibliothèque* (repr. of the 1644 ed.), Paris, Klincksieck, 1994.

Nauert, Charles G. Jr. *Agrippa and the Crisis of Renaissance Thought*, Urbana, University of Illinois Press, 1965.

Naya, Emmanuel, and Anne-Pascale Pouey-Monou, eds. *Eloge de la médiocrité: le juste milieu à la Renaissance*, Paris, Editions Rue d'Ulm, 2005.

Neuschel, Kristen B. *Word of Honor: Interpreting Noble Culture in Sixteenth-Century France*, Ithaca, NY, Cornell University Press, 1986.

Nock, Arthur Darby. *Conversion: The Old and New Religion from Alexander the Great to Augustine of Hippo* (1933), London and Baltimore, Johns Hopkins University Press, 1996.

Norena, Carlos G. *Juan Luis Vives*, The Hague, Martinus Nijhoff, 1970.

Nugent, Donald. *Ecumenism in the Age of the Reformation: The Colloquy of Poissy*, Cambridge, MA, Harvard University Press, 1974.

O'Brian, John, and Philippe Desan, eds. *La "familia" de Montaigne (en homage à Michel Simonin)*, Chicago, University of Chicago Press, 2001.

Olin, John C. *Erasmus, Utopia and the Jesuits: Essays on the Outreach of Humanism*, New York, Fordham University Press, 1994.

Ordine, Nuccio. *Giordano Bruno, Ronsard et la religion* (1999), Paris, Albin Michel, 2004.

Orléa, Manfred. *La noblesse aux états généraux de 1576 et de 1588*, Paris, PUF, 1980.

Ozment, Steven. *The Age of Reform 1250–1550: An Intellectual and Religious History of Late Medieval and Reformation Europe*, New Haven, Yale University Press, 1980.

Pagden, Anthony. *The Fall of Natural Man: The American Indian and the Origins of Comparative Ethnology*, Cambridge, Cambridge University Press, 1982.

Parker, Geoffrey. *The Dutch Revolt*, Harmondsworth, Penguin Books, 1981.

Parmentier, Bérengère. *Le siècle des moralistes, de Montaigne à La Bruyère*, Paris, Seuil, 2000.

Pascal, Blaise. *Œuvres complètes*, ed. Michel Le Guern, 2 vols., Paris, Gallimard, 2000.

Pasquier, Estienne. *Ecrits politiques*, ed. D. Thickett, Geneva, Droz, 1966.

Pasquier, J. *L'impôt des gabelles en France aux XVIIème et XVIIIème siècles* (1905), Geneva, Slatkine, 1978.

Perniola, Mario. *Del sentire cattolico: la forma culturale di una religione universale*, Bologna, Il Mulino, 2001.

Petris, Loris. *La plume et la tribune: Michel de l'Hospital et ses discours (1559–1562)*, Geneva, Droz, 2002.

Pomeau, René. *La religion de Voltaire*, Paris, Nizet, 1995.

Popkin, Richard H. *The History of Scepticism: From Erasmus to Spinoza*, Berkeley, University of California Press, 1979.

———. *The History of Scepticism: From Savonarola to Bayle*, Oxford, Oxford University Press, 2003.

Potter, David, ed. *The French Wars of Religion: Selected Documents*, London, Macmillan, 1997.

Prevot, Jacques, ed. *Libertins du XVIIème siècle*, 2 vols., Paris, Gallimard, 1998–2004.

Quint, David. *Montaigne and the Quality of Mercy: Ethical and Political Themes in the "Essais,"* Princeton, Princeton University Press, 1998.

Reiss, Timothy. "Montaigne et le sujet politique," *Oeuvres et Critiques*, 8/1–2 (1983), pp. 127–52.

Rials, Stéphane, ed. *La déclaration des droits de l'homme et du citoyen*, Paris, Hachette, 1988.

Rigolot, François. "Montaigne lecteur européen de l'Amérique," *Diogène*, 164 (1993), pp. 3–15.

Roberts, Penny. "Huguenot Petitioning during the Wars of Religion," in Raymond A. Mentzer and Andrew Spicer, eds., *Society and Culture in the Huguenot World, 1559–1685*, Cambridge, Cambridge University Press, 2002, pp. 62–77.

Roelker, Nancy Lyman. *One King, One Faith: The Parlement of Paris and the Religious Reformations of the Sixteenth Century*, Berkeley, University of California Press, 1996.

Rousseau, Jean-Jacques. *Les Confessions*, ed. Alain Grosrichard, 2 vols., Paris, Garnier-Flammarion, 2002, vol. 2.

———. *Julie, ou La Nouvelle Héloise*, ed. Michel Launey, Paris, Garnier Flammarion, 1953.

———. *Les rêveries du promeneur solitaire*, in *Oeuvres complètes*, ed. B. Gagnebin and M. Raymond, 4 vols., Paris, Gallimard, 1959–69, vol. 1, pp. 993–1099.

Roussel, François. *Montaigne: magistrat sans juridiction*, Paris, Michalon (Le Bien Commun), 2006.

Sacerdoti, Gilberto. *Sacrificio e sovranità: teologia e politica nell'Europa di Shakespeare e Bruno*, Torino, Einaudi, 2002.

Sainte-Beuve, Charles-Augustin. *Port Royal*, ed. Maxime Leroy, 3 vols., Paris, Gallimard, 1954.

Salmon, John Hearsey McMillan. *Society in Crisis: France in the Sixteenth Century*, London, Methuen, 1979.

———. *The French Wars of Religion: How Important Were Religious Factors?* Boston, Heath,1967.

———. *Renaissance and Revolt: Essays in the Intellectual and Social History of Early Modern France*, Cambridge, Cambridge University Press, 1987.

Sanders, Jason Lewis. *Justus Lipsius: The Philosophy of Renaissance Stoicism*, New York, Liberal Arts Press, 1955.

Sanders, S. G. "Montaigne et les idées politiques de Machiavel," *Bulletin de la Société des Amis de Montaigne*, 18–19 (1976), pp. 97–98.

Sauzet, Robert, ed. *Henri III et son temps: actes du Colloque de Tours, 1989*, Paris, Vrin, 1992.

Scarano Lagnani, Emanuela. *Guicciardini e la crisi del Rinascimento*, Bari, Laterza, 1973.

Schaefer, David Lewis. *The Political Philosophy of Montaigne*, Ithaca and London, Cornell University Press, 1990.

———, ed. *Freedom over Servitude: Montaigne, La Boétie and "On Voluntary Servitude,"* Westport, CT, and London, Greenwood Press, 1998.

Schiff, Mario. *La fille d'alliance de Montaigne: Marie de Gournay*, Geneva, Slatkine, 1978.

Schmitt, Paul. *La réforme catholique: le combat de Maldonat (1534–1583)*, Paris, Beauchesne, 1985.

Schwartz, Jérôme. *Diderot and Montaigne: The "Essais" and the Shaping of Diderot's Humanism*, Geneva, Droz, 1966.

Sclafert, Clément. *L'ame religieuse de Montaigne*, Paris, Nouvelles Editions Latines, 1951.

———. "Montaigne et Maldonat," *Bulletin de Littérature Ecclésiastique*, 1951, pp. 65–93 and 129–46.

Scodel, Joshua. "The Affirmation of Paradox: a Reading of Montaigne's 'De la phisionomie,'" in Gérard Defaux, ed., *Montaigne: Essays in Reading*, special issue of *Yale French Studies*, 64, 1983, pp. 209–37.

Sealy, Robert J. *The Palace Academy of Henry III*, Geneva, Droz, 1981.

Sellier, Philippe. *Pascal et Saint-Augustin* (1970), Paris, Albin Michel, 1995.

Sévigné, Marie de Rabutin-Chantal de. *Correspondance*, ed. Roger Duchêne, 3 vols. Paris, Gallimard, 1972.

Sextus Empiricus. *Outlines of Scepticism*, ed. Julia E. Annas and Julian Barnes, Cambridge, Cambridge University Press, 2000.

Seyssel, Claude de. *La monarchie de France et deux autres fragments politiques*, ed. Jacques Poujol, Paris, d'Argences, 1961.

Shakespeare, William. *Love's Labour's Lost*, ed. G. R. Hibbard, Oxford, Oxford University Press, 1990.

Shennan, J. H. *The Parlement of Paris* (1968), Phoenix Mill, Sutton Publishing, 1998.

Shklar, Judith. *Ordinary Vices*, Cambridge, MA, and London, Belknap Press of Harvard University, 1984.

Simonin, Michel. *L'encre et la lumière: quarante-sept articles (1976–2000)*, Geneva, Droz, 2004.

Skinner, Quentin. *The Foundations of Modern Political Thought*, 2 vols., Cambridge, Cambridge University Press, 1978.

———. *Machiavelli*, Oxford, Oxford University Press, 1981.

———. *Visions of Politics*, 3 vols., Cambridge, Cambridge University Press, 2003, vol. 2, *Renaissance Virtues*.

Smith, Malcolm. *Montaigne and Religious Freedom: The Dawn of Pluralism*, Geneva, Droz, 1991.

———. *Montaigne and the Roman Censors*, Geneva, Droz, 1981.

Sol, Thierry. *Fallait-il tuer César? L'argumentation politique de Dante à Machiavel*, Paris, Dalloz, 2005.

Solnon, Jean-François. *Catherine de Médicis*, Paris, Perrin, 2003.

———. *Henri III: un désir de majesté*, Paris, Perrin, 2001.

Sorell, Tom, ed. *The Rise of Modern Philosophy*, Oxford, Clarendon Press, 1993.

Staël, Anne-Louise Germaine de. *Considérations sur la Révolution française*, ed. Jacques Godechot, Paris, Tallandier 2000.

Starobinski, Jean. *Montaigne en mouvement*, Paris, Gallimard, 1982.

Statius, Pierre. *Le réel et la joie: essai sur l'oeuvre de Montaigne*, Paris, Kimé, 1997.

Stegmann, André, ed. *Edits des guerres de religion*, Paris, Vrin, 1979.

Stouz, Francis de Crue de. *Le parti des politiques au lendemain de la Sainte-Barthélemy*, Paris, Plon, 1890.

Striker, Gisela. *Essays on Hellenistic Epistemology and Ethics*, Cambridge, Cambridge University Press, 1996.

Stroud, Barry. *The Significance of Philosophical Scepticism*, Oxford, Clarendon Press, 1996.

Strowski, Fortunat. *Montaigne: sa vie publique et privée*, Paris, Editions Nouvelle Revue Critique, 1938.

Supple, James J. *Arms versus Letters: The Military and Literary Ideals in the "Essais" of Montaigne*, Oxford, Oxford University Press, 1984.

Tantillo, Ignazio. *L'Imperatore Giuliano*, Bari, Laterza, 2001.

Thickett, Dorothy. *Estienne Pasquier (1529–1615): The Versatile Barrister of 16th Century France*, London and New York, Regency Press, 1979.

Thou, Jacques Auguste de. *Mémoires*, in Joseph-François Michaud and Jean-

Joseph-François Poujoulat, eds., *Nouvelle collection des mémoires pour servir à l'histoire de France: depuis le XIIIe siècle jusqu'à la fin du XVIIIe*, 32 vols., Paris, Chez l'éditeur du Commentaire analytique du Code civil, 1836–39, vol. 11.

Tienant, Claude. *Le gouverneur de Languedoc pendant les premières guerres de religion, Henri de Montmorency-Damville*, Paris, Publisud, 1993.

Todorov, Tzvetan. *Le jardin imparfait: la pensée humaniste en France*, Paris, Grasset, 1998.

———. "Les morales de la conquête," *Diogène*, 125 (1984), pp. 93–107.

Toulemon, André. *Etienne de La Boétie: un enfant de Sarlat: président du Parlement de Bordeaux*, Paris, Librairies Techniques, 1980.

Tracy, James D. *The Politics of Erasmus: a Pacifist Intellectual in His Political Milieu*, Toronto, Toronto University Press, 1992.

Trevor-Roper, Hugh R. *George Buchanan and the Ancient Scottish Constitution*, London, Longmans, 1966.

Trinquet, Roger. *La jeunesse de Montaigne: ses origines familiales, son enfance et ses études*, Paris, Nizet, 1972.

Tuck, Richard. *Philosophy and Government, 1572–1651*, Cambridge, Cambridge University Press, 1993.

Turchetti, Mario. "Concorde ou tolérance? Les Moyenneurs à la veille des guerres de religion en France," *Revue de théologie et philosophie*, 118 (1986), pp. 255–67.

———. "Une question mal posée: la tolérance dans les édits de janvier (1562) et d'Amboise (1563): les premiers commentaires et interprétations," in Henry Méchoulan et al., eds., *La formazione storica dall'alterità*, Florence, L. S. Olski, 2001, vol. 1, pp. 245–94.

———. "Une question mal posée: l'origine et l'identité des 'Politiques' au temps des guerres de religion," in Thierry Wanegffelen, ed., *De Michel de l'Hospital à l'édit de Nantes: politique et religion face aux églises*, Clermont-Ferrand, Presses Universitaires Blaise Pascal, 2002, pp. 357–90.

Ulph, O. "Jean Bodin and the Estates General in 1576," *Journal of Modern History*, 19 (1947), pp. 289–96.

Van Kley, Dale K. *The Religious Origins of the French Revolution: From Calvin to the Civil Constitution, 1560–1791*, New Haven, Yale University Press, 1996.

Viennot, Eliane. *Marguerite de Valois: histoire d'une femme, histoire d'un mythe*, Paris, Payot, 1993.

Villey, Pierre. *L'influence de Montaigne sur les idées pédagogiques de Locke et de Rousseau*, Paris, Hachette, 1911.

———. *Les livres d'histoire moderne utilisés par Montaigne: contribution à l'étude des sources des "Essais": suivi d'un appendice sur les traductions françaises d'histoires anciennes utilisées par Montaigne* (1908), Geneva, Slatkine, 1972.

———. *Montaigne devant la postérité*, Paris, Boivin, 1935.

———. "Montaigne et Shakespeare," in Sir Israel Gollancz, ed., *A Book of Homage to Shakespeare*, London, Shakespeare Association, 1916, pp. 417–20.

———. *Les sources et l'évolution des "Essais" de Montaigne*, 2 vols., Paris, Hachette, 1933.

Vincent, Hubert. *Education et scepticisme chez Montaigne, ou pédantisme et exercice du jugement*, Paris, L'Harmattan, 1997.

————. "Scepticisme et conservatisme chez Montaigne, ou qu'est-ce qu'une philosophie sceptique?" in *Le scepticisme au XVIème et XVIIème siècle: le retour des philosophies antiques à l'age classique*, ed. Pierre-François Moreau, 2 vols., Paris, Albin Michel, 1999–2001, vol. 2, 132–63.

Vindiciae, contra tyrannos, concerning the legitimate power of a prince over the people, and of the people over a prince [1570s?], trans. and ed. George Garnett, Cambridge, Cambridge University Press, 1994.

Viret, Pierre. *L'interim fait par dialogues (1565)*, ed. Guy R. Mermier, New York and Bern, Peter Lang, 1985.

Vivanti, Corrado. *Guerre civile et paix religieuse dans la France d'Henri IV*, Paris, Desjonqueres, 2006.

Vives, Juan Luis. *D. Aurelii Augustini Hipponensis episcopi De civitate Dei libri XXII*, Geneva, Jacobus Stoer, 1610.

————. *The Selected Works of J. L. Vives*, ed. Constantin Matheeussen, Leiden and New York, E. J. Brill, 1987– .

Voltaire, François-Marie Arouet de. *Correspondance choisie*, ed. Jacqueline Helleguarc'h, Paris, Librairie Générale Française, 1990–97.

————. *Dictionnaire philosophique*, ed. René Pomeau, Paris, Garnier Flammarion, 1986.

Waele, Michel de. "Henri IV, politicien monarchomaque? Les contrats de fidélité entre le roi et les Français," in Jean-François Labourdette, Jean-Pierre Poussons, and Marie-Catherine Vignal, eds., *Le traité de Vervins*, Paris, Presses de l'Université de Paris-Sorbonne, 2000, pp. 117–31.

————. *Les relations entre le parlement de Paris et Henri IV*, Paris, Editions Publisud, 2000.

Walzer, Michael. *On Toleration*, New Haven and London, Yale University Press, 1997.

Wanegffelen, Thierry. *Catherine de Médicis: le pouvoir au féminin*, Paris, Payot, 2005.

————. *L'édit de Nantes: une histoire européenne de la tolérance*, Paris, Librairie Générale Française, 1998.

————. *Ni Rome, ni Genève: des fidèles entre deux chaires en France au XVIème siècle*, Paris, H. Champion, and Geneva, Slatkine, 1997.

————, ed. *De Michel de l'Hospital à l'édit de Nantes: politique et religion face aux églises*, Clermont-Ferrand, Presses Universitaires Blaise Pascal, 2002.

Wheland, Ruth and Carol Baxter, eds. *Toleration and Religious Identity: The Edict of Nantes and Its Implications in France, Britain and Ireland*, Dublin, Four Courts Press, 2003.

Whitfield, John Humphreys. "Machiavelli, Guicciardini, Montaigne," *Italian Studies*, 28 (1973), pp. 31–47.

Wilcox, Donald J. "Guicciardini and the Humanist Historians," *Annali di Italianistica*, 2 (1984), pp. 110–22.

Williams, Bernard. *Moral Luck*, Cambridge, Cambridge University Press, 1981.

————. *Truth and Truthfulness: An Essay in Genealogy*, Princeton, Princeton University Press, 2002.

Winter, Ian J. *Montaigne's Self-Portrait and Its Influence in France: 1580–1630*, Lexington, KY, French Forum, 1976.

Wittkower, Rudolf. "Chance, Time and Virtue," *Journal of the Warburg Institute*, 1 (1937–38), pp. 313–21.

Wolfe, Michael. *The Conversion of Henri IV: Politics, Power and Religious Belief in Early Modern France*, Cambridge, MA, Harvard University Press, 1993.

Yardeni, Myriam. *La conscience nationale en France pendant les guerres de religion (1559–1598)*, Louvain and Paris, Nauwelaerts, 1971.

Yates, Frances A. *The French Academies of the Sixteenth Century*, Nendeln, Kraus Reprint, 1973.

Zemon Davies, Natalie. *The Gift in Sixteenth Century France*, Oxford, Oxford University Press, 2000.

———. *Society and Culture in Early Modern France*, Stanford, CA, Stanford University Press, 1965.

INDEX